PRAISE FOR *DOCTORS AND DISTILLERS*

"At last, a definitive guide to the medicinal origins of every bottle behind the bar! From prehistoric beer to exotic French liqueurs, a swig of alcohol has always served as tonic and treatment. With a cocktail nerd's love of obscure ingredients and a passion for odd historical details, Camper English illuminates the murky, confounding, and even grotesque history of booze as medicine. This is the cocktail book of the year, if not the decade." —Amy Stewart, author of *The Drunken Botanist* and *Wicked Plants*

"Mr. English has written a fascinating book that makes a brilliant historical case for what I've been saying all along: alcohol is good for you. . . . Okay, maybe it's not technically good for you, but he shows that through most of human history, it's sure beat the heck out of water." —Alton Brown, creator of *Good Eats*

"Camper English is the booze writer's booze writer—the one we all turn to for true histories, unassailable facts, and clarity (of both explanation and ice). *Doctors and Distillers* puts his magnificent brain on full display, laying out the coiled-together histories of drinking and medicine. Every page has at least three 'wait, I didn't know that!' moments, and the bibliography will launch 1,000 magazine-article history sections." —Adam Rogers, author of *Proof: The Science of Booze*

"*Doctors and Distillers* is an eye-opening compendium of the unlikely, often dodgy, always colorful alchemical-medicinal backstories of alcohols in all their stupefying variety: it'll bring a little something extra to whatever you sip." —Harold McGee, author of *On Food and Cooking* and *Nose Dive*

"I must tell you that I fully believe that fermentation is actually magic. At the very least I think we can all agree that alcoholic drinks, properly administered by a judicious hand, can be medicine. Dive into these pages and you will learn the raucous and unlikely true tale of how every alcoholic drink from beer, wine, and bitters to the vanished and banned cocaine drinks of the nineteenth century, were once thought to banish all manner of ills. Better yet, you'll be grandly entertained. I predict that by the last page you'll find yourself feeling oddly . . . better." —Garrett Oliver, editor in chief, *The Oxford Companion to Beer* and brewmaster of The Brooklyn Brewery

"When the Roman philosopher Seneca wrote that 'reading nourishes the intellect and study banishes fatigue,' I'm pretty sure he was thinking about *Doctors and Distillers*, or at least would have been if he'd stuck around to read it. In any case, Mr. English has written as an instructive and entertaining a book as I can conceive."
—David Wondrich, editor in chief, *The Oxford Companion to Spirits and Cocktails*

"Equal parts science textbook and historical narrative, *Doctors and Distillers* is a beautifully researched and thoroughly engaging trip through the story of some of our most beloved libations."
—Jeffrey Morgenthaler, author of *The Bar Book*

"Camper has always written with the rare combination of eye-opening insight and delightful wit, and in *Doctors and Distillers* he outdoes himself masterfully. A globe-spanning and impeccably researched work that reaches deep into humanity's relationship with alcohol, this is no dry textbook—*Doctors and Distillers* pulls the veneer off of subjects clouded in mystery and hyperbole, exposing the history of beer, wine, spirits, and cocktails as critical in understanding modern health, medicine, and our persistent human desire to understand the universe and our place in it."
—Alex Day, partner at Death & Co., and author of *Cocktail Codex*

"Want a prescription of gin, whiskey, beer, or cocaine? Well, you'll need to travel back in time for these doctor-given elixirs. And that's exactly what Camper English does in *Doctors and Distillers*. He beautifully tells the story of how alcohol kept the world healthy and provides recipes for you to make at home. You know, just in case you get a case of 1800s-era hay fever."
—Fred Minnick, author of *Whiskey Women* and *Bourbon Curious*

"A boozy and breezy romp through medical history, *Doctors and Distillers* is an intoxicating read. Buy two copies: one for your bar and one for your bookshelf."
—Nate Pedersen, coauthor of *Quackery: A Brief History of the Worst Ways to Cure Everything*

"Channeling the witty satire of Mencken, to-the-point prose of Hemingway, and unsentimental wit of Embury, English overlays meticulously researched histories of medicine, spirits, and mixology chronologically, revealing eyebrow-raising insights about the anthropological context that's propelled the inseparable relationship between spirits, mixed drinks and medicine dating back to antiquity."
—Jim Meehan, author of *Meehan's Bartender Manual* and *The PDT Cocktail Book*

PENGUIN BOOKS

DOCTORS AND DISTILLERS

. . . .

Camper English is a cocktails and spirits writer and speaker who has covered the craft cocktail renaissance for more than fifteen years, contributing to more than fifty publications around the world, including *Popular Science*, *Saveur*, *Details*, *Whisky Advocate*, and *Drinks International*. With a focus on the nerdy side of mixology, he has studied everything from the history of carbonation to the science of clear ice cubes. He has been awarded International Cognac Writer of the Year by the Bureau National Interprofessionnel du Cognac and Best Cocktail Writer at the Tales of the Cocktail Foundation Spirited Awards, and he has been voted as one of the one hundred most influential people in the global drinks industry for several years running. He lives in San Francisco.

DOCTORS

···· AND ····

DISTILLERS

THE REMARKABLE
MEDICINAL HISTORY *of*
BEER, WINE, SPIRITS,
and COCKTAILS

CAMPER ENGLISH

PENGUIN BOOKS

PENGUIN BOOKS
An imprint of Penguin Random House LLC
penguinrandomhouse.com

An earlier version of the chapter "Tonic: Malaria, Mosquitoes, and Mauve" was
originally self-published, in different form, as *Tonic Water AKA G&T WTF*, in 2016.

LIBRARY OF CONGRESS CATALOGING-IN-PUBLICATION DATA
Names: English, Camper, author.
Title: Doctors and distillers : the remarkable medicinal history of beer,
wine, spirits, and cocktails / Camper English.
Description: New York : Penguin Books, [2022] |
Includes bibliographical references and index.
Identifiers: LCCN 2021058521 (print) | LCCN 2021058522 (ebook) |
ISBN 9780143134923 (paperback) | ISBN 9780525506591 (ebook)
Subjects: LCSH: Alcoholic beverages—Therapeutic use—History. |
Drinking of alcoholic beverages—Health aspects--History. |
Therapeutics—History. | Medicine—History.
Classification: LCC RM257.A42 E54 2022 (print) |
LCC RM257.A42 (ebook) | DDC 615.7/828—dc23/eng/20220209
LC record available at https://lccn.loc.gov/2021058521
LC ebook record available at https://lccn.loc.gov/2021058522

Printed in the United States of America
6th Printing

DESIGNED BY MEIGHAN CAVANAUGH

To your health

CONTENTS

....

PREFACE

·······················

onsider the Negroni. The bittersweet cocktail dating to the
early 1900s is made of equal parts gin, sweet vermouth, and
Campari. Gin takes its name and flavor from a berry-shaped
cone of a tree once used to ward off bubonic plague. "Vermouth"
comes from the German word for wormwood, famous for its ability
to rid the body of intestinal parasites. Campari is a brand of liqueur
dating to 1860 with a secret recipe probably containing gentian
(proven effective against indigestion) and rhubarb root (used in traditional Chinese medicine as a laxative), and until recently colored
red with cochineal insects once thought to cure depression. The cocktail is often consumed as an aperitif, specifically to stimulate the appetite in preparation for a meal.

Early on, alcohol and medicine were interchangeable: distilled
spirits were called "eau-de-vie," meaning "water of life," speaking to
their healing (or at least invigorating) powers. Before modern sanitation, alcoholic beverages were usually safer to drink than water, and

low-ABV beer was served to laborers for hydration the way Gatorade is to football players today. Alcohol is an analgesic and disinfectant (whiskey would simultaneously numb the pain and sterilize the wound), as well as a preservative, employed to extend the useful life of medicinal herbs.

Spirits were used to regulate body temperature in both hot and cold climates, to treat gout and arthritis, and to awaken someone suffering from shock. During US Prohibition, one could procure a prescription for medicinal whiskey or cognac that was just regular whiskey or cognac sold by the pharmacist rather than served by the bartender.

A spoonful of sugar added to a bitter-tasting medicine can transform it into a palatable liqueur. A large number of liqueur brands sold today have their roots as cures for cholera, dysentery, fevers, indigestion, constipation, or as all-purpose health elixirs and pain relievers. Some were (and still are) used like a daily multivitamin, taken in small doses every morning or evening to prevent illness. Others were used to buy time during any sort of injury or illness until the doctor could be fetched from the village.

Mixers were medicines too. Fizzy, mineral-rich bottled soda waters were first created to mimic natural spa waters believed to cure everything from leprosy to optical disorders. Fresh citrus juice makes for a nice Daiquiri and also contains the vitamin C necessary to stave off scurvy. Favorite rum-mixer Coca-Cola has its origins in coca (as in cocaine) wine, once considered so good for you that it was endorsed by two popes.

Even alcohol not meant to cure serious diseases was designed to ease everyday discomfort: rock and rye was cough medicine, bitters were designed to soothe stomach ailments and seasickness, and the mighty cocktail itself was not originally an evening beverage but a morning pick-me-up, particularly recommended the day after a big night of drinking.

By studying alcohol, scientists made discoveries in medicine as well as in microbiology, biochemistry, and other disciplines. Alchemy, the proto-science that gave us alcoholic distillation, is a root of modern chemistry. The study of carbonation and fermentation led to the understanding and identification of elements, gases, and the germ theory of disease. The search for a quinine alternative led to the development of chemotherapy.

There were a few bumps along the way. In the days before the regulation of food, alcohol, and medicine, all three were often mislabeled and infused with unsafe botanicals, (other) addictive drugs like cocaine and morphine, toxic dyes, and preservatives, including embalming fluid.

Only relatively recently have alcohol and medicine become uncoupled. We think of the 1950s soda fountain as a wholesome milkshake shop, but a few decades earlier you could buy your laudanum there and chase it with a wine spritzer. In Ireland, the practice of giving blood donors a free pint of Guinness ended only in 2009. Alcohol is an important part of modern herbal medicine, used as a solvent with which to extract the active properties of botanicals. And as part of family traditions around the globe, parents still rub a little whiskey (or rum or the local spirit) on their babies' gums to soothe the pain from teething.

· · · · ·

The idea for this book began to take shape several years ago. I was writing an article about the Gin and Tonic and wanted to cite the creation date of the drink. I couldn't find any specific date, just the general information that the cocktail was first consumed in 1800s India by Brits who loved gin and needed the quinine in the tonic water to ward off malaria. A few years and about twenty books read later, I didn't learn anything much about the cocktail, but I did learn a great deal about malaria in particular and medicine in general. Unlike the history of cocktails, the history of medicine is well documented. As I continued to research, I learned more about the antimalarial properties of tonic water, juniper in gin as a diuretic, absinthe as a water purifier, brandy to revive a patient from shock, ferro china to treat anemia, and how root beer's sarsaparilla was once used to soothe syphilis. Pretty soon, I could trace the medicinal origins of so many of today's drinks I realized they could fill a book, so here we are.

What you are (hopefully) about to read is the interconnected history of alcohol and medicine, and not even close to the complete history of one or the other. Luckily, a lot of those books exist already; have at it. This book is also not an exhaustive study of the medicinal uses for alcohol. I have probably neglected to mention your favorite family folk medicine, and no doubt soju and slivovitz found their way into medicinal use just as sherry and soda water did. Some alcoholic cures I missed, others I passed over, and surely there were many more that I never discovered. Some wines, beers, and spirits have a more direct medicinal lineage than others, but it should be clear by the end of the book that all alcohol and many mixers were used as medicine or with medicine at some point.

Most of the time, a drink is just a drink, to sip and enjoy with friends. As it turns out, there can be health benefits to that, but this book isn't trying to be prescriptive. Alcoholic beverages are not health drinks, despite what modern electrolyte-added beers and herb-infused vodka brands might try to imply. This book is merely meant to give the reader an appreciation of alcohol's long and lush medicinal history.

NEGRONI

1 ounce (30 ml) Campari

1 ounce (30 ml) gin

1 ounce (30 ml) sweet vermouth

Add all ingredients to an ice-filled Old-Fashioned glass. Stir and garnish with an orange twist.

DISCLAIMER

This is most definitely *not* a book of natural cures or recipes for booze-based remedies, but one about the inseparable history of alcohol and medicine, of bartenders and pharmacists, of cocktails and cures. If you need medicine, talk to your doctor. If you need a cocktail, see your local mixologist.

Schlitz

THE BEER THAT MADE MILWAUKEE FAMOUS

Beer is barley-malt and hops --- a food and a tonic. Just a touch of alcohol in it.

Not a beverage known to man is more healthful, if the beer is right.

'Tis the national beverage, from childhood up, with the sturdiest peoples of the earth.

To the weak, it's essential; to the strong it is good.

———

BUT— the beer must be pure.

Impurity means germs, and germs multiply rapidly in any saccharine product like beer.

And the beer must be old.

Age means perfect fermentation. Without it, beer ferments on the stomach causing biliousness.

Schlitz beer is brewed in absolute cleanliness.

It is cooled in a plate glass room, in filtered air.

Then it is filtered; then aged for months in refrigerating rooms. After it is bottled and sealed every bottle is sterilized.

Not a germ can exist in it.

These costly precautions have made Schlitz the standard for purity wherever beer is known.

You can get it just as well as common beer if you ask for it.

———

Ask for the Brewery Bottling.

FERMENTATION

GREEKS, GALEN, *and* GUINNESS

> Men who have been intoxicated with wine fall down face
> foremost, whereas they who have drunk barley beer lie
> outstretched on their backs; for wine makes one top-
> heavy, but beer stupefies.
>
> *Aristotle, according to Athenaeus's* Deipnosophistae

I n what is known as the "drunken monkey" hypothesis, ancestors of humans ate fallen fruit fermenting naturally on the forest floor. They liked it: alcohol has readily digestible calories
and lots of them, the fruit was easy to find via its amplified aroma,
and ethanol is antimicrobial, so it was relatively healthy. It was a win
all the way around. This theory is used to claim that humans are "pre-
adapted" for consuming alcohol.

Humans have been fermenting beverages on purpose since probably around 10,000 BCE. Pottery was found in Jiahu, northern China,
dating to 7,000 BCE with a fermented combination of rice, honey, and
fruit. Grapes were probably domesticated around 6,000 BCE, and

evidence of grape wine in the mountains in modern-day Iran dates to the mid-5000s BCE. The tomb of King Tutankhamun, who died in 1323 BCE, contained wine jars labeled with their year and vintner.

As grapes don't store well year-round, wine in ancient Mesopotamia and Egypt was a luxury product. Beer, on the other hand, was an everyday drink. A religious festival site in Turkey from around 9500 BCE may have been used for brewing a sort of beer from grasses, and evidence of a brewery was found from a semi-sedentary, foraging people living in the tenth to twelfth centuries BCE in Israel. One of the oldest known literary works in cuneiform is the *Instructions of Shuruppak*, dating to around 2500 BCE, which includes advice such as a warning not to "pass judgment when you drink beer."

Fermented beverages enter the historical record around the time that nomads settled down and became farmers in different parts of the world, leading some archaeological researchers to conclude that the domestication of grains was developed specifically to make beer—not bread—as would be assumed. Some early recipes for beer, including that in the Sumerian "Hymn to Ninkasi" (a poem, written down around 1800 BCE, invoking the Sumerian goddess of brewing), list bread as an ingredient. Bread could have been both ready-to-eat food and a stored ingredient for beer, like a box of breakfast cereal that you can eat with or without the milk.

BETTER THAN WATER

The brews of ancient times did not resemble the clear beer we know today but were more like a gruel with coarsely filtered solids still in the mix. Surviving drawings depict beer consumed from shared vessels with long straws probably made from reeds used to poke beneath the floating grain and yeast solids on top. That yeast provided healthy and nutritious proteins, vitamins, and minerals, and the beer would hydrate as well as provide calories. It was the sports drink of the pyramid age.

LEMONADE SHANDY

6 ounces (180 ml) beer
6 ounces (180 ml) lemonade

Add both ingredients to a pint glass and
garnish with a lemon wedge.

A cuneiform tablet from Iraq dating to around 3100 BCE is a record of quantities of beer provided to workers, as payment or a job perk. The people who built the pyramids (not enslaved people as depicted in *The Ten Commandments* and *The Prince of Egypt*, but more likely agricultural laborers) were given beer on their shifts. The practice was by no means limited to ancient times: work beer was provided to all sorts of household, farm, and factory workers into the Industrial Revolution and beyond.

Employers were not trying to create a drunk and docile workforce. They were trying to keep people hydrated, and they certainly would not want their employees drinking *water*. Fresh water near towns and cities would usually have not-so-fresh human and animal poop and pathogens floating in it.

Beer's preparation made it safer to drink than plain water. The water was heated or boiled, killing many microbes in the process. Alcohol produced during fermentation also kills pathogens and slows spoilage. Modern scientific studies have proven alcohol's antimicrobial properties, showing that *E. coli* and *Salmonella typhimurium* grow in nonalcoholic beer but not alcoholic beer. Hops would not become a feature of beer production until the Middle Ages, but the same study also showed that while hops didn't inhibit those pathogens, they did prevent the growth of *Listeria monocytogenes* and *Staphylococcus aureus*. Before hops, other antimicrobial herbs, including wormwood, were used in beer to extend its life, to add to its flavor, and to take advantage of the herbs' medicinal qualities.

While water usually wasn't an ingredient in wine, wine has also been proven to be antimicrobial, destroying many of the same bacteria as beer—red wine more so than white. Wine kills salmonella bacteria that can survive in unfermented (nonalcoholic) grape juice. Wine with both a relatively high alcohol content and a low pH (meaning it's acidic) has shown to be more effective against microbes than wine with one or the other of those qualities.

EARLY MEDICINAL USE OF
BEER AND WINE

Fermented beverages were used both in medicine and as medicine. While the recipe for making beer in "Hymn to Ninkasi" shows up in 1800 BCE, beer appears as medicine a few centuries before that. The earliest instructions for wound care come from a Sumerian tablet from 2100 BCE that describes the "three healing gestures" of washing a wound with beer and hot water, making plasters of herbs, ointments, and oils, and bandaging the wound.

In the Indian Vedic period (2500–200 BCE) fermented beverages were prepared from raw materials including sugar, honey, and fruit juices. An important medical document of the time, *Charaka Samhita*, described wine as "invigorator of mind and body, antidote to sleeplessness, sorrow and fatigue, producer of hunger, happiness and digestion. . . . If taken as medicine, and not for intoxication, it acts as Amrita (ambrosia), it cures the natural flow of internal fluids of the body," according to the book *Wine in Ancient India*, by Dhirendra Krishna Bose.

The Ebers papyrus, a scroll acquired by a German Egyptologist in 1873, was written around 1500 BCE and is a compilation of older Egyptian medical and magical texts. It contains instructions for herbal medicine, surgical procedures, and spells and incantations to cure ailments like crocodile bites, baldness, and sweaty feet, among other problems. (It also contained directions for making antiwrinkle treatments and other cosmetics.) At the time, diseases were thought to be divine in origin or caused by hexes and witchcraft, and treatments could include prayers and incantations; extreme surgery, including trepanning (drilling a hole in the skull); or just drinking onion soup.

Medicinal ingredients mentioned in the papyrus that we find in modern alcoholic beverages include aloe resin, caraway, coriander, cucumber, elderberry, fennel, figs, juniper, and saffron. These botanical medicines were prescribed to be taken in different kinds of beer (bitter beer, warm beer, etc.), often used in combination with milk (spoiled milk, milk of a woman who has borne a son) and water (spring water, salt water, water in which the phallus has been washed), plus wine in some recipes. It even included the sage advice "rather than drinking contaminated water it is useful to use wine."

The wine, beer, milk, and water were used to wash down the solids and were medicines themselves, as demonstrated by their specificity in different preparations. Some remedies were simple, such as an onion cooked in sweet beer to drive out indigestion. Others were more complex, like the recipe to heal diseased toes that that included such ingredients as fennel, incense, wormwood, myrrh, and elderberries. These medicines also required a lot of nasty stuff: a poultice, for instance, is made of lotus, watermelon, cat's dung, sweet beer, and wine. A zoo's worth of animals were employed, including porcupine, hippopotamus, eel, and tarantula. Rubbing cat's fat on clothes was suggested to keep away mice. Opium was recommended to stop a child from crying. Ancient Egyptian medicine left a lot of room for improvement.

ANCIENT GREECE AND WINE

The ancient Greeks (roughly 1200 BCE to 300 BCE) employed wine more often than beer in their medicines, as the country's Mediterranean climate and geography is more suited to growing grapes than grains. Its mountainous terrain and lack of abundant flat plains make growing grains inefficient, while fruit trees, olives, and grapevines thrive on its hills and slopes.

The Greeks considered beer to be a foreigner's beverage and spoke disparagingly of it. Encountering it in Armenia around 400 BCE, the Greek Xenophon wrote about "barley wine in mixing bowls. The barley itself was on top, at lip-level, and in [the bowls] were reeds, some larger and some smaller, that did not have joints. Whenever someone was thirsty he had to take these in his mouth to suck. And it was very strong unless one poured in water. And the drink was very good to the one used to it."

And not very good, we can guess, to those used to drinking wine.

Typically, wine contains more alcohol than beer (which helps it last longer before spoiling), so Xenophon's comment about beer's strength may seem odd. But the Greeks didn't drink their wine neat; they usually mixed it with water, including seawater.

Though the germ theory of disease was established only in the latter 1800s, people in ancient times knew that water on its own could be unhealthy, as we saw in the Ebers papyrus. In Greece, a Hippocratic author wrote *Airs, Waters, Places* to discuss "those kinds of water that are unhealthy and those that are very healthy, the harmful effects or the benefits that normally result from water; since water contributes a very large part to good health." This text, as explained in French historian Jacques Jouanna's *Greek Medicine from Hippocrates to Galen*, was written with an intended audience of wandering physicians who would take their practice from town to town. In each new place, they would assess both specific illnesses in patients and also the healthfulness of the overall environment—whether people were breathing good or bad air depending on the way the city was facing, and the source of the local water supply.

Airs, Waters, Places specifies that the healthiest water is boiled rainwater, so it was understood at some level that fresh water is less contaminated, and that boiling water purifies it. The unhealthiest water, "harmful in all applications," comes from stagnant lakes and marshes. This was known to cause a medical condition in which "the spleen is large and obstructed all the time." This symptom is a telltale sign of malaria, which is not caught from stagnant water itself but from mosquitoes that lay eggs in it. But it wouldn't be until nearly 1900 CE before scientists figured that out. It also explains that the healthiest waters could be consumed with less wine than water from other sources, so perhaps there was an understanding on some level that wine can help sterilize water. Then again, the same author got ice wrong. He wrote that water from melted snow and ice was diminished in quality by freezing, and that the "lightest and thinnest" parts of water dissipate during the process.

The Greek physician Hippocrates (c. 460–c. 377 BCE) is best known for helping formalize the practice of medicine. One major contribution was his insistence that diseases had natural causes and cures rather than supernatural ones, so prayers and amulets were less effective than physical treatment. Hippocrates was credited as the author of *Airs, Waters, Places* and a lot of other works, but most of them were falsely attributed posthumously. Scholars refer to "Hippocratic authors" rather than Hippocrates the person for his writings.

Hippocratic authors distinguished different types of wine for its color (white, dark, straw-colored), concentration (thin, full, hard, smooth), smell (odorous, with a honeyed smell), and age (old, young). "Soft" wine was said to inflame the spleen and liver, for example, and produce wind in the intestine. For various afflictions that might occur during different seasons, physicians would recommend wine diluted to different levels, or even (gasp!) no wine at all. In winter, wine should be consumed only slightly diluted, and in summer it should be mixed with lots of water.

A Hippocratic author wrote, "The main points in favor of . . . white strong wine . . . [are that] it passes more easily to the bladder than the other kind and is diuretic and purgative, it is always very beneficial in acute diseases. For even though it is less suitable than the sweet in other respects, yet the cleansing through the bladder which it causes is beneficial so long as it is administered correctly.

These are good points to note about the beneficial and harmful properties of wine; they were unknown to my predecessors."

Wine, as beer before it, was used as a menstruum (solvent) for herbal medicine. For tetanus, the physician was instructed to "grind wormwood, bay leaves, or henbane seed with frankincense; soak this in white wine, and pour it into a new pot; add an amount of oil equal to the wine, warm, and anoint the patient's body copiously with the warm fluid, and also his head . . . also give him very sweet white wine to drink in large quantities."

In *Diseases of Women*, the Hippocratic doctor wrote of a liquid cheese and cracker plate as treatment for postpartum diarrhea. "Take a black grape, the inside of a sweet pomegranate, crush, and mix in dark wine, scrape in some goat's cheese, sprinkle with some flour from roasted wheat and, well mixed, give it to drink."

Externally, wine was used to wash lesions, fractures, and other open wounds. In *Use of Liquids, Affections, Wounds*, and in other works, much space is devoted to external uses of wine, but "a lesion in the head should not be moistened with anything, not even wine." Flour kneaded together with water or wine can work as a poultice; another is watercress, flax, and wine to reconnect the edges of a wound. Wine is used in an eye ointment when mixed with honey, and eggs boiled in "fragrant dark wine" applied to the anus can be used to treat inflammation of the rectum.

Wine was also sweetened with honey or figs, and flavored with wormwood, thyme, and tree resin. Pine resin was probably first used to seal amphorae (the oval-shaped jars with handles near the top), but it also helped preserve the wine itself and has been called "the sulfur dioxide of the ancient world." First-century CE Roman scholar

Columella made that explicit: "When we shall have, in this manner, prepared the pitch, and have a mind to preserve our wines therewith, when they have now twice left off fermenting, we must put two cyathi of the foresaid pitch into forty-eight sextarii of must."

Resinated wine lives on in the form of Greek retsina today. Beyond pine, other resins used in wine include frankincense (also used as incense and for various ailments, including as an antidote to hemlock poisoning) and myrrh (used in perfumes but also as an antiseptic, analgesic, and antiflatulent). The mastic gum resin that gives the contemporary liqueur mastiha its name was used for stomach pains, gastric disorders, and other digestive problems.

Wine was used as medicine or in medicine, but mostly it was recognized as being good in regular quantities and was treated like food, as "drinking undiluted wine dispels hunger." Sometimes wines were mixed for enhanced nutrition: for emaciation an author recommended "a mixture of three wines, a bitter, a sweet, and an acid one."

It was particularly recommended to the elderly in ancient Greece, as was alcohol in many different cultures into somewhat modern times. Then again, "elderly" to the Greeks was much younger than it is today. Plato (c. 428–c. 348 BCE) wrote, "When a man is entering upon his fortieth year he, after a feast at the public mess, may summon the other gods and particularly call upon Dionysus to join the old men's holy rite, and their mirth as well, which the god has given to men to lighten their burden—wine, that is, the cure for the crabbedness of old age, whereby we may renew our youth and enjoy forgetfulness of despair."

SANGRIA

1 bottle dry red wine

4 ounces (120 ml) cognac

4 ounces (120 ml) orange juice

Slices of oranges, lemons, limes, and
seasonal fruits

Add all ingredients to a pitcher and chill in refrigerator
for several hours before serving over ice.

GALEN AND THE FOUR HUMORS

Greek knowledge and culture spread widely in the Mediterranean
and Middle East thanks in no small part to Macedonian Alexander
the Great (356–323 BCE), who conquered the Persian Empire and
made inroads into India. He left behind many cities, including Alex-
andria in Egypt, that were ruled by generals of his army. The period
from Alexander's death until the conquest of Egypt by Rome in 30
BCE was known as the Hellenistic age of Greek culture.

Galen (129–c. 199 CE) was a Greek physician who trained in Al-
exandria, became chief doctor for a company of gladiators, and later
lived in Rome. He wrote a great deal about wine (furthering Hippocrates's categorizations and including information about specific
vineyards) and medicine, and really about everything. It is estimated
that only a third of his works survive, but those alone account for
around 2.5 million words.

While crediting Hippocrates as the father of medicine, Galen created a structured treatment regimen based on the theory of the four humors (explained below) that became the predominant medical practice for nearly two thousand years. The theory predated Galen, but his extensive writings on the matter established Galenic medicine and humoral theory as interchangeable terms.

A historian in 1910 wrote of the increasingly logical practice of medicine: "the healing art of Hippocrates was transformed into the healing science of Galen." This sounds great, but the "science" was based on a misunderstanding of human anatomy and resulted in a whole lot of bleeding and enemas.

Galen's works were continuously reinterpreted as they were discussed by different physicians in subsequent centuries, but here is a simplified version of humoral theory: everything in the universe is composed of the four elements known to Aristotle: air, fire, earth, and water, in different proportions and amounts. There is also a fifth element, an ether, or "first matter," that will become important in the later discussion of alchemy. These elements correspond to four humors, or bodily fluids: blood, yellow bile, black bile, and phlegm. Each element is associated with a humor: air (blood), fire (yellow bile), earth (black bile), water (phlegm).

There are also four qualities of people, plants, minerals, diseases, and pretty much everything: hot, cold, wet, and dry; often called warm, cool, moist, and dry. Most things exhibit two of the qualities at the same time, hot or cold and wet or dry. Spices used as medicines, for example, are hot and dry. Each of the four bodily humors displays two of the four primary qualities—blood is hot and wet, yellow bile is hot and dry, black bile is cold and dry, and phlegm is cold and wet.

People's temperaments and some physical traits are characterized by having an excess of one of the four humors: sanguine (excess of blood), choleric (yellow bile), melancholic (black bile), phlegmatic (phlegm). The humors were thought to concentrate in specific organs, during certain seasons of the year, at different age ranges (from infancy to old age), in different genders, and even at different times of the day. To diagnose and treat a patient, a physician might take the temperament of the patient into account along with these other factors, then prescribe an appropriate procedure or medicine. This highly methodical system allowed doctors to prescribe treatments for many patients without even seeing them in person. Oh, it's August and you're a man with a fever? Grab the leeches.

To restore humoral balance, a physician might take an additive approach to support a weak humor, or choose a subtractive method to reduce an overabundant one. An additive approach could be to recommend that a choleric person eat phlegmatic foods like cucumbers or veal, while a phlegmatic person should eat choleric foods like mint and garlic. Subtractive measures involved rebalancing the humors by means of bloodletting, laxatives and enemas, emetics (to induce vomiting), expectorants (to induce coughing up mucus), diaphoretics (to induce sweat), poultices (to suck out toxins), and other techniques to purge the body of specific liquids.

Galenic medicine held that illnesses are caused by imbalanced humors, so treatments were largely interchangeable—if a headache and diarrhea were believed to be caused by an abundance of the same humor, the same food might be prescribed to treat either. Likewise, if two different foods had the same qualities, the patient could eat one or the other for their condition.

If one had a (hot) fever, they'd likely be prescribed boiled foods without spices. Spices were also thought to "cook" food and make it more easily digestible, as the stomach was thought to work like an oven. Hot and dry flavorings according to Galenic doctrine included garlic, mustard, parsley, sage, leeks, fennel, caraway seeds, and more. Ginger and galangal were unique spices in that they were hot and wet.

Meal plans were prescribed for individuals and groups depending on their natural temperament, age, gender, and other factors. These diet plans, or regimens, survive in literature. Here is a brief excerpt from Galen writing about food for old men.

> Old men must not eat much of starches, or cheese, or hard-boiled eggs, or snails, or onions, or beans, or pig-meat for food, and still more that of snakes or ospreys; or all those having hard flesh difficult to digest. On this account, therefore, they should not eat any of the crustacea, or mollusca, or tunnies, or any of the cetacea, or the flesh of venison, or goats, or cattle. These also are not useful for anyone else; but for the young, mutton is not a bad food, but for old men none of these, and still less the flesh of lambs, for this is moist and viscid and glutinous and phlegmatic.

Single meals or food items could have their qualities altered. A Hippocratic author wrote, "Take away their power from strong foods by boiling and cooling many times; remove moisture from moist things by grilling and roasting them; soak and moisten dry things, soak and boil salt things, bitter and sharp things mix with sweet, and astringent things mix with oily." The next time your grandmother complains about you slathering your eggs with too much hot sauce, tell her you are merely correcting the humoral imbalances of the omelet.

SPICE AS MEDICINE

Nearly all (probably all) spices were considered medicine before they were used in food, or at least they were used as medicine within food. Spices local or known to the Mediterranean region included caraway, coriander, cumin, juniper, and saffron, while spices imported from Asia included clove, cassia, cinnamon, ginger, mace and nutmeg, and pepper. Many but certainly not all of the following medicinal properties assigned to them have recently been verified by modern science.

Caraway was long used to treat digestive disorders and relieve constipation and menstrual cramps. Coriander (cilantro) was traditionally used to treat diabetes, urinary tract infections, skin problems, and liver diseases, among other conditions. Cumin was used in ancient Egypt to help digestion, and since then against heart disease, swelling, vomiting, and chronic fever. Saffron soothed stomach issues and was employed for all sorts of eye and ear ailments and dental pain. Romans believed adding it to wine helped one avoid a hangover.

"Warming" spices from Asia had their own medicinal uses. Cloves soothed stomachaches, diarrhea, and flatulence, and were particularly specified as a numbing agent for toothaches. Spicy cassia and cinnamon were both used as circulatory stimulants against colds, chills, and coughs, which explains their association with hot wintertime drinks to this day. Cinnamon was also used to counter nausea, but ginger is still the go-to botanical for that condition. Additionally, ginger was an aphrodisiac, a stimulant protecting against colds and phlegm, used topically to soothe burns and promote healing, and considered anti-inflammatory against arthritis.

Mace and nutmeg were recommended for the digestive and nervous systems, and to fight against toothaches and coughs. Black pepper was used to help produce urination, cure chills from fevers, heal snake and insect bites, and to induce labor in the event of a stillbirth. Many of these same qualities were ascribed to juniper (while juniper was also used as an abortifacient). A fifth-century *Syriac Book of Medicines* further recommends pepper for earache, toothache, lung diseases, chest pain, constipation, diarrhea, hernias, and much more, and it was considered effective medicine all the way through one's system.

All of these spices were used in medicinal beverages that much later evolved into liqueurs and cocktail bitters. The Asian spices are included in liqueurs like Bénédictine and in cocktail bitters like Angostura. Caraway and coriander are standard botanicals in gin, while cumin and saffron have been included in the botanical mix in a few brands as well. Saffron is also found in liqueurs like Strega, Fernet-Branca, and probably Bénédictine and Yellow Chartreuse.

SINGAPORE SLING

1.5 ounces (45 ml) gin

0.25 ounce (8 ml) Bénédictine

0.25 ounce (8 ml) Cointreau

0.25 ounce (8 ml) Cherry Heering

0.25 ounce (8 ml) grenadine

1 ounce (30 ml) lime juice

0.75 ounce (20 ml) pineapple juice

2 dashes Angostura bitters

1–2 ounces (30–60 ml) soda water

Add all ingredients except soda water to an ice-filled shaker. Shake and strain over new ice in a highball glass, top with soda, and garnish with a cherry, pineapple wedge, and mint sprig.

. . . . .

In addition to their use for specific ailments, these flavoring, medicinal botanicals are found by modern science to be antimicrobial. A recent study suggested that cumin, coriander, garlic, ginger, mustard, turmeric, black pepper, cinnamon, cloves, nutmeg, and star anise be considered for herbal antimicrobial use in modern medicines. Angelica, caraway, juniper, rosemary, sage, and wormwood have been proven to thwart microbe growth as well. The antimicrobial properties of these herbs and spices would help delay spoilage of the beer, wine, and food to which they were added.

But in the Galenic mindset, hot, dry spices balance cold, moist meats. The ability of hot and dry salt to preserve meat, fish, and fruit balanced their cold natures and thus protected them from corruption. Spices were the medicine of food.

Roman scholar Pliny the Elder (23–79 CE) provided an important reference in the form of his *Natural History*, an encyclopedia in which he referenced the previous accumulated knowledge of Greeks like Aristotle and described astronomy, geographic history, zoology, agriculture, minerals, and medicine, but most important for this discussion, botany and medicine. He commented on wine for internal versus external use: "Wine has the property of heating the parts of the body inside when it is drunk and of cooling them when poured on the outside." He also seemed to express frustration about being asked about it so often. "There is no topic more difficult to handle, or more full of detail, seeing that it is hard to say whether wine does good to people rather than harming them," he wrote. This is still true.

THERIAC AND MITHRIDATE

Pliny wrote, "There is an elaborate mixture called theriace, which is compounded of countless ingredients, although Nature has given as many remedies, any one of which would be enough by itself. The Mithridatic antidote is composed of fifty-four ingredients, no two of them having the same weight, while of some is prescribed one sixtieth part of one denarius. Which of the gods, in the name of Truth, fixed these absurd proportions? No human brain could have been sharp enough. It is plainly a showy parade of the art, and a colossal boast of science."

Pliny was nonplussed at the concept of theriac and mithridates, but these medicines were in use for an exceptionally long time. According to legend, King Mithridates VI (120–63 BCE) of modern-day Turkey swallowed a daily preventative medicine made up of every known antidote against poison. On the eve of his reign being overthrown, Mithridates tried to kill himself but alas! No poison would work. The job had to be accomplished with a sword. The supposed recipe for this all-purpose antipoison became known as "mithridatium," or "mithridate."

The recipe was carried to Rome, where Galen and many other physicians tried to improve on it and add ingredients to the original. Theriac was a similar all-purpose antidote but with additional opium included, plus viper flesh substituted in place of the skink lizard in mithridate. (It was believed that snakes contained an antidote to their own venom, and thus snake parts made it into a lot of medication over the years.)

The ingredients in these medicines were pounded up and mixed with honey like a paste. This could then be taken dissolved in wine, as a sort of pill, or smeared topically on injuries. These antipoisons could take over a month to make and were recommended to be aged for at least twelve years to ensure maximum effectiveness.

These medicines were in common medicinal use from the era of the Romans all the way into the 1800s. Humoral theory mostly covered diseases rather than snakebites and stab wounds, but the reputed therapeutic powers of theriac and mithridate evolved from being effective against venoms and poisons into being universal cure-alls. They were recommended for everything from asthma, malaria, and dropsy to treating outbreaks of bubonic plague of the 1600s in England, during which the medications were both taken internally and spread on infected peoples' buboes.

These ancient medicines were the sticky semisolid precursors to herbal liqueurs we drink today. Many of the ingredients of mithridate and theriac are found in products with complex formulas like Jägermeister and Chartreuse. Around 80 BCE, Greek physician Zopyrus made a mithridate composed of costmary, frankincense, white pepper, cinnamon, cassia, saffron, myrrh, and other ingredients. A mithridate recipe from the first century CE adds acacia, sweet flag, iris, cardamom, anise, gentian, parsley, rhubarb, and ginger. It was practically a deconstructed Negroni.

In Galen's time, mithridate contained 41 ingredients and theriac had 55, but later physicians kept adding to the recipe. (Jägermeister boasts 56 herbal ingredients, and Chartreuse has 130.) The rarer and more exotic the ingredients were to customers, the higher the price that apothecaries (compounding herbalists in an occupation distinct from physicians by the Middle Ages) could charge for the medicine. A cure-all from the 1500s contained 250 ingredients, including pearls, red coral, and emeralds, plus theriac and mithridate as subingredients. A theriac recipe from the 1600s includes most of these former ingredients plus licorice, horehound, bay laurel, rose, lavender, juniper, and clove. This is all starting to sound delicious, up to a point. Newly trendy ingredients around this time included powdered mummy thrown into the mix.

In the attempt to establish trust in these medicines, apothecaries packaged them in branded and sometimes exquisitely decorated jars. Theriacs would be compounded in large quantities in grand public ceremonies by apothecary associations, acting as both advertisement for the product and transparency of the process—after all, the end medicine was probably just a sticky glob of crumbs and not easily verifiable by the consumer as authentic or not. The public preparation ceremony was particularly popular in Italy, and "Venetian treacle" became a known "brand" of theriac, like the Kleenex of its day.

There was good reason for the public to be suspicious of off-brand mithridate. Apothecaries did not have a reputation for being super-trustworthy. Sometimes their theriacs were just a mixture of all the spoiled and leftover medicines in the pharmacist's shop mixed together. To reduce the perception of deception and incompetence, unions of apothecaries established official formularies of approved medicines within a jurisdiction and hired inspectors to ensure compliance. These books of official drug preparations are called "pharmacopoeias," and the first one is believed to be from Florence in 1498. The first *London Pharmacopoeia* was published in 1618.

Theriacs were still in use in the mid-1700s, but their days were numbered. English physician William Heberden (1710–1801) studied the history of theriacs, and in 1745 published an influential essay called "Antitheriaka." He referred to the "injudicousness, the ostentation and wantoness of this heap of drugs," not because the ingredients were ineffective, but in part because they contained unnecessary components that may negatively interact with each other. He called for mithridates and theriacs to be removed from the *London Pharmacopoeia*, and they were after 1746, though they remained in other countries' official pharmacopoeias into the late 1800s.

The legacy of theriac and mithridate is found in some of the complex, supposedly medicinal herbal elixirs of Europe dating to the 1600s, as well as in the cure-all "patent medicines" sold by untrustworthy "doctors" of the eighteenth and nineteenth centuries in Europe and America. A subset of those cure-all medicines became what we now call "bitters," the defining component of the original cocktail.

SNAKEBITE

8 ounces (230 ml) hard cider

8 ounces (230 ml) lager beer

Pour the cider into a pint glass, then top with beer.

GUINNESS IS GOOD FOR YOU

Over the centuries in beer-drinking regions, the beverage was considered a healthy and family-friendly libation for men, women, and children at all hours of the day and evening. It was a safe alternative to water in days before proper sanitation, and even afterward became thought of as generally nutritious and specifically recommended in certain conditions.

Guinness was established in 1759, but the famous Irish stout's first brand advertisement in a national newspaper came quite a bit later, in 1929. It reads, "This is the first advertisement ever issued in a national paper to advertise Guinness." Along with text describing its then 150-year history and a few superlatives, there are sections titled:

ITS HEALTH-GIVING VALUE

Guinness builds strong muscles. It feeds exhausted nerves. It enriches the blood. Doctors affirm that Guinness is a valuable restorative after Influenza and other weakening illnesses. Guinness is a valuable natural aid in cases of insomnia.

ITS NOURISHING PROPERTIES

Guinness is one of the most nourishing beverages, richer in carbo-hydrates than a glass of milk. That is one reason why it is so good when people are tired or exhausted.

GUINNESS
IS GOOD FOR YOU

Other ads followed with slogans including "A Guinness a Day" and "Guinness for Strength." In the late 1800s and early 1900s, Guinness made "Nourishing Export Stout," also known as "Invalid Stout," that was bottle conditioned, meaning carbonated by adding a touch of sugar for yeasts to eat and release carbon dioxide inside the bottle. Many other beer brands also made extra-nutritious invalid stouts probably inspired by Guinness, along with oatmeal stouts and milk stouts for the same conditions. One ad from the early 1900s in Toronto advertises "Invalid Stout for the Mother," another depicts an old man drinking a glass of it and declares, "Makes You Feel Like a Boy Again," and a third states, "Everyone finds it light, wholesome and enjoyable—a safe drink even for a dyspeptic. Ask for Invalid Stout, the most suitable liquid food to choose for your home use."

The (regular) Guinness was prescribed by doctors to postoperative patients, pregnant women, and women who had just given birth, as it was reputed to be particularly high in iron and good for replacing blood. A tradition of giving blood donors in Ireland a pint or glass of Guinness after their donation continued all the way to the end of 2009. A representative for Guinness's parent company, Diageo, said around the time the long tradition ended, "We felt this style and type of donation was not best suited to us now. Guinness has long stopped promoting the product as medicinal and we want to be in full alignment with our voluntary marketing code."

BLACK VELVET

3 ounces (90 ml) champagne
3 ounces (90 ml) Guinness

In a champagne flute, fill to half with
champagne, then top with Guinness.

· · · · ·

Today fairly strict marketing codes are in place in the US and other countries to disallow promoting beverage alcohol as healthy, nutritious, or useful in medicine. Or really, even as fun. European Union television ad policies prohibit linking the consumption of alcohol to enhanced physical performance or to social or sexual success, and advertisements "shall not claim that alcohol has therapeutic qualities or that it is a stimulant, a sedative or a means of resolving personal conflicts."

Beef, Iron and Wine.

Extract of Beef, Citrate of Iron, Sherry Wine.

This Preparation is made from Liebig's Extract Beef, Citrate of Iron, and Pure Sherry Wine. It combines in a pleasant form the valuable nutritious, tonic and stimulating properties of its ingredients. Prompt results will follow its use in cases of sudden exhaustion, arising either from acute or chronic disease, and will prove a valuable restorative for all convalescents. As a tonic it would be indicated in the treatment of impaired nutrition, impoverishment of the blood, and in all the various forms of general debility.

ADULT DOSE.—1 tablespoonful between meals, and when suffering from fatigue or exhaustion. Dose for Children should be reduced according to age. Each half fluid ounce contains the strength 1 oz. of beef, with ½ oz. sherry wine, and 2 gr. citrate of iron, 20 gr. sugar flavored with oil of orange.

PREPARED BY

FRED. J. LEWIS,
PHARMACIST,
Lewis' Block,
Newport, N. H.

QUINTESSENCE

ALCHEMY *and* AQUA VITAE

> By distillation there can be extracted from wine or from
> its dregs, the *vin ardent*, which is also called *eau-de-vie*.
> This is the most subtle part of wine. . . . Certain modern
> authors say that it is golden water, by reason of the sub-
> lime character of its preparation. It prolongs life, and that
> is why it deserves to be called the water of life.
>
> —*Arnald of Villanova*

Beverage alcohol can be really tasty, but to call it "eau-de-vie," meaning "water of life," seems a bit of a dramatic overstatement. But as it turns out, the term for distilled wine was once meant literally: eau-de-vie was considered a physical manifestation of the active energy of the universe, imbued with the ability to cure all human illness. The water of life was a medicine produced by distillation in the practice of alchemy.

Distillation is the process of separating materials by their boiling points. The basic alembic, or pot still, is shaped like a lidded pot, with a straw jammed into the lid running out of the side. Put wine or beer into the pot, turn up the heat just until it starts to boil, hold the temperature there, and collect the steam running out of the straw. Because the ethyl alcohol in the beer or wine has a lower boiling point than the water, it will boil first, and the steam will be mostly alcohol. Cool that steam down back into a liquid (run the straw through a tub of ice or cold water), and the result is mostly liquid alcohol. What's left in the pot is everything with a higher boiling point—water and any solids.

This is how alcohol is freed from water in beer or wine, but distillation can be used for separating other materials. Aristotle (384–322 BCE) wrote about sailors distilling seawater to make fresh water around 300 BCE in *Meteorology*: "Salt water, when it turns into vapor, becomes sweet and the vapor does not form salt water again when it condenses. This I know by experiment. The same thing is true in every case of the kind: wine and all fluids that evaporate and condense back into a liquid state become water. They all are water modified by a certain admixture, the nature of which determines their flavor. But this subject must be considered on another more suitable occasion."

Later in history many other nonalcoholic distillates were known as "waters"—rose water, wormwood water, and so forth. Put rose-infused water into the still, and rose-scented water comes out, with rose petals left behind. Distilling infused waters is much easier than distilling wine or beer, because the separation is between the liquid (water) and solids (rose petals), whereas for wine and beer the separation is between the two liquids alcohol and water. Distilling wine requires a more delicate touch and a deeper understanding of what's happening inside the still.

That distinction, along with improvements in still design, is why distillation was used for more than a thousand years before people figured out the process could be used to turn wine into the water of life. We owe it all to alchemy.

THE THEORY AND PRACTICE
OF ALCHEMY

Metallurgists in pre-Alexandrian Egypt (before 300 BCE) were making gold and silver alloys, called "doubling," as well as gold-plating. Doubling was diluting metals with lesser ones so that the quantity of gold seemed to increase, like thinning out twenty-four-carat gold into ten-carat. Though these procedures made "more" gold and other precious metals, they were considered practical rather than magical.

Historians date Western alchemy to around 100–300 CE in Egypt, during the period when it was a Roman province. Surviving texts from this era describe many of the basic laboratory processes used in alchemy, including fusion, calcination, solution, corrosion, filtration, crystallization, sublimation, and, most important for our discussion, distillation. These are all basic processes or techniques demonstrated in high school science class (minus the distilling, most likely) that involve rehydrating, dehydrating, filtering, and boiling.

Around 300 CE, Zosimos of Panopolis described in Greek many of these alchemical processes practiced by Egyptians. It is through Zosimos that we learn of Maria the Jewess, who may have lived around 200 CE, or who may have been only a literary device. Maria, we are told, was a teacher who created equipment for sublimation (kerotakis) and distillation (tribikos). For the latter, she is credited with inventing an alembic still with three collection vessels. In the cooking world, however, Maria's name lives on in a third supposed invention, the bain-marie water bath (a double boiler) used for gentle heating.

The stills that predate Maria didn't have a lid or the straw parts as described in the beginning of this chapter. They most likely consisted of a bowl placed upside down on top of the pot, or a fleece stretched over the top of it. After boiling the liquid in the pot, the bowl full of steam on top could be tipped over, or the fleece wrung out, and the condensation collected. It would have been inefficient but functional.

What we consider a pot still, or alembic still, today is formed of three parts: the pot on the bottom, the bulbous onion-shaped cap on top, and an arm or tube coming out of the cap that leads to a collection vessel. Later improvements to distillation included cooling the out-flow arm with water, and still later versions coiled this tube through a cold-water bath—the modern condenser. But the still is simply a tool used in the practice of alchemy.

Alchemy is most associated with the transmutation of base metals into gold, but that is just one physical practice of an entire school of thought. The goal of alchemy is to purify and perfect materials—to perfect lead, for example, by transforming it into gold, and to perfect humanity by curing disease. The largely forgotten goal of alchemy was to perfect everything in its own nature.

In order to perfect materials, the alchemist had to separate the impure from the pure using the chemical processes of sublimation, distillation, and so forth, over and over, until the desired matter was isolated. For metals this could mean heating up mineral-rich rock to extract the metal from within it. For plants it could mean isolating the essential oils from the rest of the plant.

Gold was thought by the ancient Greeks and other cultures to be the perfect heavenly metal. It does not rust or tarnish, is nontoxic when consumed, is malleable and easy to work with, and is the color of the all-powerful sun. Gold was also believed to grow in the ground from lesser materials, incubating in the warm earth like an egg in a nest. It would evolve form from one metal to the next, up through silver, and then finally reach its perfect state as gold.

Alchemists therefore concluded that to make gold from lesser materials, they would only need to figure out how to speed up the natural process that was taking place underground. The transformation of one material into another might be achieved by breaking it down into its simplest building blocks and then reassembling it, like taking apart a Lego pirate ship and reforming it into the shape of a fire truck.

This concept of being able to reduce and rebuild something is based on Aristotle's theories of *matter* and *form*—that there is only one ultimate matter in the universe that can take many different forms. Copper and gold were the same matter in different forms; so were a rock and a house built of stone. To break a metal down into its base matter, an alchemist could add a corrosive acid like vinegar or urine to it. Then the corroded metal could be heated up (perhaps in a still) to imitate the earth's warmth, in the process of transforming that matter into gold.

Obviously this transmutation was not effective no matter how much urine you added, and the reason was thought to be that the process was missing a piece: a touch of the universal spirit that would give the matter the *direction* of the form to take. The universal spirit was sort of like the assembly instructions for the Lego kit, the blueprint for how matter should take a form. It was the "active essence" of the universe, the spirit or energy present in all things. This essence was known as "the fifth element" (in addition to earth, air, fire, and water), also known as "the quint essence" or "the quintessence."

Later alchemists called a physical form of the quintessence "the philosopher's stone." This mythological substance (it was often believed to be a red powder rather than an actual stone) could be added to base materials to transform them into perfect ones or make more gold from a tiny piece of it. In chemistry terms, the philosopher's stone is a catalyst. It speeds up a reaction.

So all an alchemist had to do (in theory, anyway) to make endless gold or medicine was to make the philosopher's stone, and this was thought to be achievable through a number of complex alchemical processes. One subset of instructions on making the philosopher's stone, from 1725, specified:

> Purge the mercury with salt and with ordinary salad vinegar, to sublime it with vitriol and salt-petre, to dissolve it in aquafortis, to sublime it again, to calcine it and fix it, to put away part of it in salad oil, to distill this liquor for the purpose of separating the spiritual water, air, and fire, to fix the mercurial body in the spiritual water or to distill the spirit of liquid mercury found in it, to putrefy all, and then to raise and exalt the spirit with non-odorous white sulphur—that is to say, sal-ammoniac—to dissolve the sal-ammoniac in the spirit of liquid mercury which when distilled becomes the liquor known as the Vinegar of the Sages, to make it pass from gold to antimony three times and afterwards to

reduce it by heat, lastly to steep this warm gold in very harsh vinegar and allow it to putrefy. On the surface of the vinegar it will raise itself in the form of fiery earth of the colour of oriental pearls. This is the first operation in the grand work.

If the alchemist did not complete the operations just right, the philosopher's stone wouldn't work. Spoiler: nobody ever isolated the quintessence in stone form, but there's a chance you're sipping some of the active essence of the universe on ice right now.

GOLD RUSH

2 ounces (60 ml) bourbon

1 ounce (30 ml) honey syrup (equal parts honey and water)

1 ounce (30 ml) lemon juice

Add all ingredients to an ice-filled shaker.
Shake and strain into an Old-Fashioned glass
over new ice. Garnish with a lemon twist.

ALCHEMY IN CHINA AND INDIA

The Chinese alchemist Liu An wrote circa 122 BCE that "gold grows in the earth by a slow process and is evolved from the immaterial principle underlying the universe, passing from one form to another up to silver, and then from silver to gold."

This is strikingly similar to Greek beliefs, though it's not clear if Chinese and Greek alchemy derived one from another or shared a common source. For now, historians consider them to be parallel practices.

Wearing gold and eating and drinking from gold plates and cups, and even eating gold itself, were thought to impart some of its special properties—a state of everlasting perfection. Chinese alchemists were as interested in making gold as were their Western counterparts, but with a different goal: to prolong human life or even to render one immortal, via an elixir.

In the text of *Kinship of the Three* from the second century CE (via *The Chemical Choir* by P. G. Maxwell-Stuart) is written,

> Even if the herb chü-sheng can make one live longer,
> Why not try putting the Elixir into the mouth?
> Gold by nature does not rot or decay;
> Therefore it is of all things most precious.
> When the [alchemist] includes it in his diet
> The duration of his life becomes everlasting

This mythical elixir could be made from alchemical gold (processed through the tools of alchemy into a medicinal form), or other materials. The elixir was a tool for transformation, just like the philosopher's stone but for medicine. Other life-extending elixirs were prepared with mercury, sulfur, and arsenic—all common materials in Western alchemy as well. But rather than achieving eternal life, many Chinese emperors are suspected of having died from elixir poisoning.

India had contact with China over the centuries, and also with the

Greeks, as Alexander the Great invaded the country in 325 BCE, but again it is not clear which theories of Indian alchemy were native and which were imported. In India there was less emphasis on immortality, but alchemy was still focused on the transmutation of metals, medicinal elixirs both metal and botanical, and prolonging life. Particular attention was paid to mercury and mineral elixirs to give superpowers, including the ability to fly and to topple buildings.

Recent archaeological evidence indicates both China and India were distilling alcohol earlier than in the West, where it did not happen in any significant way until after 1000 CE. Historians believe that there could have been distillation of rice, palm tree sap, sugarcane, or other materials dating to 150 BCE to 350 CE or even earlier in India. Pottery fragments have been found in modern Pakistan that could be reassembled into a still that closely resembles village stills recently in use. Additionally, terms in literature refer to an "elephant head" that is roughly the shape of the Indian-style still. In China, text references in the 800s CE seem to imply that wine was being distilled. But exactly how Eastern distillation might have fit in with alchemy and medicine is uncertain at present.

THE ISLAMIC GOLDEN AGE

In the West, Greek and Roman alchemy continued under Islamic rule. After the fall of the Western Roman Empire in 476 CE and before the High Middle Ages in Europe beginning around 1100, the center of alchemy shifted east. The Islamic Golden Age (750–1258 CE) was a five-hundred-year era beginning shortly after the founding of Baghdad in modern-day Iraq and lasting until the destruction of that city by the Mongols. United under Islam (Muhammad died in 632), Arab rulers controlled lands including Egypt, Syria, Persia (Iran), parts of northern Africa, and southern Spain.

The Islamic Golden Age was characterized by Baghdad's House of Wisdom, an intellectual center in which scholars, directed by the ruling Abbasid caliphate, attempted to translate every known book into Arabic. This included the works of the Greeks and Romans to their west and of the Persians, Chinese, and Indians to the east.

After the end of this era at the edges of the Islamic empire, these works were translated again, this time from Arabic into Latin. For this reason, the Islamic Golden Age was called "an intellectual bridge" between the Greeks and Romans of antiquity and the later Middle Ages in Europe, but that ignores the significant contributions made by the Arabs, including great achievements in algebra, algorithms, geometry, and trigonometry; astronomy, including highly accurate star charts; mechanics, including water-powered clocks, fountains, and automata; farming practices, including crop rotation techniques, grafting, fertilizers, and pest control; optics and vision; minerology; and pharmacology.

Scholar al-Kindi (801–873) called out alchemy as a get-rich scheme, but he did make use of the still. In his book *The Alchemy of Perfume and Distillation* that contains more than one hundred recipes for perfumes, the fragrant ingredients like rosemary and roses were mostly distilled in water but sometimes in vinegar. He includes this line about one preparation: "In this way one can distill wine using a water-bath, and it comes out the same color as rose-water."

Likely al-Kindi boiled all the wine in the still and the result was clear and infused with the aroma of whatever botanicals were put into it. It would not have been higher-proof alcohol if he didn't make a separation between the first part of the distillate (with mostly just alcohol) and the second (mostly water). So despite distilling wine, there doesn't seem to be an indication that al-Kindi or others in this era noticed anything particularly special about the results. (Other historians believe that alcoholic beverage distillation should in fact be credited to the distillers of this era.)

That they were using wine at all raises a question about the consumption of alcohol under Islamic rule. At least near the beginning of the Islamic Golden Age, practicing Muslims drank wine and discussed it openly. The Quran prohibits alcohol consumption, but there was some early debate as to whether the prohibition was against alcohol altogether, just against grape or date wine, or against reaching the state of drunkenness but not necessarily drinking.

One of the most important Arabic poets from this era was Abu Nuwas (756–814), who wrote not only about drinking to excess but also about dalliances with men, women, and boys in the Greek tradition. He was thrown in prison a lot. He appeared as a character in *The Thousand and One Nights* (a compilation first referenced after 800) and himself wrote such verses about wine as the one below (from Alex Rowell's *Vintage Humour*):

> Shall I spurn it, when God Himself hasn't
>   And our own caliph shows it veneration?
> Superlative wine, radiant and bright
>   Rivalling the very sun's scintillation
> While we may not know heaven in this life
>   Still we have paradise's libation.

The dominant school of medical thought during this time was still that of Hippocrates and Galen and the four humors, but recall that the Greeks used a lot of wine in their treatments. So physicians during the Islamic Golden Age wrote about wine in medicine cautiously. A character in *The Thousand and One Nights* writes of wine that it is both sinful and useful, and

> it disperseth stone and gravel from the kidneys and strengtheneth the viscera and banisheth care, and moveth to generosity and preserveth health and digestion; it conserveth the body, expelleth disease from the joints, purifieth the frame of corrupt humours, engendereth cheerfulness, gladdeneth the heart of man and keepeth up the natural heat: it contracteth the bladder, enforceth the liver and removeth obstructions, reddeneth the cheeks, cleareth away maggots from the brain and deferreth grey hairs. In short, had not Allah (to whom be honour and glory!) forbidden it, there were not on the face of the earth aught fit to stand in its stead.

In other words, it would be incredibly useful if it weren't forbidden. Moses Maimonides (1135–1204), a Jewish physician and philosopher living in the Islamic societies of Spain and Egypt echoed the sentiment: "It is well known among physicians that the best of the nourishing foods is the one that the Moslem religion forbids, i.e., wine." He did recommend it used in a poultice applied against the bite of a mad dog, cooked with asparagus to use against spider bites, or with added pulverized emeralds, but, he noted, "if wine is forbidden to a person, [medicine] should be taken in a decoction of anise."

The alchemist Jabir ibn Hayyan (721–815) was credited with hundreds of texts, though many were written by other authors in his name, and there is a fair chance Jabir wasn't a real person but more of a name of a scientific movement. To Galen's concept of a balance between the four humors of blood, yellow bile, black bile, and phlegm, Jabir added the concept of *natures* of metals (cold, hot, dry, moist). Like rebalancing the four humors to create a healthy person, the alchemist could rebalance the four natures of metals to create the perfect metal, and the "medicine" with which to do this was called "the elixir." Much like Chinese alchemists, the Jabirian writers seemed less concerned with the creation of gold for wealth than using alchemy in the practice of medicine.

Other influential scientists of the Islamic Golden Age include al-Razi and Ibn Sina. The Persian physician al-Razi (864–925) published a book called *Doubts about Galen* in which his practical experimentation cast aspersions on the leading medical theory of the time. In alchemy, his book *The Book of the Secret of Secrets* described laboratory equipment and distillation in ways that showed he had practical experience (as opposed to Jabir's theoretical alchemy), and he wrote about mineral-based drugs in his medicinal texts.

Ibn Sina (later Latinized to Avicenna) (980–1037) was a hugely influential physician whose works continued to be published and studied in medical schools in Europe as late as 1700. Ibn Sina studied mental illness, previously thought to be an act of God and thus untreatable. He also used steam distillation to produce essential oils for aromatherapy.

In Ibn Sina's *The Canon of Medicine*, he repeats and adds to Hippocratic and Galenic medical theory. He recommends distilling water as the best treatment to make it healthy. And he advocates wine for both medicinal and nutritious qualities: "Wine is the best facilitator for food penetration to all parts of the body. It stops the formation of phlegm and breaks it down, and gets yellow bile out in the urine. It slips out black bile easily and antagonizes its effect; it loosens every condensed material without excessive abnormal heating."

He recommended against drunkenness but saw alcohol's value as an anesthetic for "one who requires heavy drunkenness in order to undergo a painful treatment of an organ." He comments on how to use it as an emetic in a relatable piece of advice: "A person trying to vomit using a little alcoholic drink should drink more if it does not work with only a little." Noted.

Some of Ibn Sina's recipes in *The Canon of Medicine* show up in a famous thirteenth-century Syrian cookbook *Scents and Flavors*. The chapter on beverages includes starchy fermented soups that are both food and drink, though probably not intoxicating. Some recipes had fermented fruit beer added to them as an ingredient.

Other beverages in *Scents and Flavors* are fruit based with added perfumes or medicinal ingredients, and among the beverages is a recipe titled "A Cure for Nausea" made with lemon, pomegranate, and sour grape juices with rose water, tamarind, wine vinegar, quince, mint, spices, and agarwood (a wood used as incense).

The final chapter in the book includes a section on distillation and perfumes—the distillates were all water based rather than wine based, and included waters of rose, agarwood, sandalwood, carnation, cinnamon, and a basil-and-cucumber combination. These waters were used to perfume food, hands, and clothing, and made into breath mints.

Though the Arabs of the Islamic Golden Age don't seem to have spent much time distilling alcohol, the word "alcohol" stems from the Arabic "kohl"—antimony sulfide used for eyeliner. Adding the prefix "al " to "kohl" gives us "alcohol," but not in its current meaning yet. Alcohol first referred to this eye powder, then later to "a substance reduced by pulverization, distillation, or sublimation."

According to Seth Rasmussen's *The Quest for Aqua Vitae*, in the sixteenth century distilled wines were called "alcool vini," meaning "the alcohol of wine" or "the subtle part of wine." Then the "vini" was dropped, and "alcohol" came to mean "the subtlety of liquid spirits" or "a distilled spirit."

AQUA VITAE

While the Islamic Golden Age was waning to the east after 1000, the Roman Catholic Church replaced the Roman Empire as the dominant organizational force in Europe. In parts of southern Italy and Spain that had been ruled by the Muslim Arabs, scholars worked to translate the old Greek knowledge from Arabic (and often the original Greek if available) into Latin. Christian scientists read the alchemical texts and merged these ideas with their current religious understandings.

Leading Christian alchemical and medical writers of the early 1200s included Dominican Albert the Great (1200–1280), his pupil Thomas Aquinas (1225–1274), and Franciscan Roger Bacon (1220–1292). In the 1300s, writers included Catalonian physician Arnald of Villanova (c. 1240–1311), Franciscan John of Rupescissa (c. 1310–1360s), and the polymath Ramon Llull (c. 1232–1315), though Llull in particular was posthumously credited with works he did not author.

These scholars developed new concepts about the composition of quintessence as well as planted the seeds for medical alchemy as their beliefs evolved over these centuries. Lead was gold that suffered from leprosy, some writers proposed, and it could be cured with the philosopher's stone. So too could people be cured through the application of some sort of alchemical medicine.

The Schola Medica Salernitana, known as the earliest Western medical school, was founded in the ninth or tenth century in Salerno, in southern Italy, and had a close connection with a local Benedictine monastery and its library. It was less of a university as we define it today and more a center of learning or a community of masters and pupils. There, Constantine the African (c. 1020–1087), along with other scholars, translated into Latin Arabic manuscripts containing Greek medical theory. From there, the Greek knowledge contained in the works spread into Europe.

The school became famous particularly into the 1200s for modernizing the practice of surgery and for the written works it produced. These included a physician's reference book with a code of conduct toward patients, and the works of the twelfth-century physician Trota of Salerno, an author among others of a collection known as the *Trotula*, which dealt with women's medical issues. The *Trotula* contained many recipes that used herbs infused into (undistilled) wine. It also contained this advice: "For removing redness from the face, we put on leeches of various colors, which are in reeds, but first we wash with wine the place to which they ought to adhere; they are usually placed around the nose and ears on both sides."

Women were limited in medical careers but practiced as midwives at childbirth, and sometimes as apothecaries and barber-surgeons, but over and over when official guilds in these professions formed, women were denied entry into them. Since guilds held monopolies on certification to treat patients, women were shut out of medicinal practice. Some managed to share their knowledge of the treatment of "women's issues" in book form if not in person. Like the *Trotula*, the 1609 book first published in French *Several Observations on Sterility, Miscarriage, Fertility, Childbirth and Illnesses of Women and Newborn Infants*, by the midwife Louise Bourgeois, became a definitive text on medical matters in childbirth.

But back at Salerno we (finally!) find physicians distilling wine into eau-de-vie, and commenting on its unique qualities. Magister Salernus (who probably died in 1167) described the process: "Place in the cucurbita one pound (white or) red wine, one pound powdered salt, four ounces native sulphur, four ounces of tartar (from wine). The liquid distilling is collected. A cloth saturated with this liquid will maintain a flame without suffering injury."

It is not clear whether this technological advance was a local discovery or learned from Arabic texts in translation. The added salts in the above instructions would help retain some of the water in the wine in the pot of the still, while allowing the alcohol vapor to transfer. However that trick was stumbled on, it was a clever hack for an inefficient still in a time without awareness of the different boiling points of alcohol and water. Regardless, the result was a clear liquid that looked like water but came from wine, a liquid that looked like water but could be lit on fire. It was a big deal.

This liquid was called "aqua ardens" (fire or burning water) or "aqua flamens" (flaming water). This terminology survives in "aguardientes," the Spanish name for firewater used to describe spirits particularly in Latin and South America.

As distilling technology improved, distilled wine with a higher alcohol content could be produced, especially by repeated distillations of the resulting spirits. At high proofs, rather than "burning water," distillates were called "the water of life" (aqua vitae). This term also survives today in the forms of "aquavit," "eau-de-vie" (in French), "whiskey" (from the Scottish Gaelic "uisge beatha"), and probably "vodka" (Slavic for "little water").

PRESBYTERIAN

2 ounces (60 ml) blended scotch whiskey

2 ounces (60 ml) ginger ale

2 ounces (60 ml) soda water

2 dashes Angostura bitters

Add all ingredients to an ice-filled highball
glass and garnish with a lemon twist.

· · · · ·

Other surviving texts from the thirteenth century describe the distillation process and refer to alcohol as something to drink specifically for medicine. Italian Taddeo Alderotti (c. 1210–1295) wrote around 1280 of using wine distilled four times for medicine and recommended it to cleanse wounds, to cure a toothache, to improve sight, and to treat deafness, epilepsy, and melancholy. He also made improvements to still design and made a ten-times-distilled wine (estimated to be at least 90 percent pure alcohol) he called "perfectissima." He called aqua vitae "of inestimable glory, the mother and mistress of all medicine."

Spanish-born physician and alchemist Arnald of Villanova, often spelled Arnaud de Ville-Neuve (and in many other ways), was a celebrity doctor of his day, treating popes and kings, and penning many tracts, including *Liber de Vinis* (*Book on Wine*), which was a bestseller about wine-based medicine for centuries. He taught medicine at the University of Montpellier in France, another important early medical school. Some credit him with introducing the still to France from Salerno, while others credit him as the creator of the coiled shape of the still's condenser, though he was given posthumous credit for a lot of actions and writings that probably weren't his.

Arnald probably wrote that distilled wine was "aqua vini" (water of wine) but that some called it "golden water" or "aqua vitae." He wrote, "The name is remarkably suitable, since it really is a water of immortality. It prolongs life, clears away ill-humours, revives the heart, and maintains youth."

Beyond its invigorating powers, Arnald showed that he understood distilled wine as medicine itself, noting its utility for washing wounds. He also commented on its extractive capabilities, that it "takes on all tastes, smells and other properties," and that these extractions were useful in medicines. He recommended ginger and cinnamon bark distilled in wine to cure paralysis of the limbs and also to give women a "white, subtle and pleasant complexion."

Modern-day scientists have shown that ethyl alcohol, or ethanol, the kind we like to drink, is a compound with a polar end that dissolves hydrophilic compounds, like sugar and salt, just as water does, and a nonpolar end that dissolves hydrophobic compounds, like oils and fats, which do not mix with water. Alcohol is close to a universal solvent and thus is the most common menstruum used in herbal medicine to extract the active compounds, like resins and essential oils, from plants.

We can see this in absinthe's "louche effect" wherein it turns cloudy when water is added. Absinthe in the bottle is translucent, as the oils from wormwood and anise are bound to the ethanol molecule, but when water is added to absinthe, the oils come out of the solution (creating a "spontaneous emulsion"), and it turns a milky color. Some particularly oil-rich gins louche with added water as well.

SPIRIT AS QUINTESSENCE

The alchemists threw everything into the still. Wine, milk, eggs, urine, blood, cheese, hair, plants, animals, solids, liquids. The goal, other than "let's find out what happens," was to extract quintessences. John of Rupescissa wrote in *A Study of the Fifth Essence of Everything* (c. 1351) that if you extracted the quintessence of something via distillation, and then applied that quintessence to new matter, you could perfect it. This should, in theory, work for both metals (perfecting them into gold) and medicine (perfecting a person into health).

Some scholars thought that the aqua vitae was the quintessence itself, but experience showed that it did not grant universal life or endless gold, so perhaps it was an impure form of the quintessence with some earthly qualities still clinging to it. There was more than one way to distill a soul, however: as the quintessence was a *universal* energy giving the direction of form to all matter, John wrote that it could be extracted from anything, not just wine.

So if you distilled blood or eggs or milk correctly and enough times, you could get the quintessence out of them. Blood was the source of life, so its extracted quintessence should be the source of eternal youth. Arnald may also have written about the preparation of blood in several forms, one of which was the "distilled fire of blood" to be given to a patient on their deathbed.

Or the alchemist could take a shortcut and use the quintessence of wine to extract the quintessence of botanicals. The infused alcohol would smell and taste like the cinnamon or wormwood or juniper put into it and hold on to its medicinal powers. John of Rupescissa thought you could further improve aqua vitae by quenching hot gold leaf into it and making "potable gold," much like the Chinese elixir.

The combination of the perfect medicine and the perfect metal proved a long-lasting one—you can still buy gold-enhanced liqueurs, after all. Arnald of Villanova was said to have healed a pope with gold in alcohol around 1300. Paracelsus (whom we'll meet soon) recommended gold-enhanced medicinal spirits in the early 1500s. Danziger Goldwasser ("gold water of Gdansk" in Poland) liqueur dates to 1606 according to the brand's website, and whether it was originally intended as medicine is not mentioned, though it stands to reason that it would have been.

The cinnamon-anise-flavored herbal liqueur with gold flakes floating in the bottle was created by Dutchman (and alchemist according to one source) Ambrosien Vermöllen, and it supposedly became a hit with royalty, including Tsar Peter the Great (1672–1725). Other cinnamon-flavored gold-flake liqueurs include Goldschläger and the liqueur in the collector's item Bols "ballerina bottle," which includes a music box in the base of the bottle.

While many of the oldest medicinal liqueurs found their way into modern cocktails, gold-flake enhanced ones were more of a novelty. Probably the most famous drink, repeated in many early cocktail books, including Harry Johnson's *New and Improved Bartender's*

Manual (1882), *Modern American Drinks* (1895), and *The Savoy Cocktail Book* (1930) is the Golden Slipper. To make it (and best of luck to you if you do), pour into a small liqueur glass an ounce of Yellow Chartreuse, then an egg yolk, then float an ounce of Goldwasser on the surface. Enjoy!

THE *SMALL BOOK OF DISTILLATION*

The printing press was invented in Germany by Johannes Gutenberg around 1440. Some of the most popular books first printed, besides historical and religious texts, were how-to books that included multidisciplinary information on metallurgy, medicine, dyeing, and other technical matters. Books were addressed to "alchemists, barbers, apothecaries, and households" or to "rich and poor, learned and unlearned." Hieronymus Brunschwig (c. 1450–c. 1512) notes that his book was "for the common people that dwell far from medicines and physicians and for them that be not able to pay for costly medicines."

Surgeon and apothecary Brunschwig (who also gave us the first medical description of gunshot wounds) wrote the 1500 book *Liber de arte distillandi de simplicibus* (often called the *Small Book of Distillation*), considered the first printed manual exclusively on distillation. It was not a book on beverage alcohol but specifically for the distillation of "medicinal waters," and aqua vitae was one water out of many described.

Brunschwig was influenced by John of Rupescissa's writings on distilling different things to isolate the quintessence within them and describes the purpose of distilling as "purifying the gross from the

subtle and the subtle from the gross . . . with the intent that the cor-
ruptible shall be made incorruptible . . . and the subtle spirit be made
more subtle so that it can better pierce and pass through the body [and
be conveyed to where it is] most needful of health and comfort."

Brunschwig included the alchemical information with the practical. Part of the book was about how to build a still and to distill with
different techniques, while the rest contained specific recipes for distilling various herbs and their medicinal properties. A cross-listing
described which distilled herb water cured which afflictions. In his
writings, he didn't refer to individual distillates as *the* quintessence
but as liquids that retained the qualities of the botanicals distilled
into them—hot or cold and wet or dry. Those qualities could then be
transferred to the patient. Distilling botanicals would also preserve
them in liquid form. Distilling could render "the fragile indestructible" and transform plants into something "like a heavenly thing."

Most of these medicines were distilled in water, much like rose
water from the Islamic Golden Age, rather than infused in wine or
aqua vitae and redistilled like gin. However, when the distillates
were to be made from dry spices rather than fresh herbs, they first
were infused into wine or aqua vitae so that the alcohol extracted
their essential oils.

In recent years, "distilled nonalcoholic spirits," including those
from the Seedlip brand, have come to market as replacements for
spirits like gin in nonalcoholic cocktails. Many of these products are
made like the distillates in Brunschwig's book: botanicals are first
infused into alcohol to extract their flavoring components, then redistilled with water. The goal in this case is to separate out the alcohol while leaving the water in the final product.

GARDEN COOLER

2 ounces (60 ml) Seedlip Garden

1 ounce (30 ml) lime juice

1 ounce (30 ml) simple syrup (equal parts
sugar and water, by volume)

Mix ingredients and pour over
ice in an Old-Fashioned glass.
Garnish with a lime wheel.

• • • • •

Probably the most powerful medicine in the *Small Book* was distilled wine itself. Brunschwig wrote, "Aqua vitae is commonly called the mistress of all medicines. It eases the diseases coming of cold, it comforts the heart, it heals all old and new sores on the head. It causes a good color in a person. It heals baldness and causes the hair well to grow, and kills lice and fleas. It cures lethargy. Cotton wet in the same and a little wrung out again and so put in the ears at night before going to bed . . . is of good against deafness." Additionally, according to Brunschwig, it relieves tooth pain; promotes good digestion and appetite; stops belching; eases jaundice, gout, dropsy, and swollen breasts; is an antidote to poisoned food; and heals tertian and quartan fevers, as well as mad-dog bites.

Although Brunschwig noted that his book was "for the common people that dwell far from medicines and physicians," later books that included recipes for distilled medicines were published specifically for European gentlewomen who were the head of large households. In addition to brewing beer for the family and staff, the woman of the house might provide medicines for the local community that lacked a doctor, as a benevolent act.

In 1561 the book *The Secrets of Lady Isabella Cortese* was published by the eponymous alchemist. It contained information on making gold and creating a universal medicine but also recipes for soaps and toothpaste (made from white wine) and a recipe to "straighten out the member" consisting of quail testicles, large-winged ants, amber, musk, and oil made from elder and tree resin.

Many alchemy-infused household books written by or for women are discussed in *The Chemistry of Alchemy*. These include *The Margaret Manuscript* (probably written for and not by Lady Margaret Clifford, Countess of Cumberland, around 1600); *The Queen's Closet Opened* (1655), by W. M.; and *Benevolent and Easy Chemistry* (1666), by Marie Meurdrac.

PARACELSUS

Philippus Aureolus Theophrastus Bombastus von Hohenheim (1493–1541) was born in Switzerland and studied metals and mining as a young man. He took the name Paracelsus and became a traveling physician and scholar throughout Europe, writing, "The universities do not teach all things, so a doctor must seek out old wives, gypsies, sorcerers, wandering tribes, old robbers, and such outlaws and take lessons from them." Paracelsus wrote many books, though few were published while he was still alive.

He was described as a man who could be found "fasting in the morning, drunk in the evening, presenting exactly every idea in the order in which it came to his mind"; as an "atheist pig"; as a "jackass" who was "paranoid, repetitive, vain, and self-aggrandizing"; and also as a "rude, circuitous obscurantist . . . violently destructive, only rarely critically constructive and never original, if ever right." The author of *The Devil's Doctor*, Philip Ball, wrote of Paracelsus, "His writings abound with preposterous vanity, they are often opaque if not downright incoherent, they are rambling and strange, they seem more closely aligned to a world of fairy tales and superstition than science and reason." Even his name was a boast: it means above or beyond Celsus—a famous Roman medical writer from the first century CE. Paracelsus was not very well-liked nor well-respected even in retrospect, and yet he made a big impact on medicine.

SALTY DOG

2 ounces (60 ml) gin or vodka
4 ounces (120 ml) grapefruit juice

Salt the rim of a highball glass by moistening it
with citrus juice then rolling the outer edge in salt
on a plate. Add ice and liquid ingredients and
garnish with a grapefruit peel or wedge.

• • • • •

Paracelsus was a medical alchemist rather than a profiteering one. He wrote, "Many have said of Alchemy, that it is for the making of gold and silver. For me such is not the aim, but to consider only what virtue and power may lie in medicines." Using the tools and metal and mineral ingredients of alchemy, he helped popularize medical chemistry (iatrochemistry) as a distinct discipline.

He advocated for intervening minimally in treatment of injuries and illnesses, keeping wounds clean, and calling for less invasive treatments that allowed nature to take its course. He wrote in later works that surgery "consists in protecting Nature from suffering and accident from without, that she may proceed unchecked in her operations." Further, "if you prevent infection, Nature will heal the wound all by herself."

Modern authors speculate that Paracelsus used small portions of less harmful medicines on patients than other doctors of the time. He argued that "the dose makes the poison," or as he actually put it, "In all things there is a poison, and there is nothing without a poison. It depends only upon the dose whether a poison is poison or not."

Galen believed that imbalance between the four humors created disease, so to cure a disease meant rebalancing the humors. Paracelsus saw things differently and is said to have publicly burned Galen's books in front of a university. He thought that external agents rather than internal fluids acted on the body and disrupted its normal function. Paracelsian medicine became associated with alchemically prepared cures for disease, as opposed to Galenic cures that involved harsh laxatives, bleeding, trepanning the skull, amputation, and other forms of purging.

It seems his bad attitude was tolerated because his form of medicine was actually fairly effective. To cure illness, Paracelsus was a fan of alchemically prepared quintessences, particularly from minerals and metals using distillation, filtration, sublimation, and so forth to purify and concentrate them and to make them more useful. They were distilled, and the resultant diluted mineral acids, such as hydro-chloric and nitric acid, were used in treatments. For example, he recommended the highly dangerous "vitriol" (sulfuric acid) for epi-lepsy, gout, and other diseases, but his preparations for it diluted or neutralized it. Sulfuric acid was mixed with rosemary oil in one preparation, and in another it was mixed with wine and distilled.

Paracelsus also treated syphilis, a disease not known at the time of Galen. In a work with a not-so-subtle title, *Essay on the French Diseases: About Imposters*, he rallied against doctors who prescribed guaiac (boiled wood shavings) for the disease. He prescribed mer-cury, which had been used to treat leprosy, thought to be a related skin disease because of its external symptoms. Mercury was used as a treatment for syphilis all the way through 1910, when Paul Ehrlich developed the arsenic-based Salvarsan. More on that later.

Galenic medicine concentrated on the application of physical sub-stances (herbal medicine) and procedures (bleeding and purging) to rebalance the humors that are responsible for diseases, but Paracel-sus gave spiritual importance to the quintessences used to cure pa-tients. One rather ridiculous abstract cure was the weapons salve, or "powder of sympathy." Possibly inspired by a folk cure, the weapons salve involved treating the weapon that caused a wound rather than the actual wound. The only thing effective about it was not med-dling with the patient and letting the patient's wound heal on its own. Surprisingly, Paracelsus was influential enough that the weapons salve caught on for a while during the 1600s.

He also believed in the homunculus, an alchemically produced human being grown from putrefied semen kept in a bottle and fed human blood. Other not-so-great cures included using mummy powder that should come from "the body of a man who did not die a natural death but rather died an unnatural death with a healthy body and without sickness."

Shortly after his death—of mysterious circumstances, suggested to be cancer from metal poisoning (but rumored to be poisoned wine), the result of a drunken fall down the stairs, or a "scuffle with assassins" at the White Horse Inn, in Salzburg, Bavaria—the students and followers of Paracelsus sorted out his more sane advice from the rest of it and published analyses of his work. The practices of mineral- and metal-based medicine spread for a few hundred years.

A century later in 1651, John French (1616–1657), in his book *The Art of Distillation*, applied Paracelsian logic to distilling. Like Brunschwig's *Small Book*, it was mostly a medicinal text but featuring more sophisticated recipes plus some alchemical magic tricks, including the one "to make powder that by spitting upon shall be inflamed."

Also included are recipes for making aqua vitae out of beer and mead in addition to wine, and alcohol is used in more recipes where it was infused with animal parts, vegetables, minerals, and metals before being redistilled. These ingredients were used for both their practical and their spiritual significance.

French's book shows various ways to distill fragrant plants, such as flowers, noting that infusing them in wine first rather than water will retain more of their odor in the resulting distillate. There is a recipe to extract the quintessence of all vegetables, which consists of an infusion into aqua vitae and a process for separating out the essential oil.

A few highly complex recipes in *The Art of Distillation* are for "compound waters," including "aqua celestis" (heavenly water) that is "a very cordial water, good against faintings and infection." One might think it would do more than that, given that it includes, among other ingredients, cinnamon, cloves, ginger, nutmeg, zedoary, galangal, long pepper, citron pill, spikenard, cardamom, calamus, germander, ground pine, mace, white frankincense, juniper berries, bay berries, motherwort, fennel, anise, sorrel, sage, rosemary, marjoram, mints, pennyroyal, elderflower, rose, rue, endive, aloe, amber, rhubarb, gentian, wormwood, figs, raisins, dates, sweet almonds, sugar, honey, and oriental pearls. These are added to aqua vitae into which hot gold is quenched, left to infuse for twenty-four hours, and distilled.

Other compound waters in the book are medicines against worms, convulsions, dropsy, colic, vertigo, kidney stones, the plague, and more. A section covers distilling animal (including human) products, such as blood, brains ("a most infallible medicine against the falling sickness"), skull ("a kind of panacea"), mummy ("a wonderful preservative against all infections"), milk ("excellent use in hot distempers of the lungs and kidneys"), urine of a healthy boy ("of great virtue in the epilepsy, gout, dropsy, convulsions"), and hair ("sprinkled upon fences and hedges to keep wild and hurtful cattle from coming to do harm in any place, for such is the stink of this liquor that it does frighten them from coming to any place near it"). Nonhuman animals put into the still include parts of calves, foxes, snakes, ants, millipedes, crabs, and tadpoles, plus the dung of doves, cows, and horses.

Paracelsus's writing helped revive alchemy, which had been losing traction, and his attention to the abstract, spiritual side of alchemy and medicine took both in some interesting directions. F. Sherwood Taylor in *A Short History of Science and Scientific Thought* summarized

Paracelsus's contributions: "Paracelsus stirred up the medical faculty by urging in violent language the use of mineral medicines; but in fact more of the medicines he recommended were inefficacious and he did little more than awake the faculty of medicine to the possibility of departing from the practice of such authorities as Galen, Hippocrates, Avicenna [Ibn Sina]."

CORPSE MEDICINE

A late 1500s Chinese herbal text reports of a (likely mythological) practice of mellification in Arabic countries, in which old men sacrifice themselves by eating only honey until they die and are preserved in it to be used as medicine for others later. Herbalist author Li Shizhen (1518–1593) wrote, "Such a one takes no more food or drink, only bathing and eating a little honey, till after a month his excreta are nothing but honey; then death ensues. His compatriots place the body to macerate in a stone coffin full of honey, with an inscription giving the year and month of burial. After a hundred years the seals are removed and the confection so formed used for the treatment of wounds and fractures of the body and limbs—only a small amount taken internally is needed for the cure."

AIRMAIL

2 ounces (60 ml) aged rum

0.75 ounce (20 ml) lime juice

0.75 ounce (20 ml) honey syrup (equal parts honey and water)

1 dash Angostura bitters

2 ounces (60 ml) sparkling wine

Add still ingredients to an ice-filled shaker.
Shake and strain into a large coupe glass and
top with sparkling wine and a mint leaf.

· · · · ·

Even if mollified men did not exist, Li Shizhen mentioned plenty of other human-derived medicines, including hair, tears, earwax, newborn feces, and sweat, for different ailments. But corpse medicine was hardly exclusive to China, and in Europe the practice of drinking mummies in medicine became so popular that good mummies were hard to find. A detailed account of corpse medicine is found in Richard Sugg's *Mummies, Cannibals and Vampires*.

The practice of mummy medicine became known in Europe around the 1100s; gained popularity after 1400, with its heyday in the sixteenth and seventeenth centuries; and was occasionally still practiced until almost 1800. Constantine the African wrote that mumia "is a spice found in the sepulchers of the dead. . . . That is best which is black, ill-smelling, shiny, and massive." An early 1700s herbal described mummy as "a resinous, hardened, black shining surface, of a somewhat acrid and bitterish taste, and of a fragrant smell."

Egyptian mummies were in demand particularly after the 1400s, and the authentic ones were robbed from tombs and sold whole. The next best thing to Egyptian mummies were corpses of travelers who had died in desert sandstorms. Mummy sourcing became a profession, along with mummy reselling. And naturally what followed was mummy counterfeiting.

A trade in mummies formed out of the Middle East, with whole bodies or ground-up parts of them sent off to European apothecaries. When supply ran low, mummy moonshiners popped up to meet demand. They attempted to make fake mummies that were blackened just like the real thing. One account from Egypt described filling bodies of enslaved people or other dead with bitumen (petroleum pitch), wrapping them in cloth, then drying them out in the sun to blacken.

After the 1500s, recently deceased corpses came into the pharmacopeia as well. And the main person responsible was our old pal Paracelsus. Directions for a Paracelsus-style mummy preparation written down by one of his followers specified a man, twenty-four years old, killed by hanging, broke upon a wheel, or stabbed. (In medical history, when a corpse is called for it should always be that of someone young who died violently, as this would ensure that the body was not diseased.) The flesh should be cut into slices or pieces and sprinkled with powder of myrrh and aloes then macerated in wine. Then it was dried out and ready to be used.

John French's *Art of Distillation* (1651) gives a recipe for Elixir of Mummy. Simply infuse mummy "man's flesh hardened" into spirit of wine, filter it, and evaporate the liquid "until that which remains in the bottom be like an oil which is the true elixir of mummy. This elixir is a wonderful preservative against all infections, also very balsamical." Like many medicinal distillation recipes, mummy medicine later found its way into household recipe collections for gentlewomen.

But the entire practice of using mummies in and as medicine might be chalked up to a translation error! Variations of the word "mumia" were used to describe the sticky, black, viscous, semisolid, natural petroleum pitch bitumen, which was recorded for medicinal use by people like Pliny and Galen. Other sticky resins from trees and honey were used both internally taken in wine and externally to seal wounds. Bitumen was also used in the embalming process in Egyptian mumification, and since the substance was challenging to find in nature, people began to harvest mummies to extract the bitumen. Over time people began to confuse mumia bitumen pitch taken from mummies with actual mummified flesh.

Medicinal mummy, often infused into something alcoholic, was recommended for palsy, vertigo, internal bleeding, and gout, but more often was used to treat external injuries like bruises and bleeding from falls. Pliny wrote that bitumen taken with wine cured dysentery, coughs, and shortness of breath. Ibn Sina during the Islamic Golden Age wrote of its use for everything from abscesses, paralysis, and epilepsy to heart palpitations, and as an antidote for poison. In one preparation, it is to be taken with marjoram, thyme, elder, barley, roses, lentils, jujubes, cumin seed, caraway, saffron, cassia, parsley, honey, wine, milk, butter, and oil.

People with epilepsy were prescribed mummy along with endless forms of other human- and animal-based medicine. The condition was usually assumed to be caused by possession by evil spirits, and for some reason drinking blood was the go-to solution. Freshly felled gladiator blood, sometimes sucked straight from the bleeding wound, was the popular cure in ancient Rome. Pliny was compelled to comment on the practice.

> The blood too of gladiators is drunk by epileptics as though it were a draught of life, though we shudder with horror when in the same arena we look at even the beasts doing the same thing. But, by Heaven!, the patients think it most effectual to suck from a man himself warm, living blood, and putting their lips to the wound to drain the very life, although it is not the custom of men to apply their mouths at all to the wounds even of wild beasts. Others seek to secure the leg-marrow and the brain of infants. . . . Artemon treated epilepsy with draughts of water drawn from a spring by night and drunk out of the skull of a man killed but not cremated.

Other cures for epilepsy included various preparations of powdered skull, heart of a wolf, frog's liver, vulture's liver, weasel brain, bear testicles, camel's brain, maggots from a rotting sheep's nose, blood of a cat, urine of a black horse, dried human heart, and human brain.

John French included a recipe for an epilepsy treatment involving the brains of a man who died a violent death, along with his arteries, veins, and nerves. These were to be bruised in a mortar and infused into the spirit of wine for half a year before being distilled. Beyond man's flesh, French's book also included a recipe for "the urine of a young man drinking much wine" allowed to putrefy before being distilled. This was used for gout and other issues.

Blood was used to treat epilepsy, and the distilled quintessence of blood was used to restore health. Arnald of Villanova probably wrote a text recommending it, and centuries later, in 1651, the physician Daniel Border wrote that it restores those at the point of death. Beyond that, distilled blood apparently kept your wine fresh. Border wrote, "If you put a little of it into a hogshead of wine it will purify it, and preserve it a long time more than any other thing whatsoever."

BLOOD AND SAND

0.75 ounce (20 ml) blended scotch whiskey

0.75 ounce (20 ml) Cherry Heering liqueur

0.75 ounce (20 ml) sweet vermouth

0.75 ounce (20 ml) orange juice

Add all ingredients to an ice-filled cocktail shaker. Shake and strain into a cocktail glass. Garnish with an orange twist.

·····

Skulls and "skull moss"—that is, lichens or moss growing on skulls— were also frequently used in corpse medicine. King Charles II (1630– 1685) of England had a signature potion called "the king's drops," which was powdered human skull in alcohol. It was made popular by him but not limited to the king's use. A woman in 1686 described in a letter to her sister how she used the drops sort of like a "mother's little helper" or perhaps an antidepressant. She wrote, "I apply myself to tend my crazy health, and keep up my weak shattered carcass, broken with restless nights and unquiet days. I take the king's drops and drink chocolate, and when my soul is sad to death I run and play with the children."

UNENDING ALCHEMY

The alchemists were concerned with multiplying metals and the perfection of matter, but they always fit the practice into their existing religious (pagan then Islamic then Christian) and philosophical worldviews. The tools and methods to perform alchemical operations were very much scientific, however, and during the forthcoming scientific revolution they would be put to use in the service of chemistry. Flemish alchemist Johannes van Helmont (1579–1644) observed and improved on some of Paracelsus's cures but noted that drinkable gold, silver, and even pearls passed through the body undigested. He recommended against taking arsenic as medicine (good advice!) and for using powdered shells (calcium carbonate) against stomach acid.

Alchemy was practiced in colonial America. John Winthrop Jr. (1606–1676) studied law and alchemy at Trinity College in Dublin and moved to the Massachusetts Bay colony. The practical aspects of alchemy were welcomed there for making medicines, dyes, and fertilizers. Winthrop became governor of Connecticut, and also a defender of witches. He worked on a set of guidelines for distinguishing diabolical magic with Harvard-educated medical practitioner and practical alchemist George Starkey (1628–1665).

Starkey (under the pen name Philalethes) influenced the work back in Europe of scientific giants Isaac Newton and Robert Boyle.

Boyle (1627–1691) was a founder of modern chemistry, most famous for Boyle's Law, which describes the relationship between pressure and volume of gas. He rallied in some books against alchemy of the past, calling alchemists vulgar and rejecting much of the work of both Paracelsus and Aristotle, and yet he still believed in transmutation (believing he'd witnessed it) and wrote a book about distilling human blood. Isaac Newton (1642–1727) was a mathematician and physicist who described the laws of motion, changed the world of optics, and invented calculus. He also studied alchemy and owned a blueprint for creating the philosopher's stone.

Increasingly, alchemical beliefs that could not be supported by objective science were rejected, and the pursuit of the philosopher's stone was largely abandoned. Chemistry and medicine moved forward without the baggage of transmutations and quintessences. Today different groups borrow favorite concepts from alchemy, now mostly in the form of mysticism and the formulation of herbal and mineral tinctures and medicines. There is a Paracelsus College, "dedicated to the living oral and experiential tradition of Alchemy applied in the service of Conscious Evolution"; an Institute for Hermetic Studies, dedicated to the "study and practice of Traditional Western Esotericism"; and an Alchemy Guild, which seeks "to preserve and advance ancient alchemical principles and Hermetic wisdom and apply those teachings to the spiritual, psychological, and physical well-being of people in modern times."

MODERN METALLIC DRINKS

Milk is sometimes fortified with iron to counter anemia, and perhaps that makes it less strange that soda and liquor are too. Irn-Bru, an orange-colored soda brand founded in 1901, is advertised as Scotland's "other national drink," after whiskey. (In this text, "whiskey" is spelled with an "e" unless in a quotation.) The brand was created as a caffeinated nonalcoholic alternative beverage for steelworkers in Glasgow who had been drinking too much beer on the job. It was originally named Iron Brew and sold as "an invigorating refreshing tonic beverage" until a proposed 1946 law change required product branding to be "literally true." Irn-Bru says that the soda does contain iron but is not brewed, so the brand changed the name to its Scottish phonetic pronunciation "Irn-Bru." The soda is fortified with caffeine, quinine, and ferric ammonium citrate—that's where the iron comes in.

The cans were first decorated with the image of a famous Scottish athlete, and early advertisements included testimonials from other sports figures as to its efficacy. They (much) later released a diet version and an energy drink, and there was an outcry when the brand announced in 2018 that half the sugar would be replaced with other sweeteners. The brand reportedly outsells Coca-Cola in Scotland— no doubt in part because it has long been a popular hangover cure for Scotland's main national drink.

Ferro china, or ferro-kina, is a subcategory of bitter Italian liqueurs (amari) that include iron citrate (ferro) and quinine (quina/kina). The category was born in 1881 or 1894 depending on the brand story, with both Baliva (created by Dr. Ernesto Baliva) and Bisleri (created by entrepreneur Felice Bisleri) as early brands on the market. There will be a lot more about the category of amaro (plural: amari) in later chapters, but the rest of them are not fortified with metals. Amari were and still are consumed as digestifs after meals, against colds, or as daily health tonics, sort of like a liquid multivitamin.

Ferro china was marketed as both a digestive aid and an iron supplement for anemia, recommended for women and children in advertisements. For children, a teaspoon was recommended at bedtime, sometimes whipped up with an egg for health.

Bisleri later released a product called Esanofele that contained quinine and iron and added arsenic to the mix. Though these products had their heyday in the late 1800s, they limped along and finally fell out of favor altogether by the 1970s. Bisleri is no longer made, but Baliva is now produced by limoncello maker Pallini. Italian bitters maker Lazzaroni has a modern brand of ferro china, as does Washington, DC, brand Don Ciccio & Figli, based on a family recipe dating to 1967. Paracelsus would be proud.

···· 3 ····

MONKS

MONASTIC LIQUEURS
and THE MIDDLE AGES

We read that monks should not drink wine at all, but since the monks of our day cannot be convinced of this, let us at least agree to drink moderately, and not to the point of excess, "for wine makes even wise men go astray" (Sir 19:2).

However, where local circumstances dictate an amount much less than what is stipulated above, or even none at all, those who live there should bless God and not grumble. Above all else we admonish them to refrain from grumbling.

—*The Rule of Saint Benedict*

While the alchemists were debating quintessences and metallic medicine, most sick people during the Middle Ages in Europe were probably happy just to receive good old-fashioned herbal treatments infused into alcohol. This era between the fall of Rome in the fifth century and the Renaissance in Europe around the fifteenth included the Christian

Crusades in the twelfth to fourteenth centuries and the Black Death in the 1300s, which depopulated a third of the continent. In the following centuries in what is now called the early modern period (1500–1800), contact with and exploitation of overseas nations gave access to new and rare beverages and medicines.

During much of this era, the population of Europe was divided into about 5 percent ruling nobles and 90 percent farmers and other workers. The remaining portion was the clergy, who formed the educated class. The main centers of literacy, herbal medicine, and agricultural science were Christian monasteries.

A History of Monastic Orders

Monastic communities were first formed from colonies of hermits—people inspired by biblical ideals to seek isolation outside cities, often living separately, yet in proximity to each other. The hermetic monastic lifestyle was formalized by Saint Pachomius around 346 CE in Egypt, specifying that monks in monastic communities would spend their time in prayer and at work, in poverty and chastity, and in obedience to their superiors. These monasteries ran hospitals, orphanages, and schools to serve their communities.

Western monasticism was formalized by the rules of Saint Benedict (c. 480–550), who founded twelve monasteries in Italy. Saint Benedict's rules dictated a life of prayer, study, and manual labor; meals eaten in silence; and about half a bottle of wine a day. His prescribed regimen was too stringent for his thirsty monks, though, so according to legend they plotted to kill him. The monks put poison in Benedict's wine, but he blessed it as usual before drinking. As he did, the vessel shattered, and the poisoned wine spilled to the floor.

He later reluctantly gave in to their demands, per the quote at the beginning of this chapter.

With daily hours of reading prescribed to the monks and nuns, libraries were essential in Benedictine monasteries, and the clergy was literate at a time when even much of the nobility was not. Monasteries became oases of knowledge, places where information was shared from one cluster to the next. Books and other manuscripts to be copied were transferred between monasteries, and some orders held annual meetings at their mother churches.

Benedictine monasteries were obligated to show hospitality to travelers stopping along their pilgrimages to see holy relics, along with other religious travelers who would share news and information they picked up during their stays. Many monasteries had guesthouses for travelers and infirmaries for the sick, staffed by monks and nuns and directed by traveling or in-house physicians. (Medical schools like those in Salerno and Montpellier were not monasteries, though clergy members would often be among their teachers.) They also had herb gardens for medicinal plants and apothecaries of plant-based medicines.

Monasteries were often built on property donated by landowning nobility, and many orders enjoyed the local landlords' ongoing patronage. Some of the priests and nuns were the second sons and daughters of nobles, sent away as the first son would inherit property and titles. And because monks were forbidden to marry, any wealth they did have would go to the order upon their death. Some orders grew rich, and their founding purpose as places for quiet prayer and reflection was lost.

In reaction, new "reform" orders would splinter off from time to time, usually with the goal of restoring devotion to Saint Benedict's original directives. The Cistercians were one of these, founded around 1115 as a change of direction from the decadent Cluniacs. (One of their great promoters, Saint Bernard, alleged the Benedictines at Cluny kept warm with cat-fur rugs and sang so much they needed huge quantities of wine.) With their rededication to work and relocation into more remote areas farther removed from influential aristocrats, the Cistercians became pioneers of agricultural progress throughout Europe. (*Monks and Wine* author Desmond Seward calls them "the drainage experts of the Middle Ages.") The Trappists, who still make some of the best beer in the world, are in turn a reform order of the Cistercians.

In contrast, the Carthusians (founded in 1084) are an order of monks who looked further back to the Egyptian hermits for their inspiration—living in solitude, not just in the remote mountains but also alone in their individual cells for much of the day. They also adopted the Cistercian organization system of a motherhouse to which the individual monasteries were subservient.

To avoid the patronage system that had proved corrupting in the past, the Carthusians and other orders decided to become autonomous, paying for the items they couldn't make in-house by selling goods to the surrounding community. These usually included handicrafts, bread, cheese, honey, and, of course, beer, wine, and liquor. The liqueur Chartreuse was created and is still made by Carthusian monks who use its sales to fund their activities.

Orders like the Benedictines and Cistercians were usually attached to specific monasteries, but the mendicant (begging) orders, the Franciscans and Dominicans, were wandering orders not limited to one place. Both orders were founded in the thirteenth century and consisted of members living in poverty and with minimal possessions. These friars might serve towns that had no parish priest, provide medical advice, and generally spread their knowledge rather than keep it confined to the monastery library. Like all learned people of the time, they practiced distillation to make medicines from plants and animals.

A document from England around 1420 describes some of the practices of these friars, which includes distilling blood. It states, "Once distilled, keep it, and mix the blood with the same quantity of aqua ardens, then distill the mixture in an alembic. The water that remains is better than all other waters in the world for healing wounds."

THE BLACK DEATH

The Black Death that killed an estimated twenty-five million people in Europe between 1347 and 1351 was probably caused by rat-carried plague. The Great Mortality originated in China and traveled west along trade routes into the Middle East and then the Mediterranean region. From there it traveled north into Europe by land and on ships to England and Scandinavia.

This was the second of three major plagues; the others were in the 500s and the late 1800s (mostly in China and India), with lots of smaller outbreaks that would come in waves. The Great Plague of London in 1665–66 and plagues in other parts of Europe were better documented, as in *A Journal of the Plague Year* by Daniel Defoe (of *Robinson Crusoe* fame). The bubonic plague hasn't been entirely eliminated: in modern times, an average of seven people in the US still catch it each year from wild rodents, but now most are cured with antibiotics.

The plague is not caused by the bite of the black rat (wonderfully named *Rattus rattus*), but by the bacterium *Yersinia pestis*, which lives inside fleas that feed off the blood of rats. If rats die off, the fleas jump to humans and start biting them. The parasite in the flea blocks it from swallowing the blood it is sucking, so the desperate flea keeps biting its host and, while doing so, regurgitating some of the parasites back into the host's bloodstream. In humans bitten by plague-infected rat fleas, bacteria concentrate in lymph nodes and cause swellings called "buboes," from which we get the name bubonic.

Some theories of the Black Death's cause in its time included divine retribution and a poor planetary alignment that on Earth drew out noxious vapors, called "miasma," which spread through wind. Unhealthy, bad-smelling miasma was thought to be the cause of (what we now know as) contagious diseases, including the plague, malaria, cholera, influenza, and dysentery, from ancient times through the late 1800s when germ theory was developed.

Physicians during later plagues wore special clothing to keep the miasmic stink out. These were plague doctor uniforms you can now find in Halloween or steampunk costume shops—the long oiled or waxed trench coat, broad-brimmed hat, goggles, and a mask with a bird beak. These outfits were fairly effective as they would largely keep the fleas off the doctor, as well as prevent person-to-person infections that are possible in the pneumonic form of the plague.

Physicians would fill the beaks of the masks with nice-smelling herbs and flowers to keep out miasma, and that also helped to distract from the stench of death no doubt. Good-smelling antimiasma botanicals used included clove, cinnamon, fennel, clove-studded oranges, musk, and sandalwood. Saffron was considered a valuable plague preventative, and a fourteen-week "Saffron War" broke out over a hijacked eight-hundred-pound shipment of saffron destined for Basel, in Switzerland, in the 1300s.

One physician, John Colle, had a different opinion on protecting yourself from miasma-based plague. He publicized the idea of counteracting bad smells with even worse ones, so he suggested that people gather around latrines and huff the noxious fumes. Some people actually took this advice.

Those who weren't inhaling latrine pits would fumigate their houses with all sorts of antimiasmic smoke by burning juniper branches, rosemary, violet, lavender, thyme, oregano, sage, and pine. Juniper wood when burned is said to produce minimal visible smoke but is highly aromatic, perfect for spring cleaning, ridding a premise of witchcraft, and fumigating against the plague. (For the same low-smoke reasons, juniper wood was also said to be favored by whiskey distillers in the Scottish Highlands back when the activity was illegal. Less smoke meant less chance of detection.)

Juniper berries, used since antiquity as a spice and preservative, might truly have been an effective treatment against the carrier of plague: they are a natural insect repellent and are still found in some natural flea powders.

SOUTH LONDON

1.5 ounces (45 ml) gin

0.75 ounce (20 ml) Tio Pepe sherry

0.75 ounce (20 ml) simple syrup

0.75 ounce (20 ml) lemon juice

3 dashes Regans' Orange Bitters

Add ingredients to an ice-filled shaker. Lightly
shake and strain into an ice-filled Old-Fashioned
glass. Garnish with a mint sprig.

· · · · ·

In addition to smoke, strong-smelling liquids, including vinegar and even urine, were sprinkled about households. Medicinal vinegar was also used in personal deodorizers. A vinegar to be applied topically was infused with wormwood, meadowsweet, marjoram, sage, cloves, rosemary, horehound, and camphor, among other ingredients. People carried handheld scented "smelling apples" that were protection against noxious vapors. The all-purpose antivenoms theriac and mithridate were consumed as well.

Most plague medicines were preventative rather than curative, and treatments tended to be external rather than prescribed for internal consumption. Of course, bleeding patients was still popular, because Galenic medicine was still the leading theory. For internal use, special preventative plague beers were brewed, and "plague waters" were distilled. One surviving recipe for plague water from 1667 includes valerian, angelica, gentian, elecampane, zedoary, galangal, rue, horehound, blessed thistle, elderflower, lavender, mace, juniper, green walnuts, aniseed, plus theriac and mithridate (each of which might contain more than fifty ingredients already), distilled and then sweetened with sugar.

In Florence and other parts of Tuscany during a later bout of plague in the 1600s, bars and other shops built "wine windows" into their edifices. These tiny windows allowed for drinks and money to be passed back and forth, without additional contact. In the 2020 coronavirus outbreak, some of these windows were reopened, and Aperol Spritzes stood in as modern-day plague waters.

Depopulation by the plague is thought to have raised the quality of life for many members of the agricultural peasant class who could now negotiate better deals with their landlords in the face of labor shortages. On the other hand, it pushed some women out of the brewing business.

Throughout history, brewing beer was women's work in the home, as baking and brewing could be accomplished with the same set of ingredients. Sometimes women produced enough extra beer to give away or sell, and some opened taverns or inns in their homes or adjacent to them. But whenever brewing expanded from a small operation into a larger commercial one, men took over and women with power and independence were villainized. (A common myth is that alewives accused of witchcraft are the archetype of witches in pointy black hats and riding on broomsticks, but this imagery comes from later children's books.)

Women were ousted from the brewing business by monasteries brewing ale to sell to local communities after 1000, and again after the depopulation by the Black Death of the 1300s. Larger operations required more capital, which was inaccessible to women, as were brewers guilds that required long internships.

MONASTIC IMPROVEMENTS

Larger brewing operations needed the beer they produced to last longer, so preservative hops became an important ingredient. Hops were added to beer at least as early as the 700s but came into more common use after 1100. From its earliest days, beer, like wine, was infused with flavorings and preservatives, and sometimes those were medicinal. Before hops were widely used, Emperor Charlemagne (742–814) promoted monasteries that sold gruit, a beer made with the addition of herbs and spices such as bog myrtle, rosemary, yarrow, mugwort, heather, caraway, and, especially later, imported spices like nutmeg and cinnamon. Every one of these ingredients is antimicrobial and might have helped prevent spoilage. Other stabilizing herbs added to beer individually or in combination included juniper, wormwood, horehound, stinging nettle, buckbean, ash tree leaves, and shoots of evergreen trees. But hops largely replaced all these flavorings.

References to hops throughout the years often come from monasteries. An ordinance from a Benedictine monastery at Corbie in France in 822 links hops to brewing. Other documents from around the same time mentioned hop gardens for their cultivation. The German Benedictine abbess and composer Hildegard von Bingen documented the use of hops in brewing in the natural history text *Physica sacra* in the 1100s. She noted hops' preservative powers in addition to their use for promoting good physical health.

Hops "preserve beer, and make it more wholesome, and better tasted; and render it diuretic. Beer purges the blood, is good in the jaundice, and for hypochondriac diseases," wrote John Pechey in *The Compleat Herbal of Physical Plants* from 1694. On the other hand, John Evelyn, in the 1670 book *Pomona*, wrote that hops are a *"Medical* [rather than] *Alimental* Vegetable." He continued: "This one ingredient, by some suspected not unworthily, preserves the drink indeed, but repays the pleasure in tormenting diseases and a shorter life."

The larger size of monastic brewing operations spurred the discovery of better sanitation methods that in turn allowed for even larger production. Extra-strong beers were developed to provide nutrition during fasting days of Lent; doppelbock was dubbed "liquid bread." To this day, Trappist beers are still known for their high alcohol content.

In the early 1800s, after the French Revolution, many expelled French monks settled in the Netherlands and Belgium, and those countries are still host to some famous Trappist breweries. As was standard, the monks grew their own food, brewed their own beer, and sold crafts and goods to the public to support their orders. Today the official site of the International Trappist Association, trappist.be, lists beer, wine, liqueurs, soap, olive oil, cheese, bread, candles, yeast, and other products for sale from these abbeys.

The International Trappist Association has currently approved (as of this writing) fourteen breweries with the "authentic Trappist product" (ATP) label for products made at abbeys located in Belgium, the Netherlands, the United States, Spain, Austria, France, Italy, and the United Kingdom. For the beer (or anything else) to be given the ATP label, the products must be made within the immediate surroundings of the abbey, under the supervision of the monks or nuns (they don't have to make it themselves, just supervise), and the profits should "be intended for the needs of the monastic community, for purposes of solidarity within the Trappist Order, or for development projects and charitable works."

Trappist beers tend to be made with sugar along with grains, which raises their resulting alcohol level in fermentation. The monks produce dubbels, tripels, and quadrupels, each with successively higher alcohol content. The most famous brands of Trappist beers include Chimay, La Trappe, Rochefort, and Westvleteren. None purport to be medicinal.

Some historians assert that monks saved European winemaking during the early Middle Ages. Wine was thought to be necessary for Mass as well as for everyday drinking, so we find improvements in viniculture near former monasteries. (The labor was by no means exclusively performed by monks; they were landlords who charged tithes to the tenants farming the lands the monastery owned.) The various monastic orders established vineyards and experimented until they found grape varietals that grew the best for the soil and climate, establishing many of Europe's famous wine regions known today. When monks traveled to new lands to establish missions such as the Jesuits in America and Mexico, they planted vineyards for their use.

Dom Pérignon (1638–1715), for whom the famous champagne was named, was a Benedictine monk who made many improvements to winemaking, including aggressive pruning of vines; harvesting grapes in the cool, damp conditions of the morning hours; and pressing with a gentle touch in various ways. Pérignon did not invent champagne, but other monks may have: the oldest recorded sparkling wine was made at the Benedictine Abbey of Saint-Hilaire in southern France, in 1531.

MIMOSA

3 ounces (90 ml) champagne

3 ounces (90 ml) orange juice

Pour both into a champagne flute.

CHARTREUSE

Chartreuse is a brand of liqueur made by Carthusian monks in the French Alps that sells 1.5 million bottles annually. It contains 130 ingredients, is assembled according to a secret recipe, and was originally designed as cure-all elixir. It is so famous a beverage that the greenish-yellow color chartreuse is named after the liqueur, not the other way around.

The Carthusian order was founded by Bruno of Cologne (later Saint Bruno) in 1084. Bruno (c. 1030–1101) was a famous educator at the University of Reims, but he left to find a location to study in solitude with six companions. Bruno built a hermitage (monastery) in a mountain valley outside Grenoble, now named the Grande Chartreuse. The order was named for the Chartreuse Mountains, which became the name of the liqueur, which became the name of the color.

Six years after founding the small monastery, Bruno was called away to become an adviser to his former pupil, Pope Urban II. He remained in the Calabria region of Italy until his death. Bruno's concept of "contemplative orders" caught on though, and soon other Carthusian houses began popping up.

The story of the liqueur begins in 1605, at the Carthusian monastery at Vauvert, in what was then a suburb of Paris, at the present Jardin du Luxembourg. There, Maréchal (Marshal) d'Estrées, a military officer under King Henri IV (1553–1610), gave the monks a manuscript likely hundreds of years old already that contained the secret of an elixir. It has long been known as "the elixir for long life," but the thoroughly researched and surprisingly honest brand-created history book *Chartreuse the Liqueur* notes that this expression was never used in the original document.

The book states, "The manuscript does not even have a title page and consists of a complicated recipe written in a dry style which would probably fail to attract attention were it not for the glowing words of praise at the end boasting the as-yet unproven properties of this elixir." The Vauvert property had gardens and orchards, as well as an apothecary on site. It produced and sold a medical elixir that achieved a famous reputation, though not much is known about this incarnation of it.

In the early 1700s, there were 170 Carthusian charterhouses in several countries around Europe, and though the Vauvert order was wealthy, the motherhouse Grande Chartreuse in the mountains had many expenses. In previous centuries, it was self-sustaining, as the monastery's brothers raised cattle and ran an iron foundry using the local charcoal and timber for fuel. They also sold tall, straight trees for ships' masts. But in the late 1600s and early 1700s, the French king ordered a reduction in trees that could be harvested for industry, wiping out both the monks' foundry and their forestry businesses. They needed a new source of income.

The monks of the motherhouse Grande Chartreuse asked for and received a copy of the manuscript held at Vauvert, copies of which survive, while the original document was lost to time. At the Grande Chartreuse, some of the brothers were assigned the task of working on the recipe to reproduce the elixir to sell. It was at one point described as "slightly green in color, with a bitter, spicy, keen taste," and the monks noted that they were adapting it for flavor as well as functionality.

Apothecary brother Jérôme Maubec recorded his results in 1755 in a manuscript that survives. His text describes the harvest of the plants, and the mixture of their preparations, but he died before recording the complete method of manufacture for the elixir. After Jérôme's death in 1762, his successor, Brother Antoine, worked on the recipe further to make it less harsh in flavor and to improve "the anti-poison property of the elixir and its color." This sounds like it could be a theriac.

The recipe specified a base of good eau-de-vie, made with the best wine that can be obtained and distilled. Instructions for its distillation included cooling the still with melted ice or snow, which would have been available high up in the mountains. The color was no accident. Jérôme specified it to be "grass-green, slightly yellow color," and his successor recorded his experiments trying to re-create it exactly. He succeeded, and in 1764 this Brother Antoine recorded in a manuscript about six pages long the recipe for "Composition of the Chartreuse elixir."

As the recipe was adapted and improved locally, the monks do not claim that the elixir is the original recipe according to the 1605 document. The brand book states, "The Carthusians did not just passively preserve a recipe, which moreover was inadequate in its original version. They adopted it and developed it, adding their knowledge to the long tradition which had resulted in the Maréchal's manuscript. . . . The recipe given to the Carthusians did not originally include 130 plants, but only slightly more than half that number." The monks note, though, that every ingredient in the original manuscript is in the final liqueur, with one exception that they do not name. They refuse to name any of the botanical ingredients used in Chartreuse, in fact.

The French Revolution of 1789 decimated the power of the Catholic Church in France. The authority of the Church to impose tithes was eliminated, and monastic vows were abolished by the government. The next year, all religious orders in France were abolished outright, and soon most of the Carthusian monks fled the country. When the monks were allowed to return from exile in 1816, the monastery had been pillaged and abandoned (though their pharmacy had largely survived), and the order was quite poor. It was at this point that the elixir was really commercialized.

The finished elixir, Elixir Vegetal de la Grande-Chartreuse, was recommended "as a remedy in most surprises, ailments, or accidents which could not wait for a doctor to come." It was advertised by the monks as "unsurpassed in serious apoplexy, syncope, asphyxia, palpitations, indigestion, the fainting and weakness which accompany difficult childbirth and in general in all cases which require prompt assistance to restore strength and life."

To this day the Elixir Vegetal is sold in pharmacies in France, where it is packaged in a small round bottle enclosed in a wooden tube. Some people use it as a daily preventative medicine to ensure overall good health. The elixir is typically poured over a sugar cube on a spoon and then dissolved on the tongue. It is supposedly good in this format for a stimulating perk (it is bottled at 69 percent ABV), treating indigestion, and curing strong colds. Others apply it topically to treat skin rashes and to relieve external pain and itching. A vintage advertisement for Chartreuse shows nuns administering Elixir Vegetal to patients to treat cholera during an epidemic in the early years of the 1900s. In the 1950s, Chartreuse was advertised as a way to soothe car sickness.

While the elixir is a "health elixir" meant to be consumed a spoonful at a time, the monks also sold three herbal liqueurs based on the same plants. The product we know today as Green Chartreuse was developed by the monks as a "table elixir" that was sweeter and with a lower alcohol content than the elixir. There was for a time a White Chartreuse based on lemon balm, and there still exists a Yellow Chartreuse. All were in production by 1874. The monks sold various other liqueurs throughout the years, including, in the very bad drinking years of the 1970s, Orange, Raspberry, and Blueberry Chartreuse variants. The order also sold toothpaste and iron supplements among other products in the early days.

ALASKA

1.5 ounces (45 ml) gin

0.5 ounce (15 ml) Yellow Chartreuse

1 dash orange bitters

Add ingredients to an ice-filled stirring pitcher. Stir and strain into a cocktail glass. Garnish with a lemon twist.

. . . . .

According to *The Scientific American Cyclopedia of Formulas* (1911), imitation Green Chartreuse can be made from angelica seeds and roots, arnica flowers, balsime (balsam herb, alecost, or costmary, which is a near relative to tansy), cinnamon, genepi, hyssop, lemon balm, mace, peppermint, poplar balsam bud, and thyme. It is heaviest in the quantities of balsime and angelica, followed by cinnamon and mace. That's far fewer than 130 ingredients, but they give the impression of pungent warm spices and cooling green herbs, and that's pretty close to the mark. The Yellow Chartreuse (according to the same *Cyclopedia*) drops the peppermint, thyme, balsime, and poplar balsam bud, and adds bitter aloe, cardamom, clove, and coriander.

By the middle 1800s, the elixir had been made at the Paris monastery at Vauvert and reformulated at the Grande Chartreuse. Over the tumultuous history of the Carthusian order, Chartreuse would come to be made at five additional distilleries. The elixir and liqueurs became incredibly popular and secured the financial health of the order, but also threatened to overwhelm it. In 1864, to better separate the religious and financial activities of the order, the production of the liqueur was moved out of the motherhouse Grande Chartreuse to a dedicated distillery in the nearby town of Fourvoirie. Chartreuse was produced there until 1903, when the French government seized the distillery (and the trademark of Chartreuse) and expelled the monks once again. A new distillery was set up in Tarragona, Spain, and Chartreuse was made there from 1903 to 1989 (even after the monks again returned to France). They could no longer use the Chartreuse trademark for their product, so it was called Liqueur Peres Chartreux Tarragone. A second distillery in Marseille was operational (at the site of a closed absinthe distillery) from 1921 into the early 1930s and produced the liqueur for the French market, but the monks longed to return to their previous French distillery in the Alps.

In the meantime, the French government sold the trademark for Chartreuse to distillers who produced their own version, generally thought to be inferior to the original. After the trademark of Grande Chartreuse was taken from the monks, this new distilling company dropped the toothpaste and iron supplements or sold them off to other companies. That company collapsed in 1929, and the trademark for Chartreuse reverted to the monks.

The Carthusian distillers returned to the Fourvoirie distillery, made operational again by 1932, but a mountain landslide destroyed nearly the entire facility just three years later. Production moved yet again to a distillery built in nearby Voiron, and the liqueur was made there from 1936 until 2017, when it outgrew capacity. In 2018 a new distillery was opened in Aiguenoire, and the Voiron site was slated to be optimized for tourism.

Today the most important part of producing the liqueur is carried out by just two monks. At the motherhouse Grande Chartreuse (away from prying eyes, rather than at the distillery site), the two monks crush and mix the botanical ingredients together: around twenty tons of ingredients are delivered to the monastery each year. The monks measure dried plants and divide them into groups stored in numbered bags that are transported to the distillery site. There, the bags with different sets of herbs are infused or macerated in alcohol and distilled in separate groups. These are combined with sugar syrup, and more plants are macerated in the spirit to give Chartreuse its characteristic green or yellow color. The liqueur is then aged in large oak vats for a length of time (which is secret, as is everything, but estimated to be three to five years) before the liquid is bottled.

The dramatic four-hundred-year-old history of Chartreuse has made the liqueur a favorite of the literary set. British writer H. H. Munro (1870–1916) wrote in a short story, "People may say what they like about the decay of Christianity; the religion that produced Green Chartreuse can never really die." The liqueur was mentioned in F. Scott Fitzgerald's *The Great Gatsby*, Evelyn Waugh's *Brideshead Revisited*, and in poems by William Wordsworth, who visited the Grande Chartreuse monastery. It is also a favorite of rockstars—no doubt the 55 percent ABV of Green Chartreuse helps with its party reputation. ZZ Top wrote a song inspired by it (the liqueur's name is coupled with "You got the color that turns me loose"), Tom Waits name-checked it, and Hunter S. Thompson was a fan of it both in his writing and in his life. In a 1993 book supposedly describing Thompson's typical day, between midnight and 6:00 a.m. he consumed "Chartreuse, cocaine, grass, Chivas, coffee, Heineken, clove cigarettes, grapefruit, Dunhills, orange juice, gin, [and] continuous pornographic movies." In the 2007 film *Death Proof* by Quentin Tarantino, the director and actor shouts, "Chartreuse! The only liquor so good they named a color after it!"

Many of the brand's biggest fans buy bottles just to keep around. Collectors seek the oldest bottles from Chartreuse's closed distilleries and pay several thousand dollars to own them. For bottles made before 1990, bottle hunters use a variety of clues on the label to determine their ages, including the name of the distillery, the importer to the destination country, the proof of Yellow Chartreuse (it changed in 1972), and the presence or absence of a UPC symbol (added in 1977).

Around 1990, Chartreuse added a date code to the neck of their bottles, beginning with an "L" followed by six digits. To determine the date of bottling, add the number 1,084 (the date when the order was founded) to the first three numbers of the code to determine the year. The next three numbers are the numerical day of the year from 001 to 365. So a bottle with "L933006" (1084+933) would be from January 6, 2017.

Several bars around the world sell vintage Chartreuse by the glass. A single ounce of Green Chartreuse produced at Fourvoirie in the late 1800s, one of several rare vintages sold at the San Francisco restaurant Spruce, will set you back $1,250.

THE LAST WORD

1 ounce (30 ml) Green Chartreuse

1 ounce (30 ml) maraschino liqueur

1 ounce (30 ml) gin

1 ounce (30 ml) lime juice

Add ingredients to an ice-filled shaker.
Shake and strain into a cocktail glass.

OTHER MONASTIC LIQUEURS

Chartreuse was wildly imitated shortly after being sold commercially, by genuine monks and profiteers alike. None of the versions have the pedigree of the original, but a few brands have been around long enough to have aged into respectability. Liqueurs are made (or were until recently) by the Benedictines of Kloster Ettal in Bavaria, Samos in Spain, and Abu Ghosh near Jerusalem; by the Cistercians at La Grâce Dieu and Notre-Dame de Lérins in France; and by many other monasteries.

The story goes that centerbe liqueur was first produced in the Middle Ages at the Benedictine Abbey of San Clemente in the Abruzzo region of Italy from local mountain herbs. Centerbe (meaning "one hundred herbs") was made famous by the pilgrims who stopped in for visits on their travels. The abbey closed, but the local citizens continued to make the liqueur in the region.

In 1817 an apothecary named Beniamino Toro began production of Centerba Toro, first sold from his pharmacy. It is bright green in color and bottled at 70 percent ABV. An 1865 catalogue of the Dublin International Exposition described it: "The strong centerba is an excellent stomachic and besides its medicinal properties when taken inwardly is very useful applied externally for cuts and wounds." The medicinal qualities of centerbe were said to be particularly in demand during an early 1800s cholera epidemic in Naples.

Today centerbe is often consumed as a digestif, or mixed into coffee, hot chocolate, or milk. (Chartreuse is good that way too.) One online recipe for homemade centerbe lists ingredients such as basil, sage, laurel, peppermint, marjoram, tangerine, orange, lemon, lemon verbena, lavender, nettle, mauve, linden, thyme, rosemary, lime flowers, chamomile, rose petals, cloves, roasted coffee beans, juniper berries, aniseed or fennel, cinnamon, saffron, black tea, and nutmeg.

VERT CHAUD

1.5 to 2 ounces (45–60 ml) centerbe
or Green Chartreuse

6 ounces (180 ml) hot chocolate

Add ingredients to a heat-resistant mug or glass
and top with marshmallows or whipped cream.

• • • • •

Centerba Toro's bottles say that it is still made according to an ancient secret (of course) recipe. It is sold in a little glass jug with straw wrapping around the outside, playing up its two-hundred-year heritage. One website's tasting notes describe Toro as a liqueur that is "fluorescent lime green and offers attractive, semi-sweet aromas that are primarily herbal, including thyme, oregano, spearmint, pine sap and fresh liquorice strap."

Another product, Stellina, is very much like Chartreuse in that it comes in yellow and green versions, and it is made about twenty-five miles from Aiguenoire, according to a secret recipe by the Sainte Famille order. The Stellina Green is made from twelve plants and is bottled at 50 percent ABV, while the Yellow is made from twenty-four plants and is sold at 42 percent ABV.

The Sainte Famille (Holy Family) order was founded in 1829. Unlike the hermetic Carthusians, Sainte Famille members interact with the outside world, using their profits to build schools, teach agricultural skills, and install water pumps in various impoverished countries. Like the Carthusians, the order was expelled from France in 1903. After expulsion, the monks relocated to the Piedmont area of Italy, south of Turin, and turned to viticulture. There, Brother Henri-Marie Berger-Billon, an experienced botanist, created the recipe for Stellina. It was his goal to make a liqueur both "pleasant and beneficial," and the recipe was finalized in 1904. In 1939 the monks returned to France, and in the 1950s they commercialized the product.

BÉNÉDICTINE

Most often mentioned alongside Chartreuse in the category of monastic liqueurs, Bénédictine is not produced by monks but inspired by a monastic elixir. In Fécamp, France, to the northwest of Paris on the shores of the English Channel, a nunnery built in 658 became a major pilgrimage site, as it housed a holy relic—the Holy Blood of Christ, which was hidden in a fig tree that washed up on shore. The nunnery was destroyed by Vikings in 842, and later the site became a grand Benedictine monastery after being rebuilt from 1175 to 1220.

According to the brand, in 1510 the Benedictine monk Dom Bernardo Vincelli created a medicinal elixir at Fécamp, and existing records cite a "drink prepared by the apothecary which costs a lot of money" from the abbey. The elixir was not commercialized at the time but was produced for the monks' use until the French Revolution, when the monks were expelled. One of the monks preserved a recipe book in which the formula for the elixir was written and passed it on to a friend during the Revolution. The grandson of said friend, Alexandre Le Grand (1830–1898), is the person responsible for Bénédictine liqueur.

"He adapted it to modern taste, making a pleasant liqueur from what was used as a medicinal remedy. He completed the re-creation of the recipe, still based on 27 herbs and spices and following the same production process, in 1863," according to heritage curator Sébastien Roncin of Bacardi, which now owns the brand.

Le Grand built an ornate palace in which to produce the liqueur. The Palais Bénédictine in Fécamp still stands and is a tourist attraction (it also houses Le Grand's art collection) where one can visit the winter garden and "taste the subtle aromas of Bénédictine and its cocktails." The most famous cocktails that include the liqueur are the Bobby Burns, the Singapore Sling, and the New Orleans classic Vieux Carré. Bénédictine was often served with cognac, so the company launched B&B, Bénédictine and Brandy, in 1938.

Bénédictine liqueur tastes primarily of honey and baking spices. Sources outside the company estimate Bénédictine's ingredients as including angelica, hyssop, juniper, myrrh, saffron, mace, fir cones, aloe, lemon balm, black tea, thyme, coriander, clove, lemon, vanilla, honey, cinnamon, and nutmeg. Others add apricot, genepi, cardamom, and maidenhair fern or orange peel and arnica to this list.

According to *The Scientific American Cyclopedia of Formulas*, imitation Bénédictine can be made from clove, nutmeg, cinnamon, lemon balm, peppermint, angelica, genepi, calamus (sweet flag), cardamom, and arnica flowers, macerated in alcohol, then distilled and sweetened.

Bénédictine is still used in traditional medicine, primarily among Chinese communities in Singapore and Malaysia. It is considered a "confinement tonic" or health tonic to be used in the thirty- or forty-day rest period after childbirth. The liqueur is added to soups or sipped neat, and some believe that a full bottle of Bénédictine should be consumed within the confinement period.

At one time the brand was promoted medicinally. A Singaporean newspaper advertisement from 1866 describes the liqueur as "tonic, anti-apoplectic, digestive, and of an exquisite flavor . . . and one of the most efficacious preservatives against epidemic diseases. Latterly the French medical men have almost unanimously prescribed it for patients who by their gastric tendency were more subject to attacks of fever and cholera."

Closer to 1950, the brand was advertised to middle-class Chinese laborers overseas who worked outdoors in inclement weather. It also caught on with women, perhaps owing to the angelica in the recipe, though it is probably *Angelica archangelica*, a different species from *Angelica sinensis*, known as "dong quai," or "female ginseng," in traditional Chinese medicine. One modern recipe online for "Essence of Chicken with DOM Benedictine Liqueur" adds a few extra slices of dong quai to the broth and liqueur. An ad from 1964 states, "Fortify your blood and your whole body after childbirth with the 27 specially selected, health giving herbs in Benedictine D.O.M." As late as the 1980s, a gift pack was advertised in Singapore (the type you see today around Christmastime with branded glassware in a gift box), but in this case it contained a bottle of Bénédictine packaged with baby powder and two bars of baby soap.

An alternative liqueur used similarly in these communities is the Japanese "herbal health tonic" Yomeishu, which contains 14 percent alcohol. The product contains fourteen herbs, including safflower, clove, ginseng root, Chinese foxglove, turmeric, cinnamon, peony, and other directly medicinal botanicals, plus some venomous snake for good measure. The Yomeishu website contains food recipes such as "Prosperity Chicken" and "Yomeishu Drunken Prawns."

VIEUX CARRÉ

1 ounce (30 ml) rye whiskey

1 ounce (30 ml) cognac

1 ounce (30 ml) sweet vermouth

0.25 ounce (8 ml) Bénédictine

2 dashes Peychaud's Bitters

2 dashes Angostura Bitters

Add ingredients to an ice-filled stirring pitcher. Stir and strain into an Old-Fashioned glass over new ice.

BUCKFAST

Buckfast Tonic Wine, also known as "Buckie," or "wreck the hoose juice," has been called a "drink with almost supernatural powers of destruction" and "the UK's version of Four Loko." It is an inexpensive caffeinated fortified wine that has become strongly associated with wayward Scottish youth. The standard bottle comes with the caffeine equivalent of eight cans of Coca-Cola, according to one report, and the flavor has been described as "a palatable mixture of berry-flavored cola and cough medicine."

Buckfast's base is not actually a wine but a mistelle: a fortified, rather than fermented, grape juice, similar to pineau des Charentes from the Cognac region, floc de Gascgone from the Armagnac region, and pommeau from the Calvados region of France. It is bottled at 15 percent ABV and has become a favorite tipple of "neds" (hooligans, more or less) in Glasgow, Scotland. According to a 2017 story in the *Telegraph* newspaper, Buckfast had been "linked to 6,500 reports of antisocial behaviour and violence in just two years."

Buckfast is named for an abbey in Devon in southern England that dates to 1018. The abbey was populated by sheepherding monks in its early years, but in 1882 it was sold to a group of Benedictine monks from Dijon fleeing persecution in their home country. For their income the monks had been selling liniments and medicines, one of which was a pick-me-up that became the basis for Buckfast. (Other orders produced tonic wines as well; a record from 1241 in Wiltshire, where Stonehenge is located, notes a Cluniac order providing a portion of iron-flavored wine.) The dosage advice for Buckfast was "three small glasses a day, for good health and lively blood." Newspaper ads declare TO AVOID COLDS AND INFLUENZA TAKE BUCKFAST TONIC WINE.

In 1927 the monks struck a deal with wine merchants J. Chandler & Company Limited, because they were having trouble acquiring the proper licensing to continue selling the wine. The monks continue to produce the wine at Buckfast Abbey (with mistelle imported from France), and the Chandler company is responsible for selling it. At the time of this agreement, the formula was changed as well; the brand acknowledges that the recipe was altered from its purely medicinal roots into a more commercial form.

One theory of why an English beverage became so popular with Scottish youth is that strict laws about alcohol sale hours (ending at 10:00 p.m. on weekdays, never for sale on Sundays) in Glasgow made the "medicinal" wine sold in pharmacies an attractive alternative to beer. Sales of Buckie reached £43.2 million in 2017, bringing the Buckfast Abbey Trust almost £12 million tax-free in 2016. Because of its association with crime in Scotland, various groups have moved to have Buckfast banned, or the tax-exempt status stripped from the abbey, to no avail.

Monks and nuns of the Middle Ages were the keepers and promoters of medical, agricultural, and alchemical knowledge in Europe and did much to improve beer, wine, and medicinal liqueurs. But at the end of this era, scientists studying alcohol would soon make world-changing medicinal discoveries.

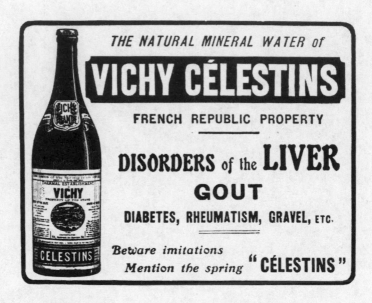

SCIENCE

PHLOGISTON, PYRMONT, PASTEUR, *and* PATHOGENS

I have removed life, for life is the germ, and the
germ is life.

Louis Pasteur

hile the monks were busy mixing up herbal cure-alls,
other intellectuals of the era were soon to shift scientific thought away from the ancient Greco-Roman
view of the world toward a more modern one. The scientific revolution of the sixteenth and seventeenth centuries was facilitated by the
increased spread of information transfer after the invention of the
printing press; an interest in industrial technology particularly among
the rising merchant (and later manufacturing) class; and new information, materials, and even diseases brought to Europe from the Americas that could not be understood by ancient knowledge.

Astronomy, physics, optics, and mathematics were combined into
an understanding of mechanics. Nicolaus Copernicus (1473–1543)

proposed the heliocentric system, that the sun is the center of our universe. Johannes Kepler (1571–1630) discovered three major laws of planetary motion. Galileo Galilei (1564–1642) made use of the telescope to contribute further to the study of motion. Isaac Newton developed calculus and the law of universal gravitation. Since more of the world could be understood as an orderly machine following universal rules, French philosopher René Descartes (1596–1650) theorized that all physical bodies, including the human one, are machines that operate by mechanical principles.

By the mid-sixteenth century, though, the pure science of chemistry was still mired in the protoscience of alchemy, and medicine still included nonsensical treatments like green lizards cooked in olive oil to close wounds and wine-washed earthworms with tree resin to heal them. Paracelsus's medical chemistry, despite its symbolic and often ineffective treatments, introduced a more rational approach to diagnosis of illness based on physical symptoms rather than temperament and planetary alignment. Paracelsus treated the disease, not the humors.

While Paracelsus spurned (and burned) the works of Galen and moved medicine forward, he was not completely responsible for killing off humoral theory. Rather, it was the reality of human anatomy that did it. Galen's idea of circulation was that blood was created in the liver, then flowed to all parts of the body where it was used up. Dissection was sometimes prohibited and sometimes encouraged for physicians in the centuries after Galen lived (and Galen dissected apes rather than humans), but few people doubted his conclusions.

Flemish physician Andreas Vesalius (1514–1564) published *De humani corporis fabrica* (On the construction of the human body) in 1543, after a study of many corpses, and showed that the body's structure probably precluded blood flow from working in the way Galen thought it did. Then English physician William Harvey (1578–1657) identified circulation of the blood in 1628 (though Arabic physician Ibn al-Nafis had reached similar conclusions in the 1200s) and importantly demonstrated his theory in front of audiences so it could not be denied. Since it was shown that blood flows in a loop rather than being constantly created and used up by the body, it became clear that there was a limited amount of it. Thus doctors should probably not spend so much time ridding their patients of "excess" quantities of that humor in particular.

As tends to be the case, physicians did not change their ways overnight, nor even over a century: doctors continued to practice bloodletting into the late 1800s, with various justifications for doing so.

GAS AND PHLOGISTON

Beer and wine inspired crucial advancements in chemistry, microbiology, and medical science in the 1700s. In the process of fermentation, yeasts eat sugars and produce alcohol and carbon dioxide. The alcohol, as discussed, has been used medically on its own and in partnership with botanicals. The discovery of carbon dioxide led to the understanding of gases generally, as well as their use in beverage carbonation and medicinal anesthesia. And the study of yeast would lead to the understanding of microorganisms, germ theory, disease transmission, and antiseptic surgery.

English scientist Robert Boyle was not fully convinced by Aristotle's theory in which there were only four elements and each element is present in some quantity in all things. He worked on an analysis of mineral water, proposed distilling seawater to desalinate it on voyages (not the first person to think of that), and studied the physical characteristics of air. This resulted in Boyle's Law of the relationship between pressure and volume of a gas. The next set of scientists differentiated between types of gas mixed up in air.

Many of the gas experiments of the 1700s were performed under glass bulbs or bell jar domes, the kind used as a terrarium or to cover a display cake at a restaurant. Often the whole experiment would take place inside a dome with its open bottom end submerged in water. A candle lit inside this bulb would use up oxygen, and the water level inside the globe would rise, showing that the volume of gas in the dome was reduced as the air was consumed by flame.

Eventually, however, the candle would go out, even though there was still some air in the globe. The early explanation for the phenomenon was that it was due to phlogiston, a concept left over from alchemy formalized by Georg Ernst Stahl (1660–1734) in 1703. Phlogiston was thought to be present in things that burned; it wasn't fire itself but the property of flammability.

Things that no longer burned, such as wood ash, were thought to be depleted of their phlogiston. The self-extinguishing candle burning under the globe went out not because it was depleted of phlogiston, but because it released phlogiston during burning and the surrounding air supposedly became saturated with it. Water that burned, aqua vitae, was for a time thought to be a compound of water and phlogiston.

But phlogiston didn't make sense (spoiler: it doesn't exist) in all ways. Stahl believed that oxidation (such as rusting) was related to combustion, yet when metal oxidized it gained weight rather than lost it. This would only be possible if phlogiston had a negative weight. Despite this being extremely unlikely, it took most of a century to disprove.

In other experiments, a magnifying glass held in the sun outside the glass bulb was used to ignite the materials on a platform within, and then the resulting solids and gases were weighed and tested. Mice were placed in the resultant gas to see how long they could continue breathing. In other experiments, plants were placed in the gas until they died, and then rodents afterward, and then the experiment was repeated in the reverse order. (Gas scientists of the 1700s suffocated a lot of rodents.) Scientists catalogued the properties of gases and showed that air contains two kinds of gases but that only one of them was combustible.

Scottish chemist Joseph Black (1728–1799) demonstrated in the 1750s a version of today's elementary school volcano science class experiment of adding baking soda to vinegar and watching it fizz: Black studied how limestone (chalk) effervesces with acids and releases "fixed air," and was able to measure the inputs and outputs and even reverse the experiment. He showed that the air created in certain reactions had different properties from common air. His "fixed air" would later be known as carbon dioxide.

Joseph Priestley (1733–1804) was a minister who began studying gases after moving next to a brewery and noticing that beer in fermentation vats created air with the same properties as those described by Black. He found that this air would kill mice that were suspended in it. This too was fixed air.

Priestley made maybe the first force-carbonated water by pouring water back and forth between two vessels over the mouse-killing fixed air above a beer vat. He then created equipment to make this bubbly water in a lab: His *Directions for Impregnating Water with Fixed Air: In Order to Communicate to It the Peculiar Spirit and Virtues of Pyrmont Water, and Other Mineral Waters of a Similar Nature* (1772) showed how to make artificially carbonated water.

He designed many different apparatuses to conduct experiments with gases, one of which evolved into the "gasogene" in 1774. It was meant to produce carbonated water from what is now baking powder (tartaric acid and sodium bicarbonate), which reacts with water inside the canister. The gasogene evolved into the soda siphon we recognize today. It also evolved into a device to administer anesthesia.

As for the "Pyrmont" in the title of Priestley's paper, this was a well-known naturally fizzy mineral spring. Priestley wrote that by adding minerals to the water and fixed air, you could make the water more like this spa, but the "peculiar spirit and virtues" of the waters came from the fizz.

Priestley thought this CO_2-impregnated water would relieve scurvy and fevers. He wrote, "I would not interfere with the providence of the physician, but I cannot entirely satisfy myself without taking this opportunity to suggest such hints as have occurred to myself, or my friends, with respect to the medicinal uses of water impregnated with fixed air. . . . The diseases in which water impregnated with fixed air will most probably be serviceable, are those of a putrid nature, of which kind is the sea-scurvy." He went on to suggest this water might be good for use in enemas (whoo!) and to treat ulcerated lungs and soothe cancers, among other "putrefying diseases."

The fact that citrus could prevent or cure scurvy was learned and forgotten many times over the centuries, but in the later 1700s a series of somewhat controlled experiments to find a remedy were attempted. Among many different suggested cures for what we now know as a vitamin deficiency were fermented food and beverages, particularly sauerkraut. The disease was thought to be an internal putrefaction (since one of the early symptoms was swollen gums and teeth falling out), and thus vegetables that fermented but did not readily spoil might confer their antiputrefactive properties to the sailors. With this in mind, Irish doctor David MacBride (1726–1778) advocated for bringing on board concentrated malted barley, which he thought would ferment internally once sailors ate it. Fermenting beer produces carbon dioxide (fixed air), so perhaps water imbued with fixed air would stop putrefaction.

Priestley was awarded the Copley Medal, and in 1773 the president of the Royal Society said it was

> for having learned from Dr. Black that this fixed or mephitic air could in great abundance be produced from chalk by means of diluted spirits of vitriol; from Dr Macbride that this fluid was of a considerable antiseptic nature; from Dr Cavendish that it would in a large quantity be absorbed by water; and from Dr Brownrigg that it was this very air which gave the briskness and chief virtues to the Spa and Pyrmont waters; Dr Priestley, I say, so well instructed, conceived that common water impregnated with this fluid alone might be useful in medicine, particularly for sailors on long voyages, for curing or preventing the sea scurvy.

GIN RICKEY

2 ounces (60 ml) gin
0.5 ounce (15 ml) lime juice
5 ounces (150 ml) club soda

Pour all ingredients into a highball glass with ice.

· · · · ·

The medal was premature because of course soda water doesn't work to cure scurvy. (The actual cure for scurvy is discussed in chapter 6.) But Priestley did foretell the future of the utility of his impregnated water: "By this process may fixed air be given to wine, beer, and almost any liquor whatever: and when beer is become flat or dead, it will be revived by this means; but the delicate agreeable flavor, or acidulous taste communicated by the fixed air, and which is manifest in water, will hardly be perceived in wine, or other liquors which have much taste of their own."

Priestley went on to identify new gases, including nitrous oxide, ammonia, sulfur dioxide, nitrogen (known as "phlogisticated air"), and oxygen ("dephlogisticated air" or "vital air"). Oxygen was independently discovered by Carl Wilhelm Scheele (as "fire air").

Priestley also recognized that plants restore the air that humans and animals respire, and wrote, "The injury which is casually done to the atmosphere by the respiration of such a large number of animals . . . is, in part at least, repaired by the vegetable creation." Further, after he experimented with oxygen and found that a mouse could live twice as long in oxygen than in the same volume of common air (before suffocating), he decided that oxygen too could be useful in medicine. He wrote, "In time, this pure air may become a fashionable article in luxury. Hitherto only two mice and myself have had the privilege of breathing it."

LAVOISIER

History leaves the impression that Priestley was a humble desktop experimental scientist, with the opposite temperament of his contemporary Antoine Lavoisier. Lavoisier (1743–1794) was a wealthy nobleman who worked for a private tax-collection agency that reported to the French government. Lavoisier performed experiments but didn't make a lot of experimental discoveries of his own. His own experiments were often re-creations of those of Priestley and others (that he pretended not to have heard about), performed with better equipment (he could afford the best). But he came to brilliant conclusions from these experiments that had eluded others.

His wife, Marie-Anne (1758–1836), acted as an illustrator, translator, and overall partner, and was the rare example of a woman of this era recognized for her contributions to science. In a portrait that hangs in the Metropolitan Museum of Art in New York, Antoine is sitting at a table writing in a scientific notebook, while Marie-Anne is standing to his side with her hand on his shoulder and her easel of drawings behind her.

Lavoisier believed that matter was neither created nor destroyed in chemical reactions (a hugely important idea on its own), a principle that he first fully stated as an aside in a book chapter on the chemical processes of wine fermentation. In his experiments he sought to demonstrate this idea by collecting and weighing all the substances involved in reactions before and after. This would show not just conservation of matter but how much of each was involved—for example, the relative quantity of nitrogen to oxygen in common air.

Lavoisier recognized oxygen's elementary nature, and that the supposedly necessary phlogiston that enables a substance to burn was better explained as the oxygen in the air. This way oxygen would have a positive weight rather than phlogiston needing to have a negative one. Priestley on the other hand was not a believer, publishing *Doctrine of Phlogiston Established, and That of the Composition of Water Refuted*.

Lavoisier also repeated experiments by Henry Cavendish (1731–1810), combining hydrogen and oxygen together with an electric spark. Though Cavendish believed phlogiston was present in both the hydrogen and oxygen, Lavoisier recognized that phlogiston was not needed at all to explain the reaction.

Lavoisier wrote in *Reflections on Phlogiston*, "In this essay, I beg of my readers to shed themselves of all prejudices as far as possible, to see in the facts only what they show, to banish all that reasoning has assumed, to transport themselves to a time before [phlogiston's definer] Stahl and to forget for a moment that his theory ever existed, if that is possible." It turns out that it *was* possible, and soon enough phlogiston passed out of the scientific literature, and most people did forget that it ever was theorized.

Lavoisier named oxygen, cocreated the system for naming chemical substances still used today, and made a list of the thirty-three suspected elements of the time. He interpreted oxygen's role in combustion and respiration. Other scientists shortly thereafter showed that plants convert carbon dioxide into oxygen in the presence of light, and by the end of the 1700s, these great experimentalists had taken the idea of air as a single element to an understanding of elemental and combined gases, human and animal respiration, combustion, and photosynthesis. It was a very productive century.

As for Lavoisier, despite his genius, his job in the French government's service would result in his death. He was imprisoned, then guillotined, in the French Revolution in 1794, the same day as his wife Marie-Anne's father. She organized the publication of Lavoisier's final memoirs after his execution.

Gases were examined for medicinal uses at places such as the Pneumatic Institution at Bristol. There, a young scientist named Humphry Davy (1778–1829) had the job of testing them. (Davy had acquired a bit of a reputation for a demonstration of rubbing two pieces of ice together to melt them, showing that friction generates heat.) He performed gas experiments on himself and huffed carbon monoxide that almost killed him. He preferred the nitrous oxide that put him into fits of giggles. This laughing gas became a hit at his parties, and he published a great work on it in 1800.

It was suggested that nitrous oxide could be used as anesthesia, and this found favor with American physicians. In 1846 Boston dental surgeon William Morton (1819–1868) demonstrated the use of inhaled liquid ether (prepared from a mixture of alcohol and sulfuric acid). Chloroform soon followed and became a preferred form of anesthesia, in part because unlike ether it is not flammable. Ether too was a hit at scientists' parties for a bit, but because in medical practice it has a "narrow margin of safety" and people tended to die while taking it, the gas has since been replaced by other anesthetics.

Today gases are used in medicine in various ways. Oxygen is

used to supplement deficient patients, nitrous oxide is used for anesthesia, and carbon dioxide is used to inflate the abdominal cavity and colon for certain medical procedures. Dry ice (solid carbon dioxide) and liquid nitrogen are also used in medicine, not just in molecular mixology. In beverages, carbon dioxide is used to carbonate most liquids, while nitrogen is used to give Guinness its signature foam, and argon and nitrogen in combination or individually are used to preserve open wine bottles.

VODKA SODA

2 ounces (60 ml) vodka

4 ounces (120 ml) soda water

Add ingredients to an ice-filled glass.
Garnish with a lime wheel.

TAKING THE WATERS

In 1542 Andrew Boorde (c. 1490–1549), a physician and the author of the first English guidebook to Europe, wrote that "water is not wholesome, sole by itself, for an Englishman." Anywhere near a populated area, water was not safe to drink and people would avoid it unless they were extremely poor.

Mineral springs in remote idyllic settings, on the other hand, were more appealing. Paracelsus studied them, and it may have influenced his mineral-forward medical approach. Spas based around natural springs date to pre-Roman times, though the Romans had a particular affinity for building baths in the home country and around the parts of Europe they conquered. Bath, in England, is a hot spring with its public facilities built by the Romans in the first century CE. Its restorative powers (legend has it) were discovered by an exiled prince in 863 BCE who wallowed in the same warm mud in the region as he witnessed pigs doing, and this cured his leprosy.

The practice of "taking the waters" at places like Bath—or like Apollinaris or Selters (from which we get the word "seltzer") in Germany, Badoit in France, and Spa in Belgium—would provide both good clean miasma-free air and water pure enough to drink. There were different types of mineral springs: wells would provide healing waters to drink, baths offered therapeutic bathing and recreation, and at spas one could drink the water *or* swim in it.

In the 1700s, the upper-class practice of visiting the baths caught on with the newly wealthy tradesperson class. Visiting spas for extended periods was like the present-day version of taking the family to a summer resort in the Catskills. Drinking water from health spas became fashionable for specific medical conditions as well as for general health.

German professor of medicine Friedrich Hoffmann (1660–1742) wrote in the late 1600s that the curative power of mineral waters was limited to the sparkling ones alone, and he went on to categorize the different springs as being rich in iron (for strengthening limbs and healing ulcers) or neutral salts (for intermittent fevers). Chalybeate (iron-containing) springs were often recommended by doctors for "impoverished blood." Iron-deficiency anemia impacts a large percentage of the population globally, particularly pregnant women, children, and the elderly, but it can also be caused by parasites like hookworms. Iron-rich spas were a natural treatment for anemia.

Some waters were high in magnesium; Epsom salts are magnesium sulfate that are still used both externally to soothe soreness, and internally as a laxative. Other waters high in bicarbonate were used to soothe the stomach. Yet other springs were recommended to cure goiter (swollen thyroid in the neck), which was usually caused by a lack of iodine in the days before iodized salt.

In the 1875 book *On the Curative Effects of Baths and Waters: Being a Handbook to the Spas of Europe*, the author Dr. Julius Braun considers matters of general health in diet, exercise, country air, and elevation, before discussing the therapeutic uses of warm versus cold baths, and then describes the salt, sulfur, sea, mud, alkaline, chalybeate, and other types of waters found at various spas. Apollinaris water is described in this book as "very useful in chronic bronchial catarrh [mucus buildup] in tendency to gall stone to gout and to the lithic acid diathesis [predisposition]. This and other highly gaseous alkaline waters form also an useful and agreeable vehicle for some medicines and a desirable addition to aperient [laxative] bitter waters the effect of which is in many cases decidedly increased thus allowing a diminution of the aperient dose and of its weakening effect."

The most famous mineral waters were bottled and sold as medicinal thirst quenchers, and also specified for mixed drinks. Apollinaris was the Perrier of its day, calling itself "The Queen of Table Waters." A "Scotch and Polly" was a Scotch and Soda with Apollinaris water, made popular in part by a comic song of the same name from 1900. In the 1862 book *The Bar-Tender's Guide* (also known as *How to Mix Drinks, or the Bon-Vivant's Companion*) by Jerry Thomas

(1830–1885), the author specifies Selters and later Apollinaris water in recipes. Vichy water is named in Harry Johnson's 1882 *New and Improved Bartender's Manual*.

Perrier comes from a spring near Vergèze, France, where Carthaginian general Hannibal supposedly rested his army's horses and war elephants on the way to Rome around 200 BCE. Much later, in 1863, Napoleon III approved its official status as natural mineral water, and it became a health spa. The spring was later sold to a Dr. Perrier who promoted the virtues of thermal water, and then to a businessman who closed the spa and decided to compete with the soft drink industry after 1900. The bottle shape of Perrier was meant to resemble an Indian club, once used for exercise (connecting the product to the idea of fitness) and now used for juggling.

The water for the brand Badoit was known in pre-Roman times, and in 1778 the physician to King Louis XVI prescribed Badoit's naturally sparkling water to "enhance the appetite, soothe digestion and make cheerful the spirit," according to the brand's website. In 1841 it was sold in bottles as "hydrotherapy at home," and ads in the 1930s featured a cartoon of "Docteur Bien-Vivre" speaking to its invigorating properties.

Evian "was discovered by a local French nobleman, the Marquis de Lessert, in the town of Évian-les-Bains," in 1789, according to the website. The water was sold locally, and a thermal health spa was opened at the site in 1806, followed in 1826 by the first bottling facility. It was first imported to the US in 1978 and marketed as a luxury item, with special edition bottles created by fashion designers.

In the United States, modern bottled water sources (or at least their brand names) often have histories as health spas as well. The

Iroquois and Mohawk peoples frequented Saratoga Springs, and the Wappo peoples of Napa Valley visited the geysers that became Calistoga Water. Poland Spring's source water in Maine supposedly cured a farmer of kidney stones in the early 1840s, and the spring became a steam bath and therapeutic water-cure retreat. The water labeled under brand names like these today is more likely to be tapped from elsewhere in the water system than at the specific springs that were made famous from people bathing in it.

In Texas, a town that became known as Mineral Wells saw more than 150,000 annual visitors by 1900, and the local "Crazy Water" was said to make a sane person insane and vice versa. (It turns out that some of the wells had high levels of lithium, which is sometimes prescribed as a mood stabilizer for bipolar disorder.) Bottled lithia water became a major health craze in the late 1800s.

Topo Chico, the extra-bubbly mineral water from Monterrey, Mexico, has been bottled since 1895 and is now owned by Coca-Cola. The website once told the legend of a "beautiful Aztec princess" in the 1400s. "After spending some time there, taking baths and drinking from the water, the daughter of Moctezuma I, his priests, and chiefs returned to the Anahuac lands optimistic, strong, happy, and refreshed. The news about the Princess's recovery spread throughout the kingdom and has passed from generation to generation up until modern times."

Topo Chico became the preferred sparkling water in a drink known in Texas as Ranch Water, though the original form of the cocktail was probably closer to a sparkling Margarita. Today several canned hard seltzer and cocktail brands sell a premade Ranch Water for those who don't want to do the mixing themselves.

RANCH WATER

2 ounces (60 ml) 100 percent agave blanco tequila

1 12-ounce bottle chilled Topo Chico sparkling water

1 lime wedge

Drink about three ounces of Topo Chico. Pour the tequila
into the bottle and squeeze in juice from the lime.

. . . . .

The purity, rather than the healthfulness, of water is used as a marketing point by spirits companies around the world, particularly
whiskey distilleries. On the tour of Jack Daniel's Tennessee Whiskey,
guides point out the cave from which the limestone water was sourced.
The Yamazaki Distillery location was chosen "where the Katsura,
Uji and Kizu rivers converge, providing a unique misty climate and
one of Japan's softest waters." At Glenmorangie, in Scotland, a visit
to the Tarlogie Springs is part of the press tour.

Most of the time, though, the special water you hear about from
distilleries is only used to ferment the base malt or other material. After
distillation, most spirits are reduced from distillation proof down to
bottle strength by mineral-free, reverse-osmosis filtered municipal tap
water.

SCALING UP FIZZY WATER

As mineral spa waters were considered healthy, entrepreneurs set
about selling them to those people wisely choosing to avoid drinking

out of the Thames or other polluted municipal sources. The first artificial mineral waters were attempts at re-creating those of famous spas, and they were produced with similar mineral contents as their inspirations. Robert Boyle published in 1685 *Short Memoirs for the Natural Experimental History of Mineral Waters*, which explains various methods for analysis of spa waters to determine their mineral content and thus their medicinal qualities.

Naturally carbonated mineral springs become fizzy from trapped gases released from volcanic magma underground, which flow up into the water sources above them. These waters were especially prized, so after Priestley showed the world how to force carbonate, the race was on to re-create these waters.

William Bewley (1726–1783), an apothecary from Norfolk, published a recipe for Bewley's Mephitic Julep. It was not a cocktail but a sparkling water with added sodium bicarbonate: "julep" was an Arabic term for a medicinal beverage before it became known as a word for a refreshing one. Bewley's drink was prescribed by doctors to treat "putrid fevers, scurvy, dysentery, bilious vomiting, etc."

Thomas Henry (1734–1816) was another apothecary who expanded on Priestley's method in an attempt to make bulk quantities of fizzy, spa-imitating waters, along with Bewley's Mephitic Julep, and is credited with being the first commercial seller of artificially carbonated water. He followed Priestley's advice to employ a pump to concentrate the gas, using a pig's bladder to hold it. Thankfully, someone suggested replacing the pig's bladder with household fire bellows, probably improving the taste of the resulting beverage significantly.

Jacob Schweppe (1740–1821) of Geneva was an amateur scientist who read about these new methods to impregnate water with gas and reproduced and expanded on the experiments at home. He assembled a commercial-scale apparatus by 1783 and started giving his bubbly waters away to local doctors at first. Later, as the business grew, he sold both a generic "acidulous soda water" and mineral waters imitating those of Pyrmont, Selters, Spa, and others, some of which were available in single, double, and triple strength with increasing amounts of mineral salts. The Selters (seltzer) water was recommended as a cooling drink for "persons exhausted by much speaking, heated by dancing, or when quitting hot rooms or crowded assemblies."

BUGS AND BEER

While Joseph Priestley's observation of fermenting beer led to an understanding of gases, the wine and beer studies of French chemist and microbiologist Louis Pasteur (1822–1895) inspired the germ theory of disease. Germ theory was not first proposed by Pasteur— Italian physician Girolamo Fracastoro (c. 1478–1553) usually gets the credit for that. Fracastoro was the author of the 1530 classic *Syphilis, or the French Disease*, which was written in Latin rhyme. In his later work *On Contagion* (1546), he explained how "little seeds of disease" could spread not by miasma but by direct contact with an infected person or contact with intimate items like clothing worn by an infected person. Unfortunately, Fracastoro lacked the microscope to prove it.

Microscopy took off in the 1600s but was vastly improved in the 1800s, and Pasteur capitalized on the advanced technology. He earned a doctorate in sciences in 1847 and in 1848 published his first of many discoveries that changed the understanding of the world. He studied wine tartrates (crystalline deposits that drop out of wines during fermentation and aging) and figured out the existence of molecular asymmetry—that molecules can have the same formula but different configurations, like left versus right shoes. This was the foundation of the discipline of stereochemistry, the part of chemistry concerned with the three-dimensional properties of molecules.

Next Pasteur studied fermentation with the intent of showing that it was a biological process rather than a chemical one. Recall that chalk or other alkaline substances when combined with vinegar or other acids in the presence of water fizzes up and releases carbon dioxide—the volcano science experiment. If this was purely a chemical reaction, then fermentation, which is also bubbly and also releases carbon dioxide, surely must be a chemical process too.

MICHELADA

1 bottle Mexican lager beer

0.5 ounce (15 ml) lime juice

2 dashes Tabasco hot sauce

1 dash Tapatío hot sauce

Small pinch of salt

Add all ingredients to a pint glass with ice.

· · · · ·

But Pasteur had the idea from his studies of wine tartrates that only living things could produce optically active asymmetrical compounds (meaning that polarized light that shines through them is rotated at different angles). He studied fermentation with the idea that it could be shown to be a microbial process, and about ten years after his crystallography discovery he published his first work toward proving it. The paper was on lactic fermentation, the thing that makes milk taste sour or turns it into yogurt, ferments pickles and sauerkraut, and makes sour beer sour. Pasteur wrote that he had discovered a specific type of fermentation that produced lactic acid from sugar, and he insisted that the process was due to a living microorganism.

He further extracted grape juice from a grape without it coming into contact with the skin and saw that it did not ferment. Pasteur believed that these experiments implied living organisms were required to cause the biological process of fermentation (as well as putrefaction), and that without those organisms the fermentation would not occur. This implied that the leading theory of spontaneous generation must be false.

Spontaneous generation held that life came from nonliving materials, like maggots "sprouting" from a leftover piece of meat, or mold growing or "coming to life" on soup left out on the counter a long time. Pasteur wasn't the first to doubt the theory of spontaneous generation, but his work helped disprove it. He publicly demonstrated that without existing life (microorganisms) present, the maggots and the mold would not appear.

Pasteur boiled in a series of flasks sugared yeast water that would ferment quickly if left exposed to the elements. Some flasks he left open to the air, while other flasks had their necks bent so that no air could get in afterward. As expected, the sealed flasks remained unspoiled, as they were uncontaminated by living microbes. He had shown that living things come only from living things. He claimed, "Never will the doctrine of spontaneous generation recover from the fatal blow that this simple experiment delivers to it."

Spontaneous generation was so ingrained in the science of the day that it would take years of advocacy to fully discredit it, so Pasteur's discovery was more like a long-term injury than a fatal blow. He repeated his experiments with other liquids, including urine and milk (not together), to show that heating them to certain levels would preserve them from spoilage as well. The process of heating food products to kill microorganisms and extend shelf life became known as "pasteurization."

Over a twenty-year period (with a five-year break in which he studied silkworm diseases and saved France's entire silk industry), Pasteur figured out the various ways beer and wine could spoil in fermentation, storage, and transport, and came up with standardized procedures for preventing spoilage and extending the life of these products. He understood that microorganisms competing with the preferred yeast strain could lead to spoilage or off flavors. As a result, in modern beverage alcohol production a specific strain of yeast is typically added to the grapes or grain, enough to vastly outnumber the natural yeasts floating around in the environment. The temperature of fermentation is controlled so that the desired yeast thrive and competing bacteria don't get a foothold. In 1866 Pasteur published *Études sur le vin*, about the diseases of wine, and in 1876 he published *Études sur la bière*, wrapping up this era of his work. He then went on to study infectious diseases in animals and people, and again he changed the world.

Smallpox is a disease estimated to have killed three hundred million people in the twentieth century alone. In the early 1700s, Lady

Mary Wortley Montagu (1689–1762) traveled with her husband to Turkey, where she learned of variolation (inoculation). She had previously contracted and survived smallpox herself but was disfigured by it, and in Turkey she had her son inoculated, followed by her other children upon returning home. Inoculation involved taking a sample from the pus of a smallpox blister and introducing it to a scratch on the arm or leg of a healthy person to induce a smaller, usually harmless case of the disease. Lady Mary became an advocate for the practice, but she was met with resistance from the medical establishment because it was a folk medicine. Even so, she convinced other members of the ruling class, including Catherine the Great of Russia in 1768, to inoculate themselves and their children.

The Turkish method was inoculation, meaning the dangerous organism was introduced to the patient in a controlled way, while vaccination means introducing a weaker version of the pathogen instead. By the end of the century, Dr. Edward Jenner (1749–1823) had vaccinated people using cowpox rather than actual smallpox to create immunity, with great success. It was one of the first diseases to be controlled by a vaccine, and it was accomplished without an understanding of infectious microorganisms.

In the next century Pasteur helped discover vaccines for other diseases. German physician Robert Koch (1843–1910) isolated the anthrax bacterium in 1876, and both he and Pasteur confirmed it spread the disease. This established the germ theory of disease, a natural progression from the germ theory of fermentation. Germ theory is usually credited to Pasteur, Koch, and Joseph Lister, who promoted antiseptics. Pasteur then developed a vaccine for rabies, which was first applied to a human in 1885.

LISTER

The miasma theory held that diseases were associated with foul-smelling air, which could be caused by stagnant water of swamps in the countryside or human sewage in more populous locations, including overcrowded slums. Hospitals of the 1800s were no great exception to overcrowding nor to foul smells of putrefying flesh and bodily fluids. Florence Nightingale (1820–1910) showed that sanitary conditions improved the survival rate during the Crimean War (1853–1856). Hospitals were redesigned, when possible, for more space between patients and increased air circulation to minimize miasma-based illness.

But because disease was supposedly caused by the air, there was no need to clean equipment. Surgeons, as opposed to educated physicians, were trained through apprenticeships. Throughout most of history, surgery was divorced from medicine, with barber-surgeons performing menial tasks such as bloodletting, haircutting, shaving, and extracting teeth. Many still didn't attend university in the early 1800s, not that they would have learned germ theory there until the latter part of the century.

Surgeons would perform operations on patient after patient without changing or cleaning their tools, their clothes, or the bed linen. Hospitals were rightfully feared, and people checked themselves in only in extreme distress. Surgery inside a hospital was a last resort, and some patients chose to run (literally get up and run) after learning they were headed in for surgery. The mortality rate was incredibly high from infection, even if the patient survived the initial cutting.

The miasma theory of disease was problematic when it came to explaining cholera, an infection of the small intestine caused by bacteria and characterized by extreme diarrhea with rapid depletion of body fluids. Cholera clearly followed populations, came and went in outbreaks, and often showed up when there was nothing especially smelly around. Attempted cures for cholera's diarrhea included vinegar, camphor, wine, horseradish, mint, mustard plaster, leeches and bloodletting, laudanum, calomel (mercury salts), and steam baths.

A surgeon named John Snow (1813–1858) showed in 1854 that most of the people who died from a particular cholera outbreak were all collecting water from the same Broad Street pump in London. Yet a brewery was also located on Broad Street, and none of the men working there died of cholera. The brewery had its own well. The workers at another factory a few yards away did get sick of cholera; so these workers in two different factories were breathing the same air but drinking different water. It couldn't be miasma. As it turns out, the Broad Street pump was located only a few yards from a sewer. John Snow is now known as the father of epidemiology for his work tracking the disease.

Another contemporary argument against the miasma theory was that in the summer of 1858, a "Great Stink" floated over London owing to human excrement piled up on the shores of the river Thames. It polluted the air so thoroughly that people fled the city to avoid its sure-to-follow cholera epidemic. And yet no epidemic came.

Later, professor Alois Pick (1859–1945) in Vienna showed that wine when added to water killed the cholera and typhoid bacilli within it, and that the more wine added, the quicker it worked. This finding was announced in 1892 while there was a cholera epidemic in Hamburg, so citizens were advised to add wine to their water several hours before drinking it.

WINE SPRITZER

White wine or dry vermouth

Soda water

To an ice-filled wineglass add 75 percent wine and
25 percent soda water. Garnish with a lemon slice.

• • • • •

Joseph Lister (1827–1912) was a British surgeon with more practical
knowledge of medicine and familiarity with microscopic studies than
most people in his profession. His father was a wine merchant and amateur scientist who made an important improvement in equipment for
the microscope. Lister became familiar with the microbiological work
of Pasteur's germ theory of fermentation and thought that germs might
be introduced into surgical wounds like yeast into crushed grapes.

While Pasteur's work showed how sterility could be achieved by
heat, filtration, or antiseptics, Lister focused on the only one of these
that would work on skin. He wrote, "When I read Pasteur's article,
I said to myself: just as we can destroy lice on the nit-filled head of a
child by applying a poison that causes no lesion to the scalp, so I believe that we can apply to a patient's wounds toxic products that will
destroy the bacteria without harming the soft parts of this tissue."

A few antiseptics were being considered and promoted by other
surgeons (though they did not share the belief in germ theory), but
Lister settled on carbolic acid. Carbolic acid was extracted from coal
tar, which is an important substance that comes into play in the history of both tonic water and syphilis. More on that in chapter 8.

Carbolic acid was used to clean sewers and kill the smell of sewage dumped onto animal fields. Beginning in 1865, Lister used it to sterilize the wounds, the doctor, the instruments, and even the air in the operating room during surgeries. Carbolic acid was a very harsh skin irritant, though, so Lister diluted it with water and later with olive oil to reduce its impact on a patient's skin. This was instantly successful at dramatically reducing the postsurgery death rate of patients, though Lister still had to argue that it worked because of germs. He then toured several countries, including the United States, to show off the new technique.

Robert Wood Johnson (1845–1910) attended one of Lister's talks in Philadelphia and was inspired by it to go into the business of making sterile dressings and sutures, along with his brothers. They named the company Johnson & Johnson.

Dr. Joseph Joshua Lawrence was there in Philadelphia too. In 1879 he launched the honorific Listerine antiseptic "for use in surgeries and bathing wounds." Initially an alcohol-based formula that was promoted as an all-purpose germicide, it was recommended as a deodorant, as an athlete's foot and dandruff treatment, as a floor cleaner, and as a preventative against smallpox, gonorrhea, and other diseases. It was specifically marketed to dentists and was later sold as the first over-the-counter mouthwash in the United States.

Much of the overlapping history of alcohol and medicine concerns the use of alcohol *as* medicine, but beer, wine, and fizzy spa water inspired great progress in medical science. By studying and replicating the natural processes of carbonation and fermentation, scientists begun to understand the nature of gases and the existence of invisible microbes. These inspired new theories about the cause of diseases and methods to kill germs, sometimes using alcohol itself to do so.

Along the way, we were rewarded with longer-lasting beer and minty fresh breath.

GREEN BEAST

3 slices peeled seedless cucumber

1 ounce (30 ml) simple syrup

1 ounce (30 ml) Pernod absinthe

1 ounce (30 ml) lime juice

4 ounces (120 ml) chilled water

Muddle cucumbers with simple syrup in a cocktail shaker.
Add ice and other ingredients. Shake and strain into a
highball glass with new ice. Garnish with a cucumber slice.
This cocktail, created by Charles Vexenat, could be
said to resemble the color of mouthwash.

BITTERSWEET

APERITIF, ABSINTHE, *and* AMARO

LONDON, April 24. Cocktails with "kicks," otherwise with drops of absinthe in its pure form, which are being freely served at London bars, though their sale is prohibited in France, Germany, and Italy, have caused *The Lancet*, a medical paper, to publish a grave warning of their effects.

The *Lancet* article states that absinthe is liable to cause hallucinations and delirium and set up a craving not unlike that experienced by morphine and cocaine addicts. It urges that a prohibition of absinthe be immediately imposed, apart from a general prohibition of alcohol.

—The New York Times, *April 25, 1930*

The human nose has around four hundred scent receptors, and recent studies estimate we can sense one trillion different odors, up from the previous estimate of a mere ten thousand. The tongue, on the other hand, is more of a blunt instrument that can detect the "five basic tastes," of sweet, salty, sour, bitter, and umami, as much as we know so far. The tongue is a probe, the final checkpoint for food acceptance or rejection. First we use our other senses: we look at food to see if it is the right color and seems edible, then we smell it and feel it to estimate if it's ripe or rotten, but then we taste it to determine if we should spit it out or swallow.

When we taste something sweet like sugar or honey, we know it contains carbohydrates like sucrose. Glutamate receptors on the tongue detect umami, the savory flavor of meat, seafood, or fermented items like soy sauce. These pleasant flavors, especially in conjunction, let us know that we have just licked a high-energy or protein-rich food source.

Sour flavors identify acids that can be delightful or extremely unpleasant. They warn us against underripe fruit and rotten meat. Sour candies make us scrunch up our face and pucker—a sure sign that we should reject them if we didn't already know better. The balance between sweet and sour tells us when fruit is just right to eat, or when a Daiquiri's lime and sugar are perfectly balanced. Salt too can go either way—a little bit is great, but too much is terrible. Humans need a balance of salt and water in the body, which is why we get thirsty after eating a whole bag of potato chips.

Bitterness alerts us to the presence of poisons in food, like strychnine in nux vomica tree seeds, which were taken to induce vomiting. Bitter flavors can become pleasant once we are accustomed to them and associate them with positive side effects, like the energy that accompanies tea and coffee and the buzz of alcohol infused with wormwood and gentian. When we eat or drink something bitter, we naturally salivate, then our stomach juices start churning. Higher doses of the same bitter foods can cause diarrhea or be abortifacient. Everything from salivation to purging is our body trying to quickly process and eliminate poisons.

Humans and other animals have adapted their diets to take advantage of bitterness. The main bittering plants used in alcoholic drinks are wormwood, gentian, quinine, and rhubarb root, but dozens of other botanicals are employed. Slightly bitter vermouth and other aperitifs are typically consumed before a meal to stimulate appetite and "open the palate." Bitter amari and other digestifs help us process foods after a meal and soothe the pain of overeating. Bitter drinks are functional beverages.

SUGAR AND CAFFEINE

But before the bitter, the sweet. Sugar and honey were both used as medicine, and both have current medicine-related uses. Honey is antibacterial and was used to seal and help heal wounds, and even today there are medical honey "wound and burn dressing" products available commercially. It was further used externally against sores and snakebites.

Honey mixed with wine was called "mulsum" and came highly recommended by Pliny, among others, as an appetite stimulant, against jaundice, as a heart stimulant, for fevers and coughs, and as a purgative if one drank poison (which seemed to happen a lot in olden times). Honey mixed with vinegar and water is called "oxymel," and it was used medicinally, particularly to treat smallpox. A brand from the 1800s, Bake's Oxymel of Horehound, was advertised as "invaluable for coughs, asthma, whooping cough."

Sugarcane is probably native to New Guinea and was propagated from there. Writing of India in 325 BCE, Nearchus, a general in Alexander the Great's military, said, "A reed in India brings forth honey without the help of bees, from which an intoxicating drink is made though the plant bears no fruit." Pliny wrote of sugar, "It is a kind of honey that collects in reeds, white like gum, and brittle to the teeth; the largest pieces are the size of a hazelnut. It is only employed as a medicine."

Sugarcane crops were transplanted from India westward to the Middle East, North Africa, Sicily, and southern Spain—the lands of the Abbasid caliphate of the Islamic Golden Age. During this era, sugar became a luxury food, like truffles or gold-foil-covered steak today: it was added to all sorts of dishes and even molded into sculptures for feasts and celebrations. From the Arab world, it was next transported to the Canary and Madeira Islands, and from there it was taken to the New World by the Spanish and Portuguese and propagated in Brazil and in the Caribbean.

Medicinal sugar was commonly but not always prescribed to treat conditions of the respiratory system. Constantine the African, known for transcribing Arabic texts into Latin at Salerno in the eleventh century, commented on sugar's internal and external medicinal uses. During his lifetime it was prescribed for coughs, chest ailments, and stomach ailments. In 1748 *A Complete History of Drugs* was translated from French and mentioned that sugar was good for the lungs, coughs, asthma, kidneys, and the bladder.

Thomas Aquinas in the thirteenth century decided that spiced sugars did not violate religious fasts because they were "not eaten with the end in mind of nourishment, but rather for ease in digestion; accordingly, they do not break the fast any more than taking of any other medicine." Arnald of Villanova recommended sugar cooked into various foods for medicinal purposes, and soon after it was an ingredient in many plague medicines. Into the Middle Ages and beyond, sugar was sold in apothecary shops, and a good number of recipes in cookbooks that included sugar were specifically intended for the sick; it was the chicken soup of its day.

As it became more readily available to Europeans, sugar was used as a spice, food, and preservative. After 1500, sugar from the New World was sent back to Europe. Soon afterward, chocolate, tea, and coffee were also sent to Europe and England from abroad, and all were paired with sugar there, despite usually being consumed unsweetened in their homelands. All these caffeinated beverages had medicinal qualities also and often provided alternatives to alcohol.

Chocolate was known to the Aztecs, who used it as a currency and beverage, and various Europeans in the 1500s reported that it was used in South America to build strength and to treat angina, constipation, dysentery, dyspepsia, fatigue, gout, hemorrhoids, and kidney problems. In Europe it was assigned humoral properties and given a host of medicinal uses.

Coffee from Ethiopia became a popular beverage in Arab lands, and cafes specializing in coffee consumption were opened by the mid-1500s. The coffee craze hit Europe the next century, and in the 1700s the European superpowers were planting coffee plants in their own territories. When the drink was first introduced to England, it was described as medicinal against sore eyes, headache, coughs, dropsy, gout, scurvy, miscarriages, and, of course, drowsiness.

Tea is native to the Himalayas and was rubbed on wounds, chewed to invigorate, and eaten in medicinal gruel in China. It is also antiseptic and kills the bacteria that cause cholera, typhoid, and dysentery, making it a safer beverage to drink than plain water or probably even beer. Plus, the water used for it is usually boiled, killing even more nasties. During the Industrial Revolution in England, tea drinking was retroactively credited with significantly reducing the incidences of waterborne diseases among workers.

ESPRESSO MARTINI

2 ounces (60 ml) vodka

0.75 ounce (20 ml) coffee liqueur

1 ounce (30 ml) espresso

Add all ingredients to an ice-filled shaker.
Shake and strain into a cocktail glass.

VERMOUTH

Artemisia absinthium (grand wormwood, or simply absinthe), is an extremely bitter plant with its name possibly coming from the Greek word "apsinthion," meaning "undrinkable." It is the darling of the wormwoods, but the *Artemisia* genus contains hundreds of species, and many are used in beverages in addition to or instead of grand wormwood. They include *Artemisia pontica* (Roman wormwood, or small wormwood), *Artemisia vulgaris* (mugwort, or common wormwood), and *Artemisia genepi* (spiked wormwood, mountain sage, or just genepi). These other wormwoods are usually less bitter and lower in the regulated compound thujone, and sometimes they are used to color spirits as well as flavor them. Pontica can be the dominant wormwood used in vermouth. Genepi flavors the category of génépi, or génépy, liqueurs, which are popular après-ski drinks near the plant's home in the Pyrenees and Alps.

"Vermouth" comes from the German "Wermut," meaning "wormwood." Today it is a fortified wine usually infused with some species of wormwood (it is not legally required in the United States) and other botanicals. Wormwood wines were popular during Roman times, recommended medicinally and sometimes recreationally. Pliny wrote about wormwood wine in the first century of the Common Era, in addition to other flavored "artificial" wines, as he called them.

These ancient wines were usually accented with other spices and sweeteners to tone down or distract from the harsh bitterness of wormwood. A 1555 book cites a wormwood wine with added nard (spikenard), cinnamon, cassia, calamus, ginger grass, and crushed date pit. Other recipes included backing botanicals like rosemary, ginger, and cinnamon, plus sweeteners including dates and sugar.

The medicinal qualities of wormwood and wormwood wines are largely related to the stomach, digestion, and purging, as are most bitter botanicals. Wormwood was used as an appetite stimulant, as a treatment for stomach pain and nausea, and as a laxative, as well as to promote urination and menstruation and to induce abortion. A 1560 German medical text described "vermouth wine" as "very good for old age, both for the cold and the hot tempers. . . . It gets rid of bad breath due to stomach upset and stimulates the liver and the pancreas. It improves the skin and the complexion and it is to be drunk before and after eating." It was also used as a vermifuge to rid the body of intestinal parasites.

The English herbalist Nicholas Culpeper (1616–1654) had a particular fondness for wormwood. He published in 1652 a tome that would be later called *The Complete Herbal*, which has been in print ever since. His goal in part was to make herbal medicine accessible to the masses, not just to the rich who could afford physicians. He cites wormwood as an effective treatment for a ridiculous number of ailments. A much-toned-down (and easier-to-read) edition from the 1800s cites wormwood's use against dropsy, jaundice, intermittent fevers, gangrene, and—mixed with vinegar—as an "antidote to the mischief of mushrooms and henbane, and to the biting of a shrew."

Wormwood was sometimes used in place of hops in beer. Dr. W. P. Worth, in the 1692 *On the New and True Art of Brewing*, wrote that "[hopping beer] may be in every respect as well performed with wormwood, and in some sense more agreeable, for wormwood is endued with many virtuous qualities, it strengthens the stomach, resists putrefaction, prevents surfeits, strengthening both the retentive and expansive faculty, and many more, as may be seen in every herbal, when as hops we do not attribute one half the virtues."

Wormwood-laced beer, called "purl," was popular in England in the 1600s, and mentioned by Shakespeare in *The Merry Wives of Windsor*. It included other spices as well and was typically consumed warm in the mornings to settle the stomach. (Later into the 1800s, the word "purl" became associated with a cocktail of beer with added gin, sugar, and ginger.) Purl-Royal was purl but with a sherry base. The historian David Wondrich writes, "If you were to taste Purl-Royal today, you'd have no trouble at all classifying it: vermouth."

Vermouth is a fortified, aromatized wine. Wines have been fortified with high-proof alcohol since the time of Arnald of Villanova. He described adding distilled alcohol to fermenting grape juice. This would stop the fermentation, resulting in a naturally sweet, extra-strength wine. This style of wine is known today as "vin doux naturel." The more common way to achieve a similar result is to fully ferment wine and add fortifying distilled alcohol, plus sugar if desired to sweeten it. But sugar is a lot easier to come by these days.

Other fortified wines include sherry from Spain, marsala from Italy, port from Portugal, and Madeira from Portugal's Madeira Islands off the coast of Africa, but unlike vermouth these are not "aromatized" with botanicals. They were all fortified to prevent spoilage during shipping, particularly for shipping to Britain, where very little wine was produced but much consumed. Many of the port houses today were founded in the 1600s and 1700s by the British, and by the mid-1800s fortification became standard in the category. Sherry used to be fortified just before shipping to preserve the wine for the trip from Spain to England, but eventually the solera system was developed in which wine is fortified, then blended with older wines successively over a series of years.

BAMBOO

1.5 ounces (45 ml) amontillado sherry

1.5 ounces (45 ml) dry vermouth

1 dash Angostura bitters

1 dash orange bitters

Stir all ingredients in a stirring pitcher with
ice and strain into a cocktail glass.
Garnish with a lemon twist.

· · · · ·

Madeira notably can remain unspoiled even after bottles have been open for up to a year, which would have been handy on long journeys across the ocean. The Madeira Islands are now part of Portugal, located along a shipping route between Europe and Asia before the Suez Canal was built. Madeira was fortified beginning in the 1700s and as with sherry, it was first done just before shipping. Now fortification happens before the end of the fermentation process. Marsala was conceived and produced by British merchants in Sicily, inspired by Madeira.

Vermouth was not fortified for shipping but designed to assist in digestion. Into the seventeenth and eighteenth centuries, wormwood wines called "Wermutwein" were popular in Germany. Paracelsus wrote about them, noting that they were to be taken in the morning as a general panacea, like purl. But the modern form of vermouth was developed in parts of present-day France and Italy mostly in the first decades of the 1800s.

Despite its Germanic name deriving from "Wermut," for "wormwood," the flavor profile of vermouth is not particularly dominated by the bitter herb—or at least not the *grand* wormwood member of the artemisia species as in the medicinal wines of Roman times. During vermouth's early existence at the end of the 1700s, there are records in Italy of bottles allocated to a wet nurse and a sick person, and other cues that it was once considered at least somewhat healthy. But like many other categories of wine and spirits, vermouth evolved into something merely helpful for digestion.

The new vermouth was fortified with distilled spirits and could include thirty botanicals in harmony with the base wine, rather than merely using wine as a menstruum for medicine. Beyond wormwood, common botanicals found in vermouth include cinnamon, cloves, coriander, elecampane, sweet flag (calamus), blessed thistle, centaury, iris, angelica, gentian, orange peel, and nutmeg, but the range is end-less. In recent years, new vermouth producers (as well as gin makers) internationally have taken to showcasing regional botanicals in their blends.

In Turin, a standard part of everyday life in the later 1800s was to drink a small glass of vermouth an hour before lunch or dinner as an aperitif to get the gastric juices flowing. It was described (as men-tioned in *The Grand Book of Vermouth di Torino*) in Turin in 1873 as follows: "The confectioners in Turin also serve liqueurs (the famous vermouth, a Turinese creation) and other drinks. It is the custom, during the day; when you feel the need for refreshment, to enter a confectioner's and take standing up a pastry (especially warm ones). Even the young ladies, even if unaccompanied, can freely take ad-vantage of the custom, which is part of everyday Turin life, without fear of breaching the laws of etiquette."

This tradition of taking a vermouth as a palate stimulant before a meal lives on in Spain and is known as "la hora del vermut," or "the vermouth hour." The ritual is practiced by some before lunch and others before dinner, and it is certainly not limited to just one drink or one hour. In Italian cities, the aperitivo hour is a similar postwork, predinner time of around 7:00–9:00 p.m., when everyone jams into the cafes to sip a quick vermouth or an aperitif cocktail or two. Small, complimentary snacks are included with the price of the drink, and the time is used to catch up on the day with others before heading off to dinner.

CHRYSANTHEMUM

2 ounces (60 ml) dry vermouth

1 ounce (30 ml) Bénédictine

3 dashes absinthe

Stir all ingredients with ice in a stirring pitcher and
strain into a coupe. Garnish with an orange twist.

ABSINTHE

In France in the mid-1800s, the predinner cafe tradition was called
"l'heure verte," or "the green hour," named for the (often) green-
colored wormwood beverage absinthe. The drink was an inspiration
to artists like Vincent van Gogh and Henri de Toulouse-Lautrec,
and writers like Charles Baudelaire and Arthur Rimbaud. It was also
rumored to make you hallucinate, cut off your own ear, or kill your
family. Then it was banned in several countries for nearly a century.

Less well remembered is that absinthe's popularity grew from its
history of medicinal use. We've already seen wormwood infused into
beer, sherry, and wine. John French commented in 1667 that it stops
wind (gas), kills worms, hinders vomiting, provokes appetite, and
strengthens the stomach. The book on which he comments is *The
Distiller of London*, a 1639 manual for physicians. It includes a recipe
for wormwood water that is merely common wormwood and aniseed
distilled and sweetened with sugar. That's pretty close to an absinthe
recipe, a spirit supposedly not invented until the middle or end of the
1700s.

The romantic version of the birth of absinthe is that it was invented by the Henriod sisters in Val-de-Travers, Switzerland, and it was promoted by an exiled French doctor, Pierre Ordinaire, in the region. He prescribed it as a medical tonic to cure everything from worms to gout to kidney stones. It was an "elixir of wormwood, composed of aromatic plants of which only he knew the secret. Many people, having made use of it, declared themselves radically cured and the doctor could not pretend to be other than pleased and to prescribe its use," according to a translated 1896 Pernod absinthe booklet.

Another version of the story is that Ordinaire invented the recipe and then it was produced by the Henriod sisters, establishing a French origin of absinthe rather than Swiss. In any case, the recipe was sold in 1797 to a Major Dubied, who scaled up production to commercialize it with his son-in-law Henri-Louis Pernod (1776–1851). Pernod built a new distillery across the French border in Pontarlier in 1805, which is the founding date used by the Pernod brand.

Absinthe is named for the grand wormwood *Artemisia absinthium*, but the dominant taste of the beverage is anise, which comes from aniseed, star anise, fennel, or a combination thereof. Fennel is used for digestion and flatulence (sugar-coated fennel seeds are often located next to the cash register at Indian restaurants) and is recommended to stimulate milk production in nursing mothers. Anise was used against flatulence too, and also for coughs and other issues with breathing and bronchitis. Star anise was taken to aid digestion and for coughs (as an expectorant), as well as for pain relief. In modern medicine, a compound in star anise is used to make Tamiflu, a drug used to treat influenza as well as bird flu.

Melissa (lemon balm) is another common additive to absinthe; it contributes citrusy mint notes. Hyssop, also minty and used in herbal medicine as an expectorant and cough suppressant, contributes to absinthe's flavoring as well as to its green coloring after distillation; so too does small wormwood *Artemisia pontica*.

France invaded and colonized Algeria in North Africa in the 1830s and 1840s, and the French soldiers there were supplied with rations of absinthe. The high-proof spirit was used to purify waters against dysentery and to prevent malaria. Dysentery is caused by either bacteria or an amoeba, transmitted through food or water contaminated by the feces of an infected person. The alcohol in absinthe may have helped kill the biological organisms in drinking water, and the wormwood was taken to rid the digestive system of parasites.

Malaria, on the other hand, is caused by a parasite that is transmitted to the blood of humans through the bite of infected mosquitoes. Though there is a compound in the artemisia species (artemisinin) that can be used against malaria, it is less present in grand wormwood used in absinthe than in sweet wormwood from Asia. Likely the absinthe consumed by French soldiers would not have delivered the artemisinin in enough quantities to be effective against that disease, but luckily there was another treatment that was known to work.

The proven antimalarial medicine known around the world was quinine from cinchona bark, which will be discussed in detail in chapter 8. The quinine-laced wine Dubonnet was supposedly created in 1846 as an entrant in a government competition to make a more palatable medicinal beverage for the French soldiers in North Africa. When it later entered the American market in 1898, it was listed as a "medicinal proprietary preparation." Today it is an aperitif wine said to be favored by Queen Elizabeth II, who takes two parts Dubonnet to one part gin as a cocktail. The standard cocktail recipe is a touch stronger with equal parts gin to Dubonnet.

DUBONNET COCKTAIL

1.5 ounces (45 ml) Dubonnet

1.5 ounces (45 ml) gin

Stir ingredients with ice in a stirring pitcher and strain
into a cocktail glass. Garnish with an orange twist.

· · · · ·

Another quinine-laced drink, Amer Picon, is a liqueur created in 1837 by a soldier and former distillery worker, also in Algiers. Gaéton Picon began producing the orange-forward product originally called Amer Africain in Algiers and later moved the distillery to Marseilles. It is typically mixed with beer in France but is also used as an ingredient in the classic cocktail Picon Punch with cognac and grenadine.

The French military took absinthe with them on other campaigns, and soldiers developed a taste for the anise beverage. Back home, they took to the predinner tradition of l'heure verte, sipping their absinthe in the cafes in Marseilles and Paris. The practice caught on with the bourgeois middle class, as well as with artists who sought out the supposed clearheaded inspirational buzz that absinthe would provide.

A few other times in history, veterans returning from military campaigns have brought their thirst for newly discovered beverages home with them. When the British fought on the side of the Dutch during the Thirty Years' War in the early 1600s, they took a liking to gin's ancestor genever and put their own spin on it when they returned. Much later, during World War I, British soldiers from Lancashire, England, were stationed near the Bénédictine liqueur distillery in Fécamp, France, and upon their return made their hometown Burnley Miners Social Club reportedly the biggest seller of the liqueur in the world. Many African American soldiers fighting in France in World War II developed a taste for cognac, and the relationship between the Black community and the spirit category has continued into modern times. In the case of absinthe, however, it was a native beverage consumed overseas that soldiers continued to drink when they returned home.

The popularity as well as the taste quality of absinthe changed dramatically throughout the mid- to late-1800s. The column still was invented in the early part of the century, and it suddenly allowed for fast and inexpensive production of high-proof spirits. This style of still can be run continuously to produce alcohol as long as fermented liquid is put into it, unlike an alembic (basic pot-shaped) still, which operates in batches and needs to be cleaned out in between. Additionally, the base of absinthe had traditionally been an eau-de-vie distilled from grapes, but Napoleon I encouraged the planting of sugar beets in the early part of the century. These, along with molasses and grain, were now distilled and used as the base of absinthe. Today sugar beet spirit is still the base of many liqueurs from Europe.

Absinthe made with these nongrape base spirits was considered lower quality than the original formula, and, further, many disreputable distillers adulterated it with unsafe agents to make it taste and look like authentic absinthe. They added artificial green coloring made with copper salts, and antimony trichloride to increase the louche effect—the cloudiness that happens when water is added. Rather than infusing wormwood into wine or eau-de-vie and redistilling it in a pot still, these producers added wormwood oils and essences to neutral alcohol.

In the 1860s and 1870s, the phylloxera vine insect tore through the vineyards of France, wiping out nearly the entire country's wine industry. This further pushed absinthe producers into using other base spirits. Absinthe's priced dropped so low during the phylloxera crisis, and wine's price increased so much, that absinthe became the less expensive liquid of the two. (Phylloxera caused a general increase in spirits consumption in Europe—scotch whiskey benefited from the lack of wine as well.)

Absinthe was very popular, and it offered a much stronger buzz for the price. Absinthe, when bottled, typically contains between 60 and 70 percent alcohol (compared with 40 percent for cognac and most spirits), which is part of the reason that the standard way of serving it is diluted with about five parts of cold water to make an aperitif. The drink, now cheaper than wine, became associated with the lower classes and alcoholism, or rather "absinthism," as it was known.

Early leaders of temperance movements only sought to ban spirits, not beer, and in France certainly not wine. Wine was considered healthy, and a liter per person per day was considered the normal amount to consume. Wine was actually prescribed as a *cure* for alcoholism.

Wine producers promoted the idea that their product was natural while absinthe was artificial. Later, after the wine industry recovered from the phylloxera epidemic, winemakers promoted the concept that it was the *quality* of industrial artificial spirits like absinthe that caused alcoholism, not the *quantity* of healthy, good old-fashioned grapes. In a *New York Times* article from 1886 an American visitor commented, "Drunkenness used not to be a French vice; but what with the destruction of the vines by phylloxera the manufacture of brandy out of beet root and potatoes, the beer devoid of malt and hops, which floods the cafes, and the drugged wine, the race is going to the dogs in the towns."

Absinthe addicts (absinthistes) were known to suffer from seizures, dementia, vertigo, hallucinations, violent outbursts, tuberculosis, spontaneous human combustion, suicide, and epilepsy as well as other mental illnesses (epilepsy was thought to be a mental illness at this point in time), and the asylums were supposedly overrun with these poor addicted creatures. One report included the statistic that people are 246 times more likely to go insane if they drink absinthe rather than wine. Absinthe impaired the health of the population, and its poisonings were passed along to children genetically, leading to a weakening of the race. Of course, nearly all these conditions can be ascribed to advanced alcoholism, sometimes concurrent with underlying mental health issues and fetal alcohol syndrome.

DEATH IN THE AFTERNOON

1 ounce (30 ml) absinthe

4 ounces (120 ml) chilled, dry champagne

Add absinthe to a champagne flute and
fill with champagne. Garnish
with a lemon twist.

· · · · ·

In public anti-absinthe demonstrations, guinea pigs were injected with wormwood essences and allowed to die while suffering horrible convulsions. Later an economist worked out the math and estimated that one of the creatures was pumped full of the human equivalent of 730 liters' worth of prepared absinthe.

The anti-absinthe movement picked up steam approaching the turn of the century, along with a rising rate of consumption of spirits in general (partially due to phylloxera) and absinthe specifically. Taxes were imposed on absinthe to make it more expensive in the hopes of keeping the low-priced, low-quality stuff out of the reach of the lower classes.

But the case that spelled absinthe's doom was that of Swiss laborer Jean Lanfray (c. 1873–1906), who shot his wife and children after drinking two glasses of absinthe in 1905. His lawyers argued that absinthe caused him to snap, and they insisted that he did not remember committing the crime. The case was a media sensation at home and internationally. The people of Switzerland passed an anti-absinthe referendum in 1908, and the ban on the drink took effect in 1910. Absinthe, the production of absinthe, and the importation or sale of absinthe was banned in the Netherlands in 1909, in the United States in 1912, and finally in France in 1915.

The active and problematic compound within wormwood is thujone, which was identified shortly after 1900. Thujone is responsible for wormwood's antibacterial properties—using it in wine and beer as in purl and vermouth helps preserve the beverages. A report from 1855 estimated that absinthe contained 260 parts per million (ppm) of thujone, and this number was used as a lower estimate of thujone quantity until recently. But after the year 2000, vintage absinthes were analyzed using modern equipment, and most were found to contain closer to a near-negligible 25 ppm of thujone.

That doesn't mean that thujone isn't dangerous; it is just not dangerous in the small quantities used in legal absinthe. At high doses, thujone can cause convulsions resembling epilepsy (as it did with the guinea pigs), renal (kidney) failure, and death. A 1997 medical report of a man who drank a small amount of essential oil of wormwood (and thus nearly straight thujone) thinking it was absinthe said he "was found at home by his father in an agitated, incoherent, and disoriented state. Paramedics noted tonic and clonic seizures with decorticate posturing. In the emergency room, he was lethargic but belligerent." He suffered congestive heart failure and spent about a week in the hospital before he was released.

Though *legal* absinthe is quite low in thujone content, it is extremely high in alcohol content. The elevated proof keeps the wormwood and other essential oils in solution. The same thing happens with ouzo and some modern gins.

For all the hysteria about thujone in the wormwood, the alcohol itself was probably the real issue for Swiss murderer Jean Lanfray. As reported, he had two glasses of absinthe, but those were at 4:30 in the morning when he first awoke, followed by crème de menthe, brandy, about six glasses of wine with lunch and then another liter of it, and a couple of coffees with brandy. It was only after that point that he committed the murders of his family. Lanfray regularly consumed extreme quantities of alcohol, but only absinthe was assigned the blame.

Despite the ban on absinthe for its supposedly maddening properties, French people in particular didn't really lose their taste for it. They decided that they could do without the wormwood during their afternoon green hour but kept enjoying anise-flavored drinks in the form of pastis. Pernod absinthe was reformulated as an anise spirit. The company later merged with its competitor Ricard in 1975. Today Pernod Ricard is one of the largest international liquor conglomerates in the world.

Driven by its allure as a dangerous drink that changes color in the glass and supposedly makes a person hallucinate, fans of the absinthe aesthetic have long sought out the forbidden spirit. In the 1990s, visitors to Prague could try "bohemian" absinthe that was available there. This style of absinthe was also imported into the United Kingdom, where absinthe had never been banned because it had never caught on in the first place.

These versions of absinthe were brightly (artificially) colored not just green, but blue, yellow, red, and black as well, and were not generally considered legitimate absinthe or of good quality. Drinkers began making their own, often simply infusing wormwood into Everclear or another high-proof spirit. Absinthe bars were regular appearances at the Burning Man counterculture festival in the Nevada desert.

As the newly formed European Union adapted common food and beverage legislation that applied to all its members, a window opened for real absinthe to hit the market again. Countries allowed absinthe to be sold as long as the thujone levels were legally negligible as measured by modern scientific equipment. This level was about the same as that of recently analyzed vintage absinthes. Everything old was new again.

In the United States, the Alcohol and Tobacco Tax and Trade Bureau took some convincing, but it finally allowed the word "absinthe" back on bottles in 2007, as long as any reference to the beverage being psychoactive was downplayed. Swiss brand Kübler became the first to reenter the US market.

Of the American producers, St. George Spirits in Alameda near San Francisco was first to market, launching in December 2007. The day it went on sale, images of the lines snaking through the parking lot were captured by a news helicopter. They sold their on-site inventory of about eighteen hundred bottles in six hours. The next batch of a thousand bottles also sold out in one day—on Super Bowl Sunday in February no less.

But it turns out that Americans in general love the appeal of absinthe and loathe the taste of anise, associating it with the "black licorice" taste of black jellybeans and Good & Plenty candy. For many, their first bottle of absinthe still sits dusty and unfinished at the back of the family liquor cabinet. Many brands launched, entered the US market, and sat on shelves. The second coming of absinthe was short-lived.

Anise has proven to be a globally popular liqueur flavor, outside the United States anyway. There is arak from Lebanon, Chinchón from Spain, ouzo from Greece, raki from Turkey, sambuca from Italy, and Xtabentún from Mexico, to name but a few.

Absinthe is still around, of course, and essential to cocktails including the Sazerac, Cocktail à la Louisiane, and the Corpse Reviver No. 2. In each of these, a mere dash of absinthe is all that is required—a little bit goes a long way. A greater quantity is called for in the Death in the Afternoon, a Hemingway-inspired combination of champagne dosed with absinthe that few people order more than once.

GENTIAN

Vermouth is an aperitif wine primarily bittered with wormwood, while quinquinas are aperitif wines primarily bittered with quinine. Americanos are aperitif wines with gentian as their bittering agent along with wormwood. It's probably not worth memorizing all these definitions, but it's worth noting that they exist to distinguish aperitifs by their main bittering agents.

Not all fortified quinine wine brands embrace the term "quinquina" instead of the broader "aperitif," most notably Lillet (formerly known as Kina Lillet), which is an ingredient in the Vesper cocktail. Other quinine-enhanced wines include Dubonnet, Byrrh, and Caperitif.

VESPER

3 ounces (90 ml) vodka

1 ounce (30 ml) gin

0.5 ounce (15 ml) Lillet Blanc

Add all ingredients to an ice-filled shaker. Shake and strain
into a cocktail glass, and garnish with a lemon twist.

· · · · ·

Brands of americanos include Cocchi Americano, Contratto Americano Rosso, and Cappelletti Aperitivo Americano Rosso. They are
typically drunk with soda water. There is also a cocktail named the
Americano, and it includes sweet vermouth and Campari (which almost certainly contains gentian), plus soda water, so the cocktail is
very much in the spirit of the americano category.

Gentian is one of the most common bittering agents in alcoholic beverages overall, possibly included more often than cinchona. Beyond its
presence in wine-based aperitifs, it is also found in spirit-based amari
Amaro Lucano, Amer Picon, Avèze, Bonal Gentiane-Quina, Fernet-
Branca, Nardini Amaro, Ramazzotti, Salers Gentiane, and Suze (of
the ones that disclose some of their ingredients). It is likely an ingredient in the secret recipes for Aperol and Campari. It is also the primary
bitter in most cocktail bitters, including Angostura and Regans'. It's
really everywhere.

Gentiana is a genus of plants with about four hundred species, but in
bitters and liqueurs mostly the great yellow gentian (*Gentiana lutea*),
and sometimes blue-flowered stemless gentian (*Gentiana acaulis*) are

used. Both the roots and the flowers of the plant are employed for slightly different flavor profiles. Gentian grows best in alpine meadows and other high-altitude locations, and much is harvested in the Alps, Jura Mountains, and Pyrenees.

German digestif liqueur Jägermeister is said to contain fifty-six secret botanicals, but one of them is a member of the gentian family: *Swertia chirayita* (often spelled "chirata" or "chiretta"), which contains the same bitter compound as other gentians. It is also known as "Indian gentian" as it was used in Ayurvedic medicine to treat fevers and malaria.

Like wormwood, gentian is extremely bitter (often described as having a tangy, radish-like note) and has a long history of use in medicine. Gentian was described in the *De materia medica* by the Greek physician Dioscorides (c. 40–90 CE) and later also by Pliny.

Species of gentian have been recommended for digestive issues including improving and stimulating appetite, curing indigestion, ending constipation, increasing urine output, discharging bile, and solving issues with menstrual flow. Its other main uses seem to be to decrease internal swelling, to treat rheumatism, and to improve functions of the liver and spleen. It was also used as a fever reducer and antimalarial. Externally, gentian was used as a poultice to soothe and cool wounds, to treat sore throat, and to cure bites of venomous beasts. In modern times, scientists have been testing these historical medical uses with modern equipment and experimental design, confirming many of them.

AMERICANO

1.5 ounces (45 ml) Campari

1.5 ounces (45 ml) sweet vermouth

3 ounces (90 ml) soda water

Add ingredients to an ice-filled double Old-Fashioned
or highball glass. Garnish with an orange twist.

APERITIFS AND DIGESTIFS

The term "aperitivo" comes from the Latin "aperire" for "open." The word was used for medicinal beverages designed to stimulate the appetite ("open the palate") and later became associated with aperitivo hour; the postwork, premealtime tradition of going for a quick drink. An aperitif beverage can really be anything consumed before a meal, but the typical drinks associated with this tradition are low in alcohol and slightly bitter or bittersweet.

Aperitif cocktails vary per country: in Spain the Gin Tonic has long been popular. In Italy the bittersweet Aperol Spritz, Americano, and Negroni are common aperitif cocktails. Vermouth and other dry fortified wines like fino and amontillado sherry, white port, and champagne are often consumed as aperitifs.

Beyond the Negroni, many people drink higher-ABV aperitifs, including the Martini and Manhattan, before dinner. Alcohol itself stimulates the appetite and enhances gastric functions, but only up to a certain amount, when it begins to have the opposite effect. The

sophisticated predinner Martini drinkers seemed to have figured it
out and typically have a single cocktail at the bar before sitting down
to dinner.

Digestifs usually contain the same bitter botanicals as aperitifs to
help with digestion but are often higher in alcohol and consumed in
smaller volumes. A Vermouth and Soda might help ready the palate
and stomach for a meal, but after filling oneself with food it is time
for a small pour of amaro. As with aperitifs, the category of digestifs
is open to interpretation. Many people drink straight spirits like cognac or scotch whiskey at the end of the meal instead of something
bitter. Others drink sweet liqueurs or dessert wines. Sugar reduces
appetite, so much like dessert, these drinks are designed to give our
stomachs the signal that we're done eating.

Amaro is the name of the category of bitter, usually spirit-based
beverages from Italy. Nearly all of them qualify as liqueurs because
they have added sugar or other sweeteners to balance the bitterness.
Non-Italian versions of amaro include Jägermeister from Germany
and Jeppson's Malört from Chicago, so the word is really shorthand
for bitter digestifs as opposed to sweet liqueurs. Amari can be further divided into categories—like alpine amaro, rabarbaro, fernet,
and ferro china, which was discussed earlier—based mostly around
the botanical mix of each.

Many of the amari on the market have histories as regional medici-
nal liqueurs, and most were commercialized in the mid- to late 1800s.
These include Averna (1868), Bigallet China-China Amer (1875),
Braulio (1875), Ciociaro (1873), Fernet-Branca (1845), Lucano (1894),
Luxardo Fernet Amaro (1889), Montenegro (1885), Ramazzotti
(1815), Santa Maria Al Monte (1892), and Sibila (1868).

FERNET-BRANCA

Fernets are very dry and very bitter, and typically close to 40 percent alcohol while other digestifs are often less boozy and lighter in flavor. Fernet-Branca is the category leader, selling over four million cases annually, so much so that most people don't know that there is a fernet category outside it. Branca contains twenty-seven ingredients, according to the brand books, including aloe from South Africa, Chinese rhubarb root, gentian from France, cinchona, zedoary, bitter orange, saffron, myrrh, and other botanicals.

The brand (and possibly the category) was founded by Bernardino Branca in 1845. Early brand stories credit the recipe to a Dr. Fernet, and then later to a group of monks from the remote Alps, so it seems likely that neither story is the exact truth. But the brand does have a strong medicinal history.

Advertisements promote Fernet-Branca as a "bitter tonic, hygienic, aperitif, digestif" that is "indispensable in all families," and as a tonic that "prevents nervousness and is a wondrous appetite stimulant. . . . It is exceptionally fast in healing the discomfort produced by the spleen, it is a remedy for anxiety, for stomachache and headache." An enlarged spleen is a key symptom of malaria, which was particularly problematic in swampy parts of Italy. Many of the amaro brands launched in the 1800s included cinchona bark or purified quinine as an ingredient to combat malaria, though cinchona was used as a general panacea in this era both in Italy and abroad.

In a cholera epidemic shortly after the brand's founding, Fernet-Branca was tested on patients, and the investigating doctor is said to have thanked the brand for inventing a "new theriac" to treat the disease. A poster from 1900 offers up a long list of ailments it assists with, when taken with water, seltzer, wine, or coffee. It claims the product prevents and relieves indigestion without weakening the stomach and digestive organs, helps with chronic attacks of the liver and spleen, and proves useful for those subject to long-standing hemorrhoidal discomfort. It is a thirst quencher when served diluted in water, is good for seasickness, and was used and commended by municipal authorities in cholera outbreaks in several Italian cities. This poster's "ANTICOLERICO" text is spelled out in a large font.

The brand's fame spread, necessitating the company to open new distilleries in several countries. In the United States, Fernet-Branca was sold during Prohibition (1920–33) as medicine with a different formula, lower in alcohol and higher in bitter aloe, which increased its laxative properties. Branca opened an American distillery in Brooklyn in 1934 to produce this medicinal version into the late 1970s.

The extremely bitter and minty liqueur is not called for in many cocktails as it quickly overpowers them, but two dashes of it are famously used in the classic Hanky Panky, created by Ada Coleman (1875–1966) at the American Bar of London's Savoy Hotel. From roughly 1903 to 1925, Coleman was the head bartender, a position so well respected in global bartending circles that some nerds can name every person who has held the job since 1893. Harry Craddock (1876–1964), author of the 1930 *Savoy Cocktail Book* (in print through many editions ever since), took over for Coleman and included her recipe for the drink in his book.

In the 1960s, the company released the extra-minty Brancamenta, supposedly inspired by how the opera singer Maria Callas sipped her fernet before going onstage—in a glass with plenty of ice and peppermint. "It was a ritual of sorts—the ice would cool her throat, the peppermint would disinfect it, and the myrrh in Fernet-Branca expanded her pylorus," according to the brand.

Currently there are two operating Fernet-Branca distilleries, one in Milan that produces most of the product for the world, and the other in Buenos Aires that makes it for much of South and Latin America. In Argentina, Italian liqueurs and vermouth are very popular, as massive immigration after 1850 resulted in most Argentinians having Italian ancestry. Fernet-Branca is usually consumed there mixed with Coca-Cola as a nightlife drink, like a Vodka Soda or Whiskey and Ginger is elsewhere. Fernet-Branca retains a loose connection to its medicinal history with American bartenders, who often reach for it as a stomach-settling hangover cure.

The aloe infused into Branca and other amari, including Amaro Lucano and Amaro Di Santa Maria Al Monte, is not the aloe vera juice found next to the coconut water and kombucha on store shelves but aloe ferox (also known as "bitter aloe" or "Cape aloe") that is crystallized and powdered. The plant contains the compound aloin, which has been used as a laxative throughout history, though the United States Food and Drug Administration banned sale of the substance for that purpose since it had not been tested for safety. It is still available for purchase as a nutritional supplement, though, with the usual disclaimer "Statements regarding dietary supplements have not been evaluated by the FDA and are not intended to diagnose, treat, cure, or prevent any disease or health condition."

Amy Stewart, author of *The Drunken Botanist*, notes of its extreme flavor, "If bitterness had a color, aloe would be black as coal." The impact of aloe is extreme in tiny quantities for some people, but because of differences in genetic makeup, others can't sense aloin at all unless it is used in high concentrations. This might help explain why people have vastly different impressions of the relative bitterness of fernets and other digestifs.

HANKY PANKY

1.5 ounces (45 ml) sweet vermouth

1.5 ounces (45 ml) gin

2 dashes Fernet-Branca

Stir all ingredients with ice in a stirring pitcher
and strain into a cocktail glass. Garnish
with an orange twist.

RHUBARB AND ANGELICA

Rhubarb root is the main flavoring agent of amaro subcategory rabarbaro, which includes brands Cappelletti Sfumato Rabarbaro (made with Italian rhubarb) and Rabarbaro Zucca (made with Chinese rhubarb). It is also found in liqueurs including Luxardo Bitter, Ramazzotti, Gran Classico, Fernet-Vallet, Fernet-Branca, Cocchi Vermouth di Torino, Barolo Chinato Cocchi, Amaro Nonino Quintessentia, Amaro Sibilla, and Amaro Dell'Erborista, and it is almost certainly in Campari and Aperol.

PAPER PLANE

0.75 ounce (20 ml) bourbon

0.75 ounce (20 ml) Amaro Nonino
Quintessentia

0.75 ounce (20 ml) Aperol

0.75 ounce (20 ml) lemon juice

Add all ingredients to an ice-filled cocktail
shaker. Shake and strain into a cocktail
glass and garnish with a lemon twist.
Created by Sam Ross.

· · · · ·

Rhubarb is native to China and other parts of Asia and was traded over the silk routes, then domesticated in Europe. In the United States and United Kingdom, it is more often used for culinary rather than medicinal purposes and is better known as a tart vegetable with a red stalk that is made into jams and baked into fruit pies. In the UK, a recent trend is to flavor gin with rhubarb stalk. The large leaves of the same plant are not used in foods, as they contain high levels of the dangerous oxalic acid.

In amaro, the root of the plant—usually just called "Chinese rhubarb" or "Turkish rhubarb"—is used and lends its smoky-mustard-like flavor. In Chinese medicine, rhubarb is known as "dà huáng," meaning "big yellow," no doubt referring to the intense yellow color of the root. It has been used as a yellow hair dye. In rhubarb liqueurs, the bright yellow is typically covered up with brown caramel coloring, but if you swirl the bottle, a yellow sheen is usually visible at the surface of the liquid.

The plant has been used for thousands of years in Chinese medicine and was mentioned in *Shen Nong Ben Cao Jing* (*Divine Husbandman's Classic of Materia Medica*) circa 200 CE. It was (and still is) used as a laxative and purgative for the treatment of constipation and diarrhea, depending on the dose. It has been used as an anti-inflammatory, to stop bleeding, and as treatment for jaundice, endometriosis, menstrual conditions, conjunctivitis, sinus infections, and nosebleeds. It was also used externally to treat burns. Rhubarb and its components have been scientifically studied for many of these uses, as well as to inhibit cancer growth and to treat severe diarrhea associated with cholera. (Since many Italian liqueurs were prescribed to prevent cholera, there might be something to it.)

Angelica (*Angelica archangelica*) root and seeds are used in fernet, absinthe, and often in gin. It is an ingredient in many liqueurs, probably including Strega, Chartreuse, Galliano, Jägermeister, and Unicum. In traditional Chinese medicine, a different species of angelica called "dong quai," "Chinese angelica," or "female ginseng" is used in medicinal elixirs. It is used to treat menstrual cramps and menopausal symptoms such as hot flashes.

In the 1597 *The Herball, or Generall Historie of Plantes*, British barber-surgeon turned herbalist John Gerard (1545–1612) wrote, "The roots of garden angelica is a singular remedy against poison, and against the plague, and all infections taken by evil and corrupt air, if you do but take a piece of the root and hold it in your mouth, or chew the same between your teeth, it doth most certainly drive away the pestilential air, yea although that corrupt air have possessed the hart, yet it driveth it out again by urine and sweat."

Gerard went on to say a decoction of the root in wine was good against witchcraft, enchantments, and the shivering of agues (the cold shakes that alternate with fever). He also noted that "it cureth the bitings of mad dogs, and all other venomous beasts." But mostly it was known to be helpful with digestion as a stomach tonic, for the lungs as an expectorant against coughs and colds, as a treatment for "diseases of the urinary organs," and for the relief of flatulence.

Hungarian liqueur Unicum uses angelica among many of the other botanicals already discussed, including gentian, cinchona, and rhubarb, plus cardamom, colombo root, sweet orange peel, lemon peel, peppermint, lemongrass, orris root, ginger, and cinnamon. It is "based on a secret family recipe and distilled from more than 40 different exotic herbs and spices."

The liqueur was created in 1790 by Dr. József Zwack, the royal physician to the court of the emperor of the Holy Roman Empire under Joseph II. The product was commercialized in 1840, and from 1899 to 1922 the bottles were labeled with the Red Cross logo, implying its medicinal use. Since then, the logo has been a gold cross on a red background. Zwack is the export name for the product in markets including the United States, and it is "similar to the original Unicum recipe, but now with enhanced spice and citrus notes."

Nearby in the Czech Republic, Becherovka was similarly created by a physician, so the story goes. Merchant Josef Vitus Becher collaborated with a Dr. Christian Frobrig on a plant-based beverage that was first called English Bitter and later Becher Carlsbad Bitter Liqueur, Becher Bitter, and other names. The product, launched in 1807, is heavy on the cinnamon; some consider it a Christmassy amaro. It was first prescribed "for curing stomach illness." By 1900 or so, Becherovka was a regular supply of the maritime transport company

Lloyd, which found "the benefits for the digestive system, heartburn, nausea, stomach cramps, and sea sickness to be benefactory."

Many other bitter liqueurs have a medicinal backstory or were created by doctors, pharmacists, or apothecaries, but this is a good enough stopping point. Paracelsus had something to say about bittersweet medicines, of course. He thought sugar was overused and reduced the effectiveness of the bitter drugs like aloe and gentian with which it was mixed specifically to counteract the bitterness. He complained of "the apothecaries, those swill-makers who do an idiot's job by mixing drugs with sugar and honey."

As usual he was a little bit right, a little bit wrong, and a lot of a jerk. Sweeteners help dampen the impact of bitterness on the tongue. The old song "A Spoonful of Sugar Helps the Medicine Go Down" was about making it palatable, after all. But though the sugar masks the flavor, the medicine is still working. Slightly bitter and not-so-sweet aperitif drinks like vermouth stimulate the appetite before a meal, while both more bitter and sweeter amari send our brains the signal to keep those digestive juices churning but also that we're done with the meal. Because they're used for functional reasons beyond intoxication, bitter and bittersweet flavored alcoholic beverages are closer to their medicinal origins than most modern spirits. And those are coming up next.

···· 6 ····

SPIRITS

GRAPES, GRAIN, AGAVE, *and* CANE

Para todo mal, mezcal. Para todo bien, también.
(*For everything bad, mezcal. For everything good, the same.*)

—*Mexican saying*

Knowledge of distilling traveled with doctors and monks from Italy, Spain, and France into new territories where grapes were less abundant, but these scholars figured out that the water of life could be derived from other base materials. In Northern and Eastern Europe, on the British Isles, and in Scandinavia grains were readily available crops and beer was distilled instead of wine. The grain-based eau-de-vie evolved into whiskey, gin, vodka, aquavit, and other spirits. Farther abroad, molasses from South America and the Caribbean was made into rum, agave in Mexico was transformed into mezcal, and corn in the American South was converted into bourbon.

Each regional spirit took shape on its own schedule from roughly the 1400s to the 1800s, but according to a pattern: The spirits were first considered pure medicine, a technological if not also divine miracle. Then doctors and herbalists added local botanicals to imbue the spirits with their medicinal qualities, and often also to cover up the flaws from rough, primitive distillation. Some spirits like gin and aquavit remained in their flavored forms until modern times, while other medicinal drinkables lost their botanicals as they began to take their present forms.

Multiple factors influenced those forms. As technology improved, stills became larger, more efficient, and specialized for the specific base materials distilled inside them. The invention of continuous distillation on column stills allowed increased production speed and efficiency for all spirits, and provided a neutral base for use in flavored spirits and liqueurs. Many spirits that had to be transported long distances in barrels on ships or overland to market were found to taste better after the journey, and so their producers began aging them in those barrels onsite as a standard part of production. Whiskey, brandy, and rum remain products often aged before sale in modern times.

Changing governance, government regulations, and taxes also influenced (and continue to influence) the base ingredients, production methods, bottle proof, and other factors of each type of spirit where it is produced and where it is sold. This chapter largely glosses over those regulatory details and sticks to spirits' uses as medicine and in medical practice.

As alcohol's inherent properties are common to all its drinkable manifestations, practical medicinal uses were repeatedly rediscovered. Every spirit was found to be useful to create a base for botanical infusions, to regulate body temperature, to invigorate the sick and tired, to sterilize wounds, and to preserve bodies and body parts, among other applications. After alternatives like rubbing alcohol and antibiotics became available, once-essential medicinal spirits were more used in home remedies. They are rubbed on teething babies' hurting gums, poured as the bedside nightcap to steer us toward slumber, and heated up to soothe colds and congestion in the form of Hot Toddies. For the most part, modern folk medicine is not covered in this text, but a few specific regional applications are described below.

ARMAGNAC AND COGNAC

Arnald of Villanova, who justified using the term "water of life" to describe distilled wine's miraculous health-giving properties, died in 1311. The previous year, Vital du Four (c. 1260–1327), prior of Eauze, in Gascony, published a book now kept in the Vatican archives called *To Keep Your Health and Stay on Top Form*. Du Four was a French Franciscan friar (later a cardinal and a bishop) who wrote texts on subjects both practical and spiritual.

A section of the book is known as the "Forty Virtues of Armagnac" and is cited by the Bureau National Interprofessionnel de l'Armagnac as the first reference to the spirit. Today armagnac is eclipsed by its big brother cognac in terms of sales and prestige, but both spirits are distilled from grapes in specific regions of France. Both are brandies, the category defined as spirits distilled from fruit. (Today "eau-de-vie" is used to refer to unaged brandy, but "brandy" can refer to aged or unaged fruit spirit.) Beyond grapes, brandies can be made from fruits like pears and apples, as in calvados, France's third great brandy.

The "Forty Virtues" text describes uses of eau-de-vie as encountered for the first time, within the era-appropriate framework of alchemy and proto-chemistry, medicine, and the behavior caused by its consumption. The virtues of the spirit are introduced: "This water, if used with moderation and according to the rules of medicine, will have many effects and it is reported that it has forty virtues or efficacies." As to the wondrous power of distilled alcohol, these virtues include the following: "It cooks an egg. It preserves raw or cooked meat keeping it from putrefaction when steeped therein. It allows the extraction of the active ingredients from plants that have been soaked in it except for violets, that do not retain their perfume."

The alchemical connection is clear. "It solidifies mercury, purifies copper, and dissolves spirits and carbonized matter." Medicinally, armagnac "removes blemishes from the eyes, takes away redness and heat. Heals wounds and any weeping, cankers and fistula if drunk and if affected areas washed in it. The burning water really helps those suffering from colic. Dissolved in wine it will crumble bladder stones. Similarly dissolved with its salt it will break down and remove kidney stones."

There is also a recipe for a compound medicine near the end of the list, made by redistilling eau-de-vie with nutmeg, cloves, galanga, cardamom, grains of paradise, ginger, and cinnamon that is "effective against all cold diseases if the patient drinks it in moderation."

Not-so-medicinally, "when kept in the mouth, it loosens the tongue, gives audacity to weak or shy people when drunk from time to time. It dries up the flow of tears. It sharpens the intellect if taken in moderation. It recalls forgotten things to memory. And above all it makes man joyous, preserves youth and retards ageing." Plus, as a bonus, it "removes bad smells from the nose, gums and armpits," and "its smell is enough to kill snakes."

A second medicinal brandy reference comes from Charles II of Navarre, also known as Charles the Bad (1332–1387), in the mid-fourteenth century. The power-thirsty ruler spent his life scheming (including with someone named Peter the Cruel), double-crossing, and then losing control of parts of Spain and France. Charles took eau-de-vie externally as prescribed by his physician for "a loathsome disease caused by his debauchery," according to one source. One can only wonder!

Charles slept wrapped in a linen cloth that was dipped in the eau-de-vie. One night the cloth caught fire from a candle, and he burned to death trapped inside it. The story became a popular tale used as an example of divine justice against the wicked.

Armagnac was commercialized in the 1400s, likely before cognac, but the cognac industry had a couple of things working in its favor. The merchants of the Cognac region benefited from easier access to the ocean and a long history of trading. The Charente River, which flows through the cities of Cognac and Jarnac, was used to transport wines and the region's salt (famously used for preserving cod, particularly in northern countries). Records show that, by the early 1500s, cognac was commercialized and sold internationally.

French brandy, like many other wines and spirits, including sherry, port, and Madeira, was optimized for export by foreign traders and the sailors on the ships along the way. Dutch and English traders purchased wines from France and shipped them back home where grapes didn't grow abundantly or produce wine of equal quality. The Dutch initially imported French wine to distill in their home country. Records of distilling in the Netherlands date to at least the mid-1300s, and the Dutch gave distilled wine the term "brandewijn" for burnt wine. This survives as "brandy."

Later, the Dutch sold copper stills to the merchants of the Cognac region who used them to distill locally, as it would make more sense to distill wine before it had the chance to spoil on the trip back to the homeland. The Dutch added eau-de-vie to water to sterilize it, and to wine to fortify it so that it would last longer on their lengthy ocean voyages. At some point, probably when distillation became more efficient and less expensive, the distilled wines became known for being drinkable on their own rather than (or in addition to) for their use as mere fortifying agents. Barrel-aged "old" brandies (most only a few years old in reality) later became prized in London and other parts of the United Kingdom, as well as in Ireland.

Perhaps because of its big head start, brandy gained and retained a reputation of being particularly medicinal and healthy compared with other spirits, all the way into the modern era. In early colonial America, medicinal plants were added to beer, wine, cider, rum, gin, or brandy, but the latter seemed to be the favorite. Brandy with water was consumed as a remedy for cholera in the 1800s.

The American Herbal from 1801 recommended brandy or rum with hops for jaundice, with bay laurel for coughs, or with beaver tree bark for dysentery. Brandy was specified (no rum option) to be infused with ash tree bark for rheumatism, fever, and ague (malaria); with powdered Guinea pepper for coughs, and with wormwood for spasms, for tertian (every other day) agues, and for killing internal worms. On its own, the book specifies that French brandy "is esteemed the best in Europe, both for drinking and for medicinal purposes. This kind of brandy, drank with moderation, well diluted with water, strengthens the tone of the nervous systems, raises the spirits, and braces the fibres; is good in the gout, and a variety of other complaints; but drank to excess, and that practice being long continued, often proves fatal."

FRENCH 75

1 ounce (30 ml) cognac (or gin)

0.5 ounce (15 ml) lemon juice

0.5 ounce (15 ml) simple syrup

3 ounces (90 ml) champagne

Add all still ingredients to an ice-filled shaker.
Shake and strain into a champagne flute. Top with
champagne and garnish with a lemon twist.

· · · · ·

Antarctic explorer Louis Bernacchi wrote in his diary during an expedition in 1898 to 1900 that the trip leader had consumed all the brandy and, "unless the doctor has a bottle or so, we have not a drop of brandy at Cape Adair for medicinal purposes. On this occasion we were obliged to use whiskey. It is really scandalous."

Medical journals of the time tended to agree with this analysis, and though whiskey was also quite commonly used medicinally, there seemed to be a preference for brandy if it could be found unadulterated. Around the turn of the twentieth century, *The Lancet*, a medical journal, declared that it is "universally regarded as superior . . . from a medicinal point of view" and furthermore "a spirit derived exclusively from grain . . . will be less ethereal, if ethereal at all, than grape-derived spirit and *a priori* a less powerful restorative."

Brandy was believed to be an especially good bracer, or as a scientific review of its use in medicine said, "Its prime use was as a cardiac stimulant as it seemed to increase the cardiac output and blood pressure." A 1935 ad in the US headlined THE BRANDY—QUICK! depicts a nurse with a cup on a tray and the text "Sudden illness . . . a frenzied telephone call for the doctor . . . then 'What do to?' while awaiting medical aid. Every moment counts. Brandy, of course! In thousands of such desperate emergencies, Three-Star Hennessy has proved its remarkable revivifying powers to sustain life until the doctor arrives. A bottle of Three-Star Hennessy is an important part of the medicine cabinet in the home of those who fully realize that emergencies can and often do arise in the middle of the night and other times when it is not possible to otherwise procure this valuable stimulant."

The association of brandy with reviving a patient may have led to the common and delightful myth about its application, that of the Saint Bernard rescue dog of the Swiss Alps that carries a mini-barrel full of brandy worn around its neck. The brandy is to warm lost travelers or those stuck in an avalanche. The part about the dogs is true, not so the brandy. Alpine mastiff dogs were trained in search and rescue and saved many lives, but the adorable little barrels were an invention of English painter Edwin Landseer in his 1820 *Alpine Mastiffs Reanimating a Distressed Traveler.*

The image became indelibly associated with the dogs and embraced in advertising by cognac brands like Hennessy and Martell, but alcohol as a hypothermia treatment would have been a bad idea. Alcohol dilates blood vessels, making the sufferer *feel* warmer but reducing rather than raising body temperature.

Brandy as well as other spirits were often prescribed for fevers, which makes better sense, as the dilated blood vessels lower the body temperature. And the patient probably didn't mind the added impression of heat since it came with a comforting buzz. Beyond the pick-me-up and cool-me-down uses, brandy and other spirits were given to patients who had trouble eating, taking advantage of the beverages' high caloric densities, ease of administration, and quick rate at which they entered the bloodstream.

During US Prohibition, Hennessy cognac was allowed to be sold as a prescription medicinal brandy, particularly through the pharmaceutical importer and wholesale drug company Schieffelin & Company. The cognac brand's owner, Moët Hennessy, bought Schieffelin in 1981.

Grappa is brandy distilled from fermented grape solids left over after the grapes have been pressed for winemaking. It is known as marc in France and by other names in different countries, and it has been used as a folk medicine through recent times. In its native Italy, grappa was consumed by workers both in the summer to lower body temperature and in the winter to make them feel warmer. When one felt a cold was coming on, they would mix grappa with hot milk before bedtime, according to Elisabetta Nonino of the eponymous grappa brand. Nonino also said that grappa was rubbed on sore muscles at the end of a day of hard work and used to numb tooth pain until one could get to a dentist. Additionally, in days before refrigeration was universal (as late as the mid-1900s in some regions), grappa was used to preserve cherries, which were then used both as a treat and as a source of vitamins and energy for people feeling ill.

SIDECAR

2 ounces (60 ml) cognac

1 ounce (30 ml) Cointreau

1 ounce (30 ml) lemon juice

Add all ingredients to an ice-filled shaker. Shake
and strain into a cocktail glass, optionally rimmed
with sugar. Garnish with an orange twist.

PISCO PUNCH

Spanish conquistadores planted grapevines in Peru in the 1500s,
probably with vines originating from the Canary Islands. Catholic
clergy used sacramental wine in their ceremonies, so it was considered important for the Jesuits and the later Franciscan missionaries
to produce it locally in case of supply shortages from the home
country. The coastal valleys of Peru turned out to be ideal locations
for growing grapes, and by the 1600s the country was producing so
much wine that Spain tried to prohibit its export to prevent competition with its homegrown products.

Wine in Peru was distilled into brandy (first called "aguardiente
de uva" meaning "grape firewater," and now "pisco") by the early
1600s, with records of a still bequeathed in a will in 1613. The distillery Hacienda La Caravedo in Ica, dating to 1684, is reputed to be the
oldest operating distillery in the Americas.

Peruvian pisco became an important spirit in young San Francisco. Ships sailing to the California Gold Rush of 1849, before the

Panama Canal was built, stopped into the port of Pisco and loaded up their ships with the local brandy. Pisco was served in the saloons of San Francisco in the 1850s, including at the fancy Bank Exchange where Mark Twain was a regular. At this famous saloon a few decades later, bartender and later coproprietor Duncan Nicol (1852–1926) served the Pisco Punch that became one of the city's most famous drinks. (It doesn't appear that he invented it, though; it predates him at the bar.) Like having a Bellini at its birthplace at Harry's Bar in Venice, or a Singapore Sling at the Raffles in Singapore, one simply could not visit San Francisco without sampling the famous Pisco Punch at the Bank Exchange.

The drink's recipe was a secret (supposedly only Nicol's deaf-mute assistant was allowed in the back room while it was being prepared) that Nicol took to his grave when he died during US Prohibition. The punch was widely reported to "make a gnat fight an elephant," which doesn't exactly sound like a recommendation, and also produced a buzz "in the region of bliss of hasheesh and absinthe," as a 1912 promotional pamphlet declared.

Clearly the drink packed a wallop, but what was in it? Bartenders have settled on pisco, pineapple syrup thickened with gum Arabic sap, and citrus. But that doesn't quite explain the reported impact of the drink. Pisco scholar Guillermo Toro Lira, as quoted in Gregory Dicum's *The Pisco Book*, thinks he figured out the missing ingredient.

"It had to be cocaine," said Toro-Lira. The theoretical cocaine could have been purified or come in the form of Peruvian coca leaves infused into pisco. Cocaine had been a wonder drug and a frequent ingredient in patent medicines (as will be covered in chapter 7) and had been used in early formulas for Coca-Cola and a wine called Vin Mariani. But a 1907 law in California made cocaine legal only via prescription. Toro-Lira said, "That's why it was a secret recipe—he didn't want it exposed. I don't know what form of cocaine he used . . . but I am 99.9 percent sure he used cocaine."

PISCO PUNCH

2 ounces (60 ml) pisco

0.75 ounce (20 ml) lemon juice

0.75 ounce (20 ml) pineapple gum Arabic syrup

Add all ingredients to an ice-filled cocktail
shaker and shake vigorously. Strain
into a cocktail glass.

GENEVER AND GIN

Juniper has appeared whenever medicine has in history: In the Ebers papyrus of Egypt, it is used along with coriander, poppy, wormwood, and honey in a remedy "by which the goddess Isis prepared for the god Ra to drive out the pains that are in his head." A Hippocratic author called for oil of juniper in treatments for conditions including fistulae and ulcers. Galen wrote that juniper berries "cleanse the liver and kidneys." Pliny recommended juniper for keeping away snakes as well as for many internal uses. Hieronymus Brunschwig provided a recipe in his book for distilled water of juniper berries against "gravel in the limbs and in the bladder."

The juniper berry (which is actually a cone) has been prescribed to be taken in beer, wine, and spirits to cure conditions including chest ailments, consumption, convulsions, coughs, cramps, gout, jaundice, nosebleeds, shortness of breath, and sudden chills; to improve sight and memory; and to dissuade vipers. It was inserted into physicians' plague mask beaks to ward off the Black Death caused by miasma. It was most commonly used to cure colic, to induce abortions (for which it was used into the mid-1900s), and most often as a diuretic to promote urination. Genever and gin were used for most of these purposes—one nickname for the latter, noted in the early 1800s, was "diddle drain" for its diuretic character.

As mentioned, the Dutch were initially distilling French grapes into burnt wine (brandewijn), and taxes were levied on brandy in Amsterdam before 1500, but when distillation became a larger-scale operation, distillers switched to malted barley and other local and reliable grains instead of grapes. Grain was called "koren" in Dutch, and the grain-based distillate was called "korenbrandewijn" (shortened to "korenwijn"), meaning "grain brandy."

"Genever" is simply "juniper" in Dutch, and the oldest known recipe for a spirit that looks like genever dates to 1495 from the Netherlands. It was a combination wine-and-beer base that was redistilled with juniper, nutmeg, cinnamon, galangal, grains of paradise, cloves, ginger, sage, and cardamom. All these botanicals show up in various modern gins. Gin is closer to vodka flavored with juniper and other botanicals, while genever is closer to unaged whiskey with the same.

The Lucas Bols company has been producing genever since at least the 1600s, as a 1664 document notes the purchase of nearly one thousand pounds of juniper berries from the VOC (the Dutch East India Company), enough to make five thousand liters. The Bols distillery itself dates to 1575 from Amsterdam, while the VOC was a trading company formed in 1602 in the same city. The VOC used its extensive fleet of ships to bring in fruits, spices, textiles, and other imports from around the world.

Before the company made genever, Bols produced liqueurs from these imported ingredients, individually and in combinations. They produced over two hundred different liqueurs for important customers, "specifically VOC officers based in various ports all over the world," according to company documents. The relationship between distillers and the VOC was important, as they could quickly process and preserve the spoils of foreign lands as ships docked back home.

The first commercial product Bols produced was kümmel, a liqueur with caraway seeds along with cumin and fennel. Other early products included crème de menthe, a digestif made with peppermint, and goldwasser with gold flakes floating in the bottle. Later toward the 1800s, single-flavor liqueurs became the more popular products.

While Bols was initially headquartered in Amsterdam, the center of genever production in the Netherlands was a town near Rotterdam called Schiedam. It was home to nearly four hundred distilleries by the end of the nineteenth century and became known as "Black Nazareth" from all the smokestack soot coating the city. The Nolet distillery, which produces Ketel One vodka, was founded in Schiedam in 1691 to make genever. The first De Kuyper distillery also opened in Schiedam in 1752 to make genever, though the company is now known for its liqueurs, which they began producing in 1920 (including the Peachtree Schnapps that made the 1980s cocktail the Fuzzy Navel a sensation). But the other legacy of Dutch genever is British gin.

IMPROVED GIN COCKTAIL

2 ounces (60 ml) genever

1 teaspoon (5 ml) simple syrup

0.5 teaspoon (3 ml) maraschino liqueur

1 dash absinthe

2 dashes Angostura bitters

Stir ingredients with ice in a stirring pitcher and strain
into a cocktail glass. Garnish with a lemon twist.

. . . . .

When the British took to juniper, they really took to juniper. Genever
was known in England because English soldiers fought as allies with
the Dutch in conflicts in the 1600s. (The term "Dutch courage" for
soldiers using alcohol to bolster confidence for battle may have originated in this century.) When the Dutch William of Orange (1650–
1702) came to rule England in 1689, the Brits adopted the spirit as
their own and started making it in bulk. Distillers were encouraged
by lowered taxes on grain distillates, as well as a temporary ban on
French brandy due to ongoing conflicts with that country. "Genever"
became "geneva," which became "gin."

Within a few decades the country was in a gin-soaked crisis known
as the "gin craze," with its peak from 1720 to 1750. Overcrowded
London slums were suddenly overwhelmed with a cheap, strong in-
toxicant. The situation was a bit similar to the introduction of absinthe
in France during phylloxera, but far worse. The annual consumption

of gin was estimated at two gallons per person, including children. The famous engraving *Gin Lane*, by William Hogarth, depicted a "gin shop" advertised with "Drunk for a penny / Dead drunk for two pence / Clean straw for nothing," inviting the guest to pass out on the premises. By all reports that happened often. Sensationalized but often true stories in the news were of husbands killing wives, mothers dropping children in the fireplace, women turning to sex work, and sickly starving infants, all due to excessive consumption of gin.

While the quantity of gin produced and consumed had taken off, the quality of the locally made product did not. The spirit that became gin was first roughly distilled from grain, then sold to rectifiers who compounded it—redistilled it with gin botanicals and diluted it for sale. The higher-quality distillers used juniper berries and actually redistilled the mixture, while the unscrupulous ones just added cheap juniper oil or turpentine to the rough spirit. Often, the retailers, such as a pub or shop owner, would sweeten it and further water it down, and then disguise their deception by adding spicy cayenne pepper, garlic, horseradish, and grains of paradise to mimic the alcohol burn. They were also recorded adding things like almond oil, sulfuric acid, carbonate of potash, and alum, probably to hide a poor-quality base spirit. Many of these same adulterants were used later during US Prohibition in the production of homemade "bathtub gin."

The British government imposed a series of taxes and passed laws to curb the out-of-control intake of gin, but these were ineffective for years. Eventually around 1750, taxes and regulations, combined with a decline in wages and grain crop failures, reduced gin consumption to less dramatic levels.

Modern gin took form in the late 1800s after column distillation became available. Column stills can produce spirits continually without having to stop and start batch by batch, and they can be designed to distill a nearly neutral-flavored spirit like vodka. While genever has a malty, whiskey-like base, the neutral spirit used in gin allows the other botanicals in the mix to stand out. Citrusy notes from coriander, as well as actual citrus peels, orris root, and angelica—and perhaps licorice root, calamus, and other spices—formed a supporting role in the flavor, as they do in gin today.

Though it was already infused with medicinal juniper, gin was long used as a base for medicine. As Olivia Williams points out in *Gin Glorious Gin*, gin infused with cloves was taken as a hangover remedy, as a cure for indigestion, and as a pick-me-up. It was also infused with pine bark and wormwood, or with celery root, fennel, cinnamon, and caraway in another preparation. Gin on its own was used as a reviver or stimulator much like brandy, and it was also commonly taken for worms, according to the 1856 British book *Popular Errors Explained and Illustrated*. In modern times, gin-soaked raisins eaten regularly are a common home remedy against arthritis, and a 105-year-old woman in New Jersey credited eating nine gin-soaked raisins daily with surviving her case of COVID-19.

A country's homemade spirits tended to travel with its ships: The Dutch brought genever with them around the world, and the British brought gin. Plymouth Gin alone outfitted the British Royal Navy with one thousand barrels a year in the mid-1800s. The gin on board was used in several delicious medicinal preparations, like Pink Gin (for seasickness), Gimlet (for scurvy), and Gin and Tonic (for malaria), which have evolved into purely recreational drinks today.

PINK GIN

2 ounces (60 ml) gin

3 dashes Angostura bitters

Stir with ice in a stirring pitcher and strain into
a cocktail glass. Garnish with a lemon twist.

VODKA

Today vodka is crystal clear and flavorless, but as with most spirits it
evolved over the centuries into its modern form. The beginnings of
the category are murky, with both Poland and Russia claiming to be
originators of the spirit. According to Russian food historian William
Pokhlebkin, a 1982 international copyright dispute over vodka
between the two countries resulted in an official court decision that
Russia was the originator. Unfortunately, it appears that Pokhlebkin fabricated this legal case, as well as much of his 1991 book, *A
History of Vodka*. Because so many writers have relied on this book
as a historical reference, and the author's deception is not as well-
known, most of the histories of the spirit written in English since
then have been tainted by Pokhlebkin's misinformation in one way
or another.

Proceeding cautiously: Knowledge of distillation seems likely to
have arrived in Poland first, via monks traveling between monasteries
or from physicians who trained at medical schools such as those in
Salerno and Montpellier. The word "vodka" is the diminutive form of
the word for water in Slavic, "voda," sort of like how "papacito" in

Spanish means "little dad" but is a term of affection. The 1534 herbal *Of Herbs and Their Powers* from Polish physician and botanist Stefan Falimirz included recipes for "little waters," both nonalcoholic herbal waters and some alcoholic distillates with herbs, which sounds a lot like Brunschwig's *Small Book of Distillation*, from a few decades earlier, in 1500. "Vodka" was first used to specifically refer to the medical and cosmetic preparation of alcohol, distinct from an existing word meaning "booze" in general, but over time it became the common name for the spirit as a beverage.

Like most spirits, vodka was mentioned in historical texts medicinally before recreationally. The first known written references to vodka date to the early 1400s when it was likely distilled just once, then diluted before drinking. It grew into more of a social rather than medicinal drink in the later 1500s. A fifteenth-century Swedish document claims the local version of vodka known as "brannwein" (burned wine) could cure more than forty conditions including headache, lice, kidney stones, and toothache, and was "good for women who are infertile," according to the book *Classic Vodka*.

Filtration was and still is a crucial process in making vodka, initially cleaning up imperfect distillation. Early vodka filtration methods included using fining agents like milk, egg whites, and isinglass (fish swim bladders), which are still used in modern wine production. Fining agents stick to particulates in the liquid and cause them to clump together so they can be more easily removed. (Other fining agents used in wine over the years have included gelatin, crustacean exoskeletons, and even ox blood.) Polish and Russian vodka was also filtered through river sand, paper, felt, ashes, potash, and burnt wormwood.

It may have been filtered via freeze distillation too. In this process, low-ABV vodka was left outside in winter so that the water and impurities would solidify into ice, while the unfrozen alcohol could be drained off. Freeze distillation is the process by which apple-jack was made in early America—cider was repeatedly frozen and the ice skimmed off, leaving a higher-alcohol spirit behind at each step.

Probably just before 1800, charcoal filtration came to be used in vodka, and it is still the main filtration agent used to remove color, odor, and impurities from spirits. Charcoal filtration works via ad-sorption, a process in which particles stick to the surface of the car-bon and are trapped like flies on flypaper. Charcoal is formed when wood, bones, or other plant matter is burned with limited oxygen. In Russia, charcoal from alder and particularly birch trees was valued for its use in vodka production.

Charcoal had also been used medicinally for centuries; it was rec-ommended in an Egyptian papyrus for skin conditions like foul-smelling wounds. Hippocrates, Pliny, and Galen all commented on its use, including in treatments for diseases and disorders like epi-lepsy and anthrax. *Activated* charcoal or carbon is a special prepara-tion of charcoal that greatly increases its surface area so that the same amount of charcoal can adsorb much more material. Activated charcoal is what emergency room doctors use in suspected overdoses and poisonings: The patient swallows it so it will hopefully adsorb the drugs or poison in the victim's stomach before the toxins are ab-sorbed into the bloodstream. The activated charcoal is then harm-lessly excreted with the toxins attached.

In modern times, activated charcoal has become a supposed health supplement with some products making claims about it "detoxifying" the body. The intense color has also attracted Instagram photographers seeking to make black ice cream, lemonade, and Halloween cocktails, but there is a downside: Because it adsorbs poisons, it will also do the same for any necessary medications taken around the same time, rendering them inactive. A person drinking a black cocktail might disable their medication, and it wouldn't "detox" the cocktail anyway—activated charcoal doesn't affect alcohol toxicity since ethanol doesn't bind strongly to it.

Vodka of the 1500s would mostly have been distilled from grains. (Despite the popular misconception, potatoes came into common use in vodka only in the mid-1700s, and still very few brands are made from them.) Today vodka can be and is made, depending on the country's laws, from any base material that ferments, including quinoa, molasses, sugar beets, honey, and even discarded coffee fruit.

Early vodka was flavored with local honey, anise, tree buds, leaves, cherries and other fruit, nuts, juniper, mint, and imported spices. Żubrówka, vodka flavored with "bison grass," may date to the 1500s. The grass is said to be a favorite of bison grazing in the ancient Białystok forest that was once the private hunting ground of the king of Poland. Its aroma is like a combination of white flowers, vanilla, and cinnamon. When mixed with apple juice in a cocktail called either the Szarlotka (meaning "apple pie") or Tatanka (the Indigenous American word for bison brought to wider recognition in the 1990 movie *Dances with Wolves*), the result tastes like apple pie.

Bison grass contains coumarin, which is banned as a food additive in the United States because of potential liver toxicity, so the US versions of żubrówka are flavored with other ingredients to resemble the natural version. Coumarin is also present in tonka beans, so despite the spice's common appearance in Europe and Canada, it is not legally available for food or beverage use stateside.

SZARLOTKA OR TATANKA

■

2 ounces (60 ml) bison grass vodka
4 ounces (120 ml) apple juice

Pour over ice in a glass.

· · · · ·

As with gin, vodka came into its modern form only after the column still was invented in the early 1800s, allowing for spirits to be distilled up to nearly pure, neutral alcohol. It is then watered back down to its bottle proof of usually 40 percent ABV. The neutral spirit provides the base for flavored vodka, gin, many liqueurs, and aquavit.

Aquavit, or akvavit, also derives its name from aqua vitae, and is a flavored spirit originally made from a base of distilled wine, then grain, and now sometimes potatoes. The alleged first reference to the drink from 1531 is directly medicinal. It occurs in a letter from a Danish lord accompanying a gift of "some water which is called aqua vite and is a help for all sort of illness which a man can have both internally and externally." Today the spirit is flavored with some combination of caraway, cumin, dill, fennel, anise, cardamom, and citrus peel mostly in its native Sweden, Denmark, and Norway. Like other formerly medicinal flavored wines and spirits, today aquavit is often taken as a digestif accompaniment to food.

Because household cleaners, cosmetics, and other industrial products essentially use vodka as their base, the spirit in modern times is often dismissed as nothing but a flavorless alcohol-delivery mechanism. David A. Embury (1886–1960) in *The Fine Art of Mixing Drinks* (1948), which was written when vodka was relatively new and exciting on the American scene, wrote, "If, therefore, you need grain alcohol to dilute your tincture of iodine or to rub on your back and the corner drug store is closed, just use vodka. Of course the vodka is half distilled water but that won't harm your back at all."

For other applications in medicine and cosmetics, higher-proof and nearly pure alcohol is needed. Antiseptic hand sanitizers contain 60–80 percent ethanol. Typically, this industrial alcohol is produced specifically for nonbeverage use in separate distilleries from those that make vodka and other spirits. However, at the beginning of the global COVID-19 crisis in 2020, many beverage alcohol brands, including Buffalo Trace, Bayou Rum Distillery, and Tito's Handmade Vodka, donated their alcohol for use in hand sanitizers.

This was not the first time beverage distilleries were recruited in the service of medicine when times were tough. During World War II, American bourbon distilleries grew penicillin in their fermentation tanks. They also produced industrial alcohol, which could be used for smokeless powder, chemical warfare materials, rubber, and other medicinal supplies.

According to Patricia Herlihy's *Vodka: A Global History*, vodka is used today in Eastern Europe in home remedies, including as a topical treatment for dry sores or as a gargle for sore throats. It was also believed to be a prophylactic against radiation poisoning and was consumed by Ukrainians after the Chernobyl nuclear power plant explosion.

Modern-day vodka stories on the web also emphasize its nonbeverage uses. With headlines like PASS THE BOTTLE FOR THE 8 HEALTH BENEFITS OF VODKA, 15 USES OF VODKA YOU MAY HAVE NEVER IMAGINED, and 10 WEIRD USES FOR VODKA, these stories advise readers to use vodka to soothe poison ivy, jellyfish stings, and skin after shaving; to kill bathroom mold and odor-causing bacteria on worn clothing; or to keep flowers fresh. Vodka is effective for most of these purposes, but so is rubbing alcohol.

WHITE RUSSIAN

■

2 ounces (60 ml) vodka

1 ounce (30 ml) coffee liqueur

1 ounce (30 ml) cream

Pour the vodka and coffee liqueur over ice
in a rocks glass. Top with cream and
give it a gentle stir.

RUM

Sugarcane juice and molasses (rum can be made from either) were possibly distilled in India in the centuries around the start of the Common Era, according to archaeological findings, as discussed in chapter 2. That's over fifteen hundred years before distilling came to the Western Hemisphere, the part of the world with which we most associate the spirit. Sugarcane cultivation spread over the centuries via the trade routes westward from its native Asia and India into the Middle East, then to the Arab-controlled regions of Sicily and Spain. It was transplanted to Madeira and the Canary Islands, and from there to the New World with Columbus and others.

Distillation of sugarcane probably did not follow the same path. Cane had been planted in Europe when distillation technology was available, but there isn't much evidence that molasses, the by-product of sugar production, was distilled on the continent. It is generally assumed that the stills used in Brazil, the dominant New World sugar provider in the 1500s, came from Europe. However, it is possible that the Portuguese took a shortcut and brought stills or knowledge of distillation from India directly to the New World, but so far that remains only an enticing theory.

In any case, in the 1600s, the British, Dutch, and French all established Caribbean sugar plantations and expanded quickly. The sugar industry grew in the Caribbean as well as in Brazil, with Barbados and later Jamaica particularly profitable islands for the British. Molasses supplemented animal and human food and was used in various ways including as mortar. Then as part of standard operations, a still would be employed on plantations to produce rum from molasses combined with the "skimmings" of the boiled sugarcane juice in the early days. The rum was consumed by laborers as "a booster, a medicine, a salve to the pains of toil," as writer Dave Broom put it.

The people toiling were enslaved Africans and Indigenous peoples, and to a much lesser extent European indentured servants. Slavery was not new to the world and was not limited to sugar and rum production in the Caribbean. But the enormous demand for sugar combined with racism and imperialism resulted in a huge expansion of slavery. By the time the abhorrent practice was abolished in the Americas, more than ten million people were taken from Africa across the Atlantic.

After slavery was abolished, new labor forces particularly from India and China willing to work for the promise of a better life were recruited to sugarcane-growing areas. Today, while working conditions have improved over the centuries since cane was first harvested, laborers in sugarcane fields can still endure unsafe conditions for subsistence wages. In recent decades, an epidemic of chronic kidney disease among sugarcane cutters in Central America has been reported, believed to be due to dehydration, exposure to air pollutants from burnt sugarcane, and other factors.

Rum in the early 1600s was considered a rotgut liquor only suitable for the laboring class, earning it the name "kill-devil" and descriptors such as "rough and disagreeable" and "a hot, hellish, and terrible liquor." This would change within a few decades, though, as distillers better figured out how to control molasses fermentation in hot climates.

MAI TAI

2 ounces (60 ml) aged rum

1 ounce (30 ml) lime juice

0.5 ounce (15 ml) curaçao liqueur

0.5 ounce (15 ml) orgeat

Add all ingredients into an ice-filled shaker.
Shake and dump into a rocks glass. Garnish
with a lime wheel and mint sprig.

· · · · ·

In the 1651 book *A True and Exact History of the Island of Barbados*, by Richard Ligon, the author noted that immoderate use of spirits (whether grain spirits from the British homeland, imported French brandy, or the local kill-devil) causes constipation and torment in the bowels and had killed many people, but that "strong drinks are very requisite where so much heat is; for the spirits being exhausted with much sweating, the inner parts are left cold and faint, and shall need comforting, and reviving."

Pretty much every spirit in every part of the world was used to regulate body temperature in any sort of weather. Calvados fortified soldiers fighting in World War I, and, as mentioned, grappa fortified workers on both cold mornings and hot days. In the United States, "without a mixture of rum in the winter, it is impossible to endure the cold," according to a 1757 letter sent to the British Parliament. In Brazil where the rum was distilled from sugarcane juice rather than molasses and called "cachaça," a doctor noted in 1721 that it was "very helpful in cold and humid climates, for obese people, for the elderly, and for weak-stomached people."

The new booze on the scene was compared with European spirits to test which was the better medicine. In a short 1770 text, *An Essay on Spirituous Liquors, with Regard to Their Effects on Health; in Which the Comparative Wholesomeness of Rum and Brandy Are Particularly Considered*, the author (who was likely not a neutral party in the debate), Robert Dossie (1717–1777) finds that "there is not the least foundation, nevertheless, for the belief, that (French) brandy is superior to (British) rum in any of their qualities which can effect health: on the contrary, it is evident, from the clearest proofs, which subjects of this nature can admit of, that the drinking rum in moderation is more sal-utary, and in excess much less hurtful, than the drinking brandy."

The text ends with an interesting (particularly for the later dis-cussion of scurvy) call to mix rum with less acidic citrus. "It is well known, that while the custom of drinking plentifully of small punch, made very sour with lime juice, prevailed in our West Indian colo-nies, a much greater number of bad and fatal diseases, were con-tracted than are observed at present among those, who drink punch with less acid in proportion to the spirit. The juice of oranges, and milder fruits, taken with the distilled spirits, is less detrimental: but that of lemons and limes ought always to be admitted sparingly, and with caution. Under these restrictions, the use of good spirituous li-quors, especially rum, may be deemed innocent in general; and, in some cases above-mentioned, salutary and medicinal."

The American Herbal from 1801 noted other medicinal uses for rum, here in the diluted form of grog: "Good rum properly diluted with water, sweetened with sugar, and drank with moderation, strengthens the lax fibres, increases the thin fluids, and warms the habit. It proves the most beneficial to those exposed to heat, moisture, corrupted air, and putrid diseases. It is also serviceable externally, if applied in con-junction with corroboration, anodyne, and antiseptic fomentations. Strong grog, poured down a sailor's throat, when he was apparently dead with the yellow fever in the year 1798, restored him to life and health."

Most of the medicines in *The American Herbal* are specified to be mixed with brandy, or the choice of brandy or rum, but rum is spe-cifically mentioned to be used with wood sorrel. The juice of the plant, "mixed with good rum, and sweetened with brown sugar, is esteemed to be an excellent remedy for the cure of a cough; it is an Indian discovery." It turns out that it is not a great remedy at all: wood sorrel, like rhubarb leaves, contains oxalic acid and should not be consumed in large quantities.

One way to test the medicinal quality of spirits in the 1700s was to compare their ability to preserve infused organic matter. As noted by Wayne Curtis in *And a Bottle of Rum*, a Swedish traveler in 1750 commented about the English belief in the healthfulness of rum: "They say that if you put a piece of fresh meat into rum and another into brandy, and leave them there for a few months, that in the rum will keep as it was, but that in the brandy will be eaten full of holes." This information was ignored in the case of one famous piece of meat.

British navy vice-admiral Horatio Nelson (1758–1805) was killed in the Battle of Trafalgar in 1805, and the decision was made to return his body to England for burial, instead of the usual "burial" at sea. To preserve it, the corpse was placed in a barrel that was then filled with brandy by the ship's surgeon.

The surgeon, William Beatty, wrote a book defending his decision to use brandy over rum, saying that both spirits were available onboard: "A very general but erroneous opinion was found to prevail on the [ship's] arrival in England, that rum preserves the dead body from decay much longer and more perfectly than any other spirit, and ought therefore to have been used: but the fact is quite the reverse, for there are several kinds of spirit much better for that purpose than rum; and as their appropriateness in this respect arises from their degree of strength, on which alone their antiseptic quality depends, brandy is superior."

(Alcohol of all varieties had a long past and glorious future of use as a preservative for body parts. Wine was used as embalming fluid in ancient Egypt. Outlaw Joaquin Murrieta's head was preserved in whiskey by California Rangers in the 1850s as proof to claim the reward for his execution. African explorer Dr. David Livingstone's body was embalmed with salt and brandy for its long transport back to his burial place of Westminster Abbey after his death in 1873.)

There had been a practice on board ships of sailors surreptitiously making a small hole in a barrel of spirits and sucking out the contents with a straw. It was rumored that the barrel containing Nelson's body arrived empty back in London from thirsty sailors performing this act, but the surgeon's account makes clear that the brandy in the cask was emptied and refreshed with new brandy several times along the trip. Still, the truth did not get in the way of a good story or prevent sailors using the expression "tapping the admiral" for sneaking a sip out of the cask. "Nelson's blood" became a nickname for navy rum, despite the fact that rum was not the preservative used.

Sailors in the British navy had some rum to drink on board anyway. Daily rum rations were issued, at least when sailing through the Caribbean where they controlled the spirits' production. Setting forth from the home country, ships would often be outfitted with gin rations instead. The onboard water on ships would become slimy with algae within weeks and the beer would sour, so the twice-daily portion of rum (at first served neat then mixed with water, later with citrus to make grog) was a welcome source of calories and comfort for that form of labor. The navy even had an official rum blend sourced from several islands and then distributed as part of provisioning to ships. Versions of the British navy's rum ration remained in place, with increasingly smaller quantities of alcohol, until July 31, 1970. The date of the last rum ration is known to aficionados as Black Tot Day.

DAIQUIRI

2 ounces (60 ml) aged white rum

1 ounce (30 ml) lime juice

1 ounce (30 ml) simple syrup

Add all ingredients to an ice-filled shaker. Shake and
strain into a cocktail glass. Garnish with lime wheel.

· · · · ·

Though rum is associated with tropical climates, it predates whiskey as
an American spirit. Caribbean distilleries sold their molasses cheaply
to American colonies. In Boston, New York, Philadelphia, and other
areas, distillers converted the molasses into rum beginning in the late
1660s, and by 1763 there were 159 rum distilleries in New England.
American-made rum was much less expensive than imported French
brandy, and distilling molasses reserved the homegrown grains for
food and beer. It remained popular until wars and blockades reduced
access to molasses, and American-made rye and bourbon became the
homemade specialty.

In *The American Herbal*, the author mentions that Jamaican rum is
reported to be the best but that New England rum from West Indies
molasses is improved with aging, whereas "when it is first distilled,
the odor and taste is so disagreeable that it is not fit to be drank by
the human species."

Rum's reputation improved throughout the 1700s into a respect-
able and then a superior drink, especially when compared with grain
spirits. It was the combination of barrel aging, column distillation,

and charcoal filtration that brought rum into its modern form. (Much if not most Caribbean molasses-based white rum is distilled then aged for a year or so in barrels before being filtered to clarity.) Though whiskey later became the American spirit, rum continued to be distilled regularly in New England all the way up to Prohibition.

The New England molasses distilling industry went out with a bang. Or, rather, a sploosh. On January 15, 1919, the day before the Prohibition amendment to the US Constitution was ratified, a ninety-foot-wide and fifty-foot-tall tank of molasses at the United States Industrial Alcohol Company in Boston's North End burst after a sudden temperature increase, causing more than two million gallons of liquid to rush through the streets at up to thirty-five miles per hour. The molasses tsunami was said to be twenty-five feet (eight meters) high as it ran through the city, killing 21 people and injuring 150 more.

Though rum had become a respected spirit in flavor, near the end of the 1800s the word "rum" came to be used pejoratively to refer to spirits, sort of like how "booze" is used today. A Prohibition advocate in 1895 said, "No workingman ever drank a glass of rum who did not rob his wife and children of the price of it." "Demon rum" referred to any liquor that may have been drunk by "rummies," and during Prohibition "rum runners" on groups of ships known as "rum fleets" brought any sort of alcohol into the US. A 1910 study reported in the *Boston Medical and Surgical Journal* found that unlike the earlier studies of preserved meat, rum killed rabbits injected with it and was therefore the worst liquor option compared with brandy, whiskey, and gin.

Like all spirits, rum was infused with herbs, spices, barks, and other ingredients to make medicines. Some traditional infused rums are still common, with secret family recipes passed down between generations. Guifiti, or gifiti, is made by the Garifuna peoples of mixed African and Indigenous descent living in Honduras and Belize (among other countries). It is taken as a preventative and cure to assist with digestion, reduce fevers and stress, enhance sexual performance, strengthen the immune system, and promote general health and vitality. It is consumed as a shot once or a few times each day, sometimes after work or before bed as more of a "drinking bitters" than a spiced rum.

Mamajuana is an herbal remedy from the Dominican Republic with extra emphasis on its purported aphrodisiac qualities, and supposedly once included the penis of a sea turtle in its recipe. Now it contains brazilwood and cat's claw among other dried botanicals that can be purchased mixed together on the island or online—it's a popular tourist souvenir. The mix is meant to be infused into red wine, dark rum, and honey in different proportions according to the recipe, or it can be steeped in water like a tea. Beyond its supposed sexual enhancement capabilities, mamajuana is said to help with the flu, digestion, and circulation, plus it supposedly cleans the blood, and is a tonic for the kidney and liver.

Even the spiced rum Captain Morgan has medicinal origins, or rather it has a medicinal origin story. According to one source, the recipe for Captain Morgan was licensed around 1945 from a Kingston, Jamaica, pharmacy named Levy Brothers. The rum was sourced from the local Long Pond distillery and infused with medicinal spices.

The far more likely truth is that the rum was created in a boardroom in the early 1980s by the Seagram company and made specifically to mix with Coca-Cola. It was heavy on the vanilla (the combination obviously works, as Coca-Cola later released a vanilla variant) but was given the unspecific name "spiced" that allowed people to project their own idea of its flavor onto it. It is certainly not spicy. Seagram had an existing nonspiced rum line named Captain Morgan (for which vintage ads can be found online) that was rebranded into what became one of the top-ten bestselling spirits in the world.

HEMINGWAY DAIQUIRI

2 ounces (60 ml) aged white rum

0.5 ounce (15 ml) maraschino liqueur

0.75 ounce (20 ml) lime juice

0.5 ounce (15 ml) grapefruit juice

Add all ingredients to an ice-filled shaker.
Shake and strain into a cocktail glass. Garnish
with a lime wheel. This cocktail was the
writer's preference as he believed he had
diabetes, and it is lower in added sugar
than the conventional daiquiri.

SCURVY

Humans, guinea pigs, and some fish, birds, fruit bats, and primates cannot synthesize vitamin C, yet it is essential to our survival. Scurvy, the deficiency of vitamin C, was the scourge of both the far-wandering sailors and the location-locked soldiers who lacked a balanced diet. It was a common condition in military camps, and in prisons and asylums.

During the Irish Potato Famine, which impacted many countries in the 1840s, the sudden blight wiping out a staple food source raised the prices of other vegetables and dairy. About a million people died of scurvy, typhus, cholera, or dysentery, and about two million emigrated from Ireland.

In the United States, travelers making their way to and participating in the San Francisco Gold Rush of the mid-1800s suffered scurvy owing to poor food provisioning. At Fort Laramie, Wyoming, a last stop before the Rocky Mountains on the overland route to California, scurvy in 1858 was treated by a surgeon who made medicine of "a thick greenish-brown mucilaginous mixture" from prickly pear cactus, mixed with two ounces of whiskey flavored with lemon essence. In the American Civil War of the 1860s, scurvy along with other nutritional deficiencies mostly impacted poorly supplied Confederate fighters.

By that time, the cure for scurvy was known. The condition was most thoroughly studied at sea and had impacted the voyages of Vasco da Gama, Ferdinand Magellan, Captain James Cook, and Christopher Columbus. In the 1700s, physicians and surgeons working for the British Royal Navy tackled the issue: Was it a disease (like the venereal diseases that it was sometimes confused with) or a deficiency?

The preventative and treatment for scurvy was discovered and rediscovered many times throughout history, with citrus specifically prescribed as early as 1564. Sea captains of many different countries understood that citrus prevented or cured scurvy, yet their real-world wisdom was continuously passed over in favor of some theory that usually fit in with Galenic medicine by physicians on the mainland.

Suspected causes of scurvy included an excess of salt in the diet, copper poisoning, poor ventilation or moist air (good old miasma again), dirty clothing and living conditions, lack of potassium, and parasites living on cockroaches, among other ideas. Shipboard food like salted meat, stale beer, and hard biscuit contained little or no vitamin C.

Symptoms of the disease are bleeding and swelling of gums, terrible-smelling breath, teeth and hair falling out, skin bruises, weak bones, reopening of old wounds, hallucinations, and blindness in the end. The running theory was that scurvy was a "disease of putrefaction." People were thought to be rotting on the inside.

Proposed antiscorbutics (scurvy preventatives or cures) included rice, beans, sulfuric acid, vinegar, molasses, cinchona bark, mustard, opium, mercury, rhubarb, hops, juniper berries, seal carcass oil, scurvy grass, and especially sauerkraut or horseradish. Fermented beverages like spruce beer, regular beer, and cider, plus fizzy soda water and rum punch were quite often employed. So was gargling with urine, which probably didn't help with the foul-breath issue. Other ineffective treatments included purgatives, bleeding, sweating, bathing in animal blood, and—surprisingly often—burial of a person up to the neck in sand.

John French's 1651 *The Art of Distillation* listed a recipe for "A Scorbutical Water or a Compound Water of Horseradish" that contained scurvy grass, brooklime, watercress, white wine, lemons, briony, horseradish, and nutmeg. It was to be macerated for three days and then distilled. "Three or four spoonfuls of this water taken twice in a day cures the scurvy presently."

Many of these cures centered on acidity, fermentation, or carbonation, under the theory that they prevented putrefaction of the organs. Taking "fixed air" (carbon dioxide) was suggested by one chemist who

recommended that sailors should mix lime juice and sodium bicarbonate to "be swallowed during the effervescence." They got the lime part
right anyway. Likewise, concentrated malt syrup was supposed to ferment into beer inside the stomach, with similar gas produced.

In an onboard clinical trial in 1747, Scottish doctor James Lind
(1716–1794) divided patients suffering from scurvy into six groups
who received one of the following: cider, sulfuric acid, vinegar, sea
water, citrus (oranges and lemon), or a medicinal paste of garlic, mustard seed, and horseradish. Citrus worked best, but Lind didn't dwell
on it as a preventative so much as a curative treatment, and the British
navy did not implement citrus rations for another four decades.

Captain Cook (1728–1779) was thought to have conquered scurvy
in the 1770s, but in reality he managed it well with better onboard living conditions and frequent stops for fresh food. On his second voy-
age of 1772–75, Cook's ship was supplied with many antiscorbutic
options: malt wort, sauerkraut, "elixir of vitriol" (sulfuric acid), cider,
Joseph Priestley's soda-water-creating device, evaporated carrot juice,
and a poisonous mix of antimony and phosphate of lime called Dr.
James's Powder. Cook thought concentrated malt was the solution,
and due to his stature, his insistence that it was the best scurvy preventative delayed the implementation of citrus by a couple decades.

At the same time, sea captains were taking matters into their own
hands, sourcing both citrus and other fresh vegetables when they
went on land. Finally, by the 1790s, some Royal Navy ships were
officially outfitted with lemon juice as a scurvy preventative. (The
Merchant Navy implemented it much later.) It was served as a daily
allowance with spirit, water, and sugar, or in a drink called a Negus
with fortified wine in place of spirit.

With citrus identified as the solution, there was still the problem of how to preserve the fruit or its juice on board ships already notorious for having spoiled beer and undrinkable water after a few weeks or months. Lind recommended a "rob" of lemons and oranges reduced over a fire to boil off water. This was meant to be rehydrated on board with water or alcohol such as in a punch or with wine. Unbeknownst to them, the heat of boiling would destroy much of the vitamin C in the juice, and it would deteriorate even more after storage at room temperature. Others tried concentrating the lemons by freeze distillation, or by adding tartaric acid.

Other methods to preserve citrus juice included mixing it into olive oil, brandy, or rum, sometimes with added sugar. The latter would be a Daiquiri (rum, lime, and sugar) if limes had been used rather than oranges and lemons. But limes were not the preferred citrus of the navy until the mid-1800s. To support merchants from the homeland, Britain switched from purchasing large quantities of Mediterranean lemons to buying West Indies limes (particularly from Montserrat in the Lesser Antilles) owned by British merchants. For this affectation, Americans began to call British seamen "limeys."

In both medical texts and drink recipes, there was confusion between lemons and limes, given the closeness of their names, the green color of unripe lemons, and the inability to identify which was which once squeezed. Though limes are more acidic than lemons and oranges, they contain significantly less vitamin C than either one, and the commercially prepared reduced lime juice on board was relatively useless against scurvy. Some physicians began to reverse their opinions as to whether the whole citrus thing was effective at all. Incidents of scurvy actually crept up again for a time after the switch to limes, but sea voyages became faster with the introduction of steamships, and scurvy declined again.

SPIRITS   203

The Rose family of Leith, Scotland, was in the shipbuilding business and then later in the ship-supplying business. By 1871 the family company was called L. Rose & Company, "lime juice and wine merchants." Lauchlan Rose (1829–1885) knew of the provisioning requirements of the time, which were lime juice in 15 percent Demerara rum, provided in four-gallon jars, but he didn't feel that the sailors were getting the benefits of fresh lime juice. Around 1865 Rose had the idea to create a sweet juice drink for both sailors and the general public, a less medicinal (and less boozy) preparation than what was used on board.

Preservation of food by sealing glass containers and canning was relatively recent technology at the time, and Rose used what he learned about the process in his preparation. The Merchant Shipping Act of 1867 required British ships to carry fresh lime juice on board, and in the same year Rose registered a patent for "an improved method of preserving vegetable juices." His trick was to employ sulfuric acid in an airtight container to preserve the juice, then it was sweetened and bottled as Rose's Lime Juice Cordial. It was a success both domestically and on board. By 1893 Rose was able to purchase his own estates on which to grow lime trees.

In the 1900s the company diversified and produced lime marmalade and "promoted gin and lime as a social drink and the 'discovery' that lime juice could act as a hangover cure," according to the book *Limeys*. Rose & Company later produced rum shrub, ginger brandy, and orange quinine wine. In 1957 the company was bought by Schweppes, makers of tonic water and mineral waters, which were both also used medicinally at first. *Limeys* author David I. Harvie calls Rose's Lime Juice Cordial the "world's first and still surviving branded fruit drink."

Rose's Lime Juice Cordial is used in place of fresh lime juice in some dive bars and homes, though it contains sweeteners, preservatives, and added coloring. The ingredient was immortalized in Raymond Chandler's 1953 book *The Long Goodbye*, in which a character states, "What they call a gimlet is just some lime or lemon juice and gin with a dash of sugar and bitters. A real gimlet is half gin and half Rose's Lime Juice and nothing else. It beats martinis hollow."

The sentiment of the latter sentence is disputed, as is where the Gimlet got its name. One theory is that it was named after a Captain Gimlette. The second is that the drink is named after a small tool to poke holes in casks—much like the ones supposedly used to drain Nelson's blood.

Vitamin C was not isolated until 1928, and it was finally proven to be the curative agent for scurvy in 1932. Experiments were conducted on guinea pigs, which had been found to share our common need for vitamin C through diet. This was not the first time guinea pigs have served as experimental subjects: They were shot up with wormwood until they died. Lavoisier and Pasteur both employed them in their experiments. And humans have sent them into space several times. What a ride.

GIMLET

2 ounces (60 ml) gin

0.5 ounce (15 ml) Rose's Lime Juice Cordial

Add all ingredients to an ice-filled shaker.
Shake and strain into a cocktail glass.
Garnish with a lime wedge.

WHISKEY

While vodka and the base of gin and aquavit can be distilled from grain, the grain is usually distilled to such a high ABV that the resulting spirit is nearly neutral in character. Whiskey is a spirit distilled from grain to a low-enough ABV that it retains grain flavors and aromas, and is nearly always aged in barrels. (Recall that in this text the spelling "whiskey" is used regardless of its origin.)

Beer making in the British Isles dates back several thousand years, and it wasn't at the time an ideal wine-growing environment, so it is no wonder that when the technology of distillation came to the Isles it was put to use on fermented grain. The word "whiskey" comes to us from the Gaelic "usquebaugh," meaning—once again— "aqua vitae," or "water of life." In Ireland, knowledge of distilling likely came from monks returning from pilgrimages, and evidence of distillation becoming somewhat common there starts at the beginning of the 1400s.

The first written reference to grain distilling in Scotland comes in a 1494 order of malt from the British king to be sent to a Benedictine friar to make spirit. In 1506 Edinburgh's Guild of Surgeon Barbers (predecessor to the Royal College of Surgeons) was given a monopoly in the production of whiskey for the region.

The spirit was considered purely medicinal at first. Sometime in the late 1500s Irish whiskey's virtues were listed, a writer claiming that taken in moderation it kills flesh worms, slows aging, strengthens youth, helps digestion, cuts phlegm, lightens the mind, quickens the spirit, cures dropsy, and keeps teeth from chattering, the heart from swelling, the hands from shivering, and bones from aching, among other features.

Early whiskey in the British Isles was flavored with herbs and other botanicals, like early vodka and gin. Hector Boece in 1526 wrote, "When my ancestors were determined of a set purpose to be merry, they used a kind of aqua vitae, void of all spice, and only consisting of such herbs and roots as grew in their own gardens." A traveler before 1617 wrote of Irish whiskey that it was preferred to British aqua vitae because it contained raisins, fennel seed, and other ingredients to mitigate the heat and make it taste pleasant.

The Art of Distillation lists a recipe for "Usque-Bath or Irish Aqua Vitae" with wine, raisins, dates, cinnamon, nutmeg, and licorice infused into aqua vitae. He notes, "This liquor is commonly used in surfeits [illness due to excessive eating or drinking] being a good stomach water."

Irish whiskey entered the *London Pharmacopoeia* in the 1677 edition along with other new entries: Peruvian bark (cinchona) and human urine. You win some, you lose some. Other accounts of early whiskey describe its being flavored with a species of Scottish pea, and as late as 1755 whiskey was defined as "a compounded distilled spirit, being drawn on aromatics."

IRISH COFFEE

1.5 ounces (45 ml) Irish whiskey

1 ounce (30 ml) simple syrup made with brown sugar

4 ounces (120 ml) coffee

Heavy cream, whipped

Combine all liquid ingredients and top with cream.

. . . . .

Brandy and soda had been considered a healthy drink in the Isles, but in the last decades of the 1800s the phylloxera pest epidemic caused brandy to become limited and many drinkers to switch to scotch or Irish whiskey with soda. Irish whiskey brand Kinahan's was advertised as "delicious and very wholesome . . . universally recommended by the profession," and Dunville's was "recommended by the medical profession in preference to French brandy." Kilmarnock scotch was advertised as follows: "Kilmarnock, or Old Highland Whisky, is a pure and well-matured spirit, and in combination with Rosbach water is a healthful and delicious beverage." Whiskey and soda was lauded as healthy by both the whiskey makers and the soda water bottlers, and the drink became so popular that whiskey makers changed their blends to better suit the drink.

In 1889 Queen Victoria of the United Kingdom (1819–1901) was advised by physician Sir William Jenner to give up claret and champagne and drink only scotch and Apollinaris water. The combination, which was advertised as Scotch and Polly, was popular enough that a song by the same name written by E. W. Rogers was a radio hit around 1900. The refrain went:

> *Scotch and Polly, Scotch and Polly, jolly good stuff to drink*
> *The Scotch got up in my head you know*
> *The Polly got winking at me so*
> *I lost my way, my rings, my chain, my watch*
> *I either had too much of the "Polly"*
> *Or else too much of the Scotch.*

WHISKEY IN AMERICA

Knowledge of distillation spread to the American colonies with early settlers. There may have been some distilling in New York when it was still New Amsterdam in 1640, but by the middle of the century distilling of local grain was common inland. This whiskey was made from rye, which grows well in cold climates. (Rum distilleries, reliant on Caribbean molasses, were typically located close to ports in both the US and Canada.)

Particularly after the American Revolutionary War in the late 1700s, farmer-distillers moved farther inland into Kentucky in large numbers, now distilling the native corn rather than rye. Distilling grain into whiskey made it easier to transport and trade in addition to transforming it into medicine. By one measure, a horse could carry four bushels of grain but twenty-four bushels' worth of whiskey.

The 1830 *Gunn's Domestic Medicine*, one of several American medicine books by John C. Gunn, is a nearly eight-hundred-page book of home remedies for all sorts of ailments to be cured with mostly American herbs, barks, roots, and other botanicals. The book instructed that whiskey, used alone, was a stimulant and strengthener against fevers, and that either whiskey or brandy could be taken after drinking too much cold water, but only if (opium-containing) laudanum was unavailable.

In combination, whiskey could be used in an external rub with oil and Spanish flies (a toxic blister beetle) or cayenne pepper against palsy (loss of voluntary motion in parts of the body), mixed with a "corrosive sublimate" applied externally against cancer, mixed with water and squirted into the vagina to bring on stalled menstruation, mixed with powdered red pepper to help rattlesnake bite and poisoning victims throw up, or used in a tincture with asafoetida resin against whooping cough. It could also be used in a base of bitters (poplar root, wild cherry bark, dogwood tree root bark, and black snakeroot with old whiskey or old rum) against dyspepsia in recovery, or in a Whiskey Toddy (whiskey with sugar, hot water, mint tea, or ginger, calamus, and dogwood blossom tea) to be used against cholera.

In the American Civil War (1861–65) whiskey was employed alongside quinine and morphine to treat wounds and other injuries. It was also used to preserve body parts sent to the Army Medical Museum in Washington, DC, where they'd be studied by doctors attempting to improve military medicine. The museum director sent whiskey to battlefields for surgeons to use as a preservative, but often the deliverymen drank it along the way. He ended up lacing it with an emetic to induce vomiting in anyone who snuck a sip.

As with all spirits, whiskey was used to regulate temperature, and literature is particularly rich with references to Whiskey Hot Toddies as medicine. During the 1918 influenza epidemic, staff at one hospital reported, "We could give them a little hot whiskey toddy; that's about all we had time to do." The effectiveness of whiskey against the flu was debated, but many doctors agreed it could soothe the suffering of patients in any case.

HOT TODDY

2 ounces (60 ml) bourbon whiskey

0.5 ounce (15 ml) honey

0.5 ounce (15 ml) lemon juice

4 ounces (120 ml) boiling water

Add all ingredients to a mug. Garnish with
lemon wheel and optional cinnamon stick.

• • • • •

That is, if it was legitimate whiskey. In the times before distillers created trademarked brands and custom-shaped bottles with labels,
they sold barrels to rectifiers, who would prepare it for sale to customers by diluting it. Much like gin retailers had, these rectifiers
would quite often alter it to taste stronger or look older by adding
prune juice, tobacco spit, sawdust inside a tobacco pouch, and other
flavorings and colorings.

The 1853 book *The Manufacture of Liquors, Wines, and Cordials
Without the Aid of Distillation*, by Pierre Lacour, features whiskey-
faking recipes beginning with neutral spirits. Fake Irish whiskey
called for sugar, creosote, and burnt sugar. Imitation scotch added
starch, creosote, cochineal, and coloring, while not-so-old "old bourbon whiskey" added sugar, tea, wintergreen oil, cochineal, and coloring. Other rectifiers might add glycerin or sulfuric acid.

Spirits were rectified in bulk by grocers or even by the friendly
neighborhood bartender. The back half of the first bartenders' guide
(named *The Bar-Tender's Guide* and frequently called *How to Mix*

Drinks) from 1862, by Jerry Thomas, was a section called "Manual for the Manufacture of Cordials, Liquors, Fancy Syrups, &c. &c." written by another author. In it are many recipes for faking spirits, including gin, genever, brandy, and absinthe. The scotch, Irish, and Pennsylvania whiskeys are actually the least deceitful of the bunch, merely thinned out with unaged spirit to stretch three gallons into ten.

Real aged whiskey was preferred for medicinal use, however. The Chicken Cock brand was advertised as "aged in wood for medicinal use." Instructions to convert whiskey into the cough medicine rock and rye were "take five pounds of pure white rock candy and dissolve it in a gallon of old rye whiskey—the older the better."

Rock and rye started out as just that, rock candy infused into rye whiskey. It was commonly used against coughs, including those caused by "consumption," which is better known today as tuberculosis. In the years after its debut in the 1870s, soothing ingredients — including orange peel, cloves, horehound, and balsam—were added to the recipe.

Bottled versions of rock and rye started appearing in 1878, and by 1882 Fairbanks' Rock Cordials was offering not just rock and rye but also rock and cognac, rock and Jamaica (assumedly rum), rock and Schiedam (assumedly genever), rock and New England (rum again). The ad copy boasted, "The best physicians recommend it. All leading druggists sell it. If you have trouble with your throat or lungs, it will cure it." Another brand advertised its use "for coughs, colds, sore throat, bronchitis, asthma, pneumonia, consumption and all diseases of the throat, chest and lungs." Surprisingly, some brands of rock and rye are still on the market. "America's oldest cordial producer," Charles Jacquin et Cie from Philadelphia, produces Jacquin's, which dates to 1884.

In 1870 Old Forester became the first bourbon exclusively sold in bottles, according to the brand. With product sold in labeled containers, it would both prevent tampering and allow for advertising with customers coming to know individual brands. But just because whiskey was in a bottle didn't mean that the whiskey was pure—it could still have all the coloring and flavorings added.

Three sets of legislation cleaned up the mess of adulterated and falsely advertised whiskey in America: the Bottled-in-Bond Act of 1897, which created a certification for unadulterated whiskey; the Pure Food and Drug Act of 1906 (discussed in the next chapter), which prohibited "adulterated or misbranded or poisonous or deleterious foods, drugs or medicines, and liquors"; and the Taft Decision of 1909, which finally created definitions for bourbon and other whiskeys in the US.

The requirements specified in the Bottled-in-Bond Act changed a bit over the years, but the certification guarantees that the whiskey (now all spirits) is aged for a certain length of time (now at least four years) and bottled with no adulteration at 50 percent ABV. There are some other rules in there, but those are the important ones. As an incentive to distillers to embrace the act, they didn't have to pay tax on the aging whiskey while it was under bond. The act didn't stop fake whiskey from being produced, advertised, and sold, but it provided a certification for a subset of whiskey that was guaranteed legitimate. It is a bit like today's organic food certifications—artificially flavored potato chips are still available, but consumers can find certified organic ones if they like.

The Taft Decision defined what whiskey was, with definitions that last to this day. The decision clarified that whiskey came from grain (not molasses), allowed for labels to state "straight" bourbon or rye or blended whiskey with neutral spirits and so forth, and required certain other information on the label. After this, consumers could expect to know what they were really drinking, for medicine or for pleasure.

NEW YORK SOUR

■

2 ounces (60 ml) bourbon

1 ounce (30 ml) lemon juice

1 ounce (30 ml) simple syrup

0.5 ounce (15 ml) fruity red wine

Add first three ingredients to an ice-filled shaker.
Shake and pour over new ice in a rocks glass.
Float wine on top.

BAIJIU

While Western medicine focuses mostly on treating disease, traditional Chinese medicine places more emphasis on health and wellness, and preventative medicine is an essential component. The *Huangdi neijing* (Yellow Emperor's Inner Classic), the fundamental doctrine of Chinese medicine probably composed in the third century BCE, states: "To administer medicines to diseases which have already developed and to suppress revolts which have already developed is comparable to the behavior of those persons who begin to dig a well after they have become thirsty, and of those who begin to cast weapons after they have already engaged in battle. Would these actions not be too late?"

Much of traditional Chinese medicine is concerned with balancing qi, a life force that surges through the body, as imbalance is said to lead to disease and illness. Practitioners use physical therapy such as acupuncture, cupping, massage, and tai chi, as well as herbal, animal, and mineral-based medicines. Historically, wine-based medicines were used in different ways depending on the ailment, a bit reminiscent of Greek medicine. A sixteenth-century text states, "If bitten by a serpent, the wound is to be washed with cold wine. If a person has been subjected to a great dread, and death is feared, one or two cups of hot wine must be poured down his throat at once."

The world's bestselling spirit is baijiu, and over 98 percent of it is consumed in its native China. In 2019 eleven billion liters of baijiu were sold globally, more than all of whiskey, vodka, gin, rum, and tequila combined. The first five most valuable spirits brands in 2021 as rated by the Brand Finance company are baijiu; Jack Daniel's was in sixth place.

The word for all alcohol in Chinese is "jiu." The original term for distilled spirits was "shaojiu," meaning "burned wine," just like "brandewijn," which became "brandy." There are distinct terms in Chinese for medicinal alcohol, nutritional alcohol, and healthful alcohol, according to Derek Sandhaus, author of *Baijiu: The Essential Guide to Chinese Spirits*. Now "baijiu" is the catchall term for "white liquor," referring to distilled spirits, though most is distilled from grains including sorghum and rice.

During the Chinese Civil War (roughly 1927–49), Beijing Erguotou (erguotou is a type of baijiu) started as a company making sterilizer and antiseptics. Kweichow Moutai baijiu was also used to disinfect wounds and to give soldiers the local version of "Dutch courage" to fortify them for battle. Chinese premier Zhou Enlai famously shared Moutai baijiu with US president Richard Nixon during a banquet in 1972, while telling him of Moutai's history in curing diseases and treating wounds. Nixon replied, "Let me make a toast with this panacea."

Today herbs are sometimes added in the fermentation step of making baijiu, though this is less common than it once was. More often, wine or baijiu is used as a base for medicinal infusions, whether this is done at home (stalls in food markets in modern cities like Chengdu sell jugs of bulk baijiu alongside bags of dried medicinal herbs and animal parts) or sold preinfused in the bottle. These tonics are used to increase virility and to treat and prevent everything from baldness to wrinkles.

The selection of medicinal ingredients in Chinese medicine includes many botanicals since proven efficacious, along with some that are more symbolic, and this is probably due to their preventative nature. If you eat a ham sandwich every day to prevent arthritis and don't get arthritis, for example, then it looks like the sandwich treatment may have worked.

Some common Chinese medicinal herbs that make their way into distilled alcohol, nonalcoholic teas, and fermented beverages include ginseng, angelica, cinnamon and cassia, ginger, and rhubarb root. Animal-based infusions include deer antlers, deer penis, seal penis, dog penis, ants, bees, seahorses, and snakes. The parent company of the Chuangu distillery, a prominent producer of baijiu, also breeds deer for use in medicinal tonics.

AGAVE

Mezcal and tequila are spirits distilled from agave, a genus of spiky plants with more than two hundred species that resemble, but are

not, cacti. While tequila is made from one type of agave in Jalisco
and parts of a few other states, mezcal can be made from a number of
other species of agave in other regions of Mexico. Before Spanish
colonization, the Indigenous people of today's Mexico and nearby
regions used the fibrous agave plant and its spiked leaves as rope,
thread, wood and roof tiles for housing, needles, nails, soles of shoes,
and clothing.

Aguamiel, unfermented "honey water" from certain agave, was
still used relatively recently in more remote regions as a morning
tonic for digestion and as a laxative and diuretic. Pulque is a fermented agave sap (an agave beer or wine) that could be consumed
when water was scarce, plus it has nutritional properties including
some important vitamins. According to *A Guide to Tequila, Mezcal,
and Pulque*, sixteen medicines in the first New World pharmacopoeia
contain pulque as an ingredient.

Pulque was used medicinally for snakebites and other external
wounds, as a fertility drug, as an aphrodisiac, and to soothe the aches
of old age. It was consumed by the Aztecs in ritual sacrifices on the
part of both the priests doing the sacrificing and those on the receiv-
ing end. It was generally forbidden to common people except pregnant women and the elderly, and alcoholic intoxication was considered
a great crime. Today there is a bit of a rebirth in the category, with
bars and stores called "pulquerias" selling fresh pulque flavored with
dozens of different tropical fruits and spices.

In addition to agave-based fermented beverages, Indigenous people in Mexico and elsewhere in South America made beer from corn,
and mead from honey, sometimes infused with herbs as medicinal
and ceremonial beverages.

Agaves for tequila and mezcal are different from that of pulque.

For pulque, plants are cut open to access a sweet sap that is drained multiple times daily for up to six months until the plant is exhausted. The liquid is fermented, and it is consumed within a short time period. For mezcal and tequila, the entire plant is harvested, and the fibrous core is roasted and shredded, then fermented and distilled. While documentation is unfortunately scarce, at least in English, tequila and mezcal were no doubt used as the base of medicinal infusions the same way other spirits have been throughout the world.

Recently, tequila has benefited from good press in terms of its healthfulness, with article headlines like DRINKING TEQUILA CAN HELP YOU LOSE WEIGHT, DRINKING TEQUILA IS GOOD FOR YOUR BONES, and A SHOT OF TEQUILA EACH DAY MIGHT KEEP THE DOCTOR AWAY frequently found online. These are mostly based on studies of agave sugars on mice, but it is highly unlikely that any of these components are left in tequila or mezcal after agave is fermented and distilled. It is far more likely that tequila and mezcal have identical health impacts to other distilled spirits.

MARGARITA

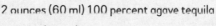

2 ounces (60 ml) 100 percent agave tequila

1 ounce (30 ml) lime juice

1 ounce (30 ml) Cointreau

Add all ingredients to an ice-filled shaker.
Shake and strain over new ice in a rocks glass.

POISON

PHOSPHATES, PATENT MEDICINES, PURE FOOD, *and* PROHIBITION

Gullible America will spend this year some seventy-five millions of dollars in the purchase of patent medicines. In consideration of this sum it will swallow huge quantities of alcohol, an appalling amount of opiates and narcotics, a wide assortment of varied drugs ranging from powerful and dangerous heart depressants to insidious liver stimulants; and, in excess of all other ingredients, undiluted fraud.

—*Samuel Hopkins Adams*, Collier's Weekly, *1905*

In the post–Civil War United States, meat and milk could be poisoned by embalming fluid, whiskey adulterated with tobacco spit, and children's medicines laced with opium and alcohol. All of this was legal, as was advertising the purity of the products that were anything but. Thanks to the muckraking journalists and progressive politicians who put public safety before corporate profit, a series of regulations, including the Bottled-in-Bond Act of 1897 and the Pure Food and Drug Act of 1906, were passed to make the worst of unsafe practices illegal.

Soon after these became laws, though, in 1920, the Eighteenth Amendment went into effect, prohibiting the manufacture, sale, or transportation of intoxicating liquors for beverage purposes. It was promoted as a societal cleanup to rid the country of slums and jails and the home of domestic abuse. In practice, though, Prohibition resulted in crime syndicates selling adulterated alcohol that poisoned and killed many. The Twenty-First Amendment, ratified in 1933, put an end to the experiment.

THE WHOLESOME SODA FOUNTAIN

The popular image of a soda fountain is something out of the 1950s: a clean, pure milkshake and hamburger counter in a Main Street family drugstore where teenagers hang out after school. That image is a far cry from the humble origins of the soda fountain as a spigot inside a druggist's shop in the first decades of the 1800s and from the dispensary of opioids, stimulants, and patent medicines they became later in the century.

Commercial-sized soda dispensing apparatuses at first were large, and quite dangerous. Beneath the pharmacy counter would be a chamber where an acid and base (sulfuric acid and calcium carbonate, respectively) were mixed to make carbon dioxide gas, the "fixed air" of old. The gas passed through a tank of ice-cooled water to carbonate it, and the water was piped up to a spigot.

Early versions of these soda dispensers might have a single tap that would be operated by the pharmacist who dispensed soda in between compounding drugs for customers. As soda water and then flavored sodas became more popular, the fountains were redesigned to be larger with multiple tap handles, marble bar tops, and brass or silver tap handles and other hardware. Soda fountains in some drug stores became the main attraction, taking up half the room and resembling a posh hotel bar of today. At the 1876 Centennial Exposition in Philadelphia, the Arctic Soda Water Apparatus on display was thirty-three feet high, could dispense twenty-eight types of water, and was decorated with ferns and statues. After the Expo, the fountain was moved to Coney Island, and then later to a department store in Saint Louis.

In Europe, soda fountains were less popular, as sparkling waters and sodas were sold in bottles. In an 1819 book about travels in America, the author wrote about summer: "the first thing every American who can afford five cents . . . takes on rising in the morning, is a glass of soda water: many houses are open for the sale of it, and some of them are fitted up with Parisian elegance." That quote is a touch unusual, given that most travelers to the young United States commented on how early risers would go out for a *cocktail* first thing in the morning. On the other hand, soda fountains were not entirely innocent either.

The earliest ones would offer a few types of fizzy water to take as a health tonic, or perhaps with which to wash down medicinal tinctures from the pharmacist. Though an alternative to the saloon, the soda fountain offered plenty of intoxicating drinks. Early soda flavoring syrups contained healthyish flavors like lemon, cherry, and violet; and natural, medicinal and herbal flavors like British dandelion and burdock or American wintergreen and sarsaparilla. Some sold wine and liqueur-based sodas and other beverages. Toward the middle of the 1800s, sodas could contain opium and cocaine. And many of the brands of soda on the market today were born as flavored medicinal syrups meant to be mixed into soda waters à la minute.

By 1900, books for soda fountain operators listed recipes for both purely recreational and purely medicinal drinks together. The medicinal syrups and tinctures included Angostura (angostura bark bitters with sweetened syrup); Beef, Iron, and Cinchona (tinctures of each with vanilla and lemon syrups); Calisaya Tonic (cinchona plus quinine sulphate, gentian, orange peel, caraway, rose oil, alcohol, and cochineal coloring); Coca-Calisaya; Pepsin and Iron; and Headache Powder.

In the beginning of the era around 1800, herbal brews available at fountains included ginger beer and root beer. The latter was initially a homemade combination of roots, herbs, berries, and barks that probably evolved from spruce tip beer, an earlier cure for scurvy. Later, root beer became more associated, as it is today, with the flavors of wintergreen, sarsaparilla, vanilla, sassafras, and licorice root.

Sarsaparilla in America was brewed in a form of "small beer," a lightly fermented, low-alcohol beverage. Alternatively, sarsaparilla root could be infused into whiskey for purely medicinal use. The slightly bitter plant had a reputation as a cure for syphilis as early as the 1500s, and in the early 1800s, it was recommended against skin ailments, hepatitis, rheumatism, and other diseases. *The American Herbal* of 1801 noted sarsaparilla's use for venereal disease, as well as promoting perspiration, and sweetening and purifying the blood and humors. It mentions that a decoction is prepared by boiling the root in water to make an extract.

Another root beer ingredient, sassafras, in *The American Herbal* is noted as a stimulant, aperient (laxative), diuretic, diaphoretic, and corroborant (invigorator). Like sarsaparilla, it was recommended to treat venereal disease but also used as an antiscorbutic (scurvy preventative or cure) and for other conditions. Its pleasant aroma was later used to disguise odors in both patent medicines and poorly distilled liquor.

ROOT OF ALL EVIL

1 ounce (30 ml) absinthe

3 ounces (90 ml) root beer

Add ingredients to an ice-filled highball glass.

SYPHILIS AND ROOT BEER

Syphilis showed up in Europe right after Christopher Columbus (1451–1506) returned from the New World in 1493. Some of Columbus's crew joined Charles VIII of France's army that then invaded Naples, Italy. Then some of those mercenaries joined a Scottish-led invasion of England, while others spread the disease back to their own homelands. By the year 1500, less than a decade after Columbus's return, syphilis was in all these countries, plus Hungary, Russia, the Middle East, Africa, and even India. It reached China and Australia within another fifteen years.

Syphilis was not the disease of friendship. The French called it "the disease of Naples," while the Italians called it "the French disease."

Most people blamed their neighbors or enemies for the presence of syphilis. The Dutch called it "the Spanish pox," Turks called it "the Christian disease," the Russians called it Polish, the Polish called it German, and in India, the Muslims blamed the Hindus and vice versa.

The "Columbian hypothesis" of the disease returning with Columbus is the most popular theory explaining syphilis's path of transmission, but another theory is that syphilis already existed throughout the world but evolved into a new virulent sexually transmitted form at this time. It might have gone unnoticed before 1500 owing to syphilis's reputation as "the great imitator" with its symptoms frequently confused with other diseases, particularly leprosy. (Leprosy was also thought to be a sexually transmitted disease or perhaps even a stage of syphilis.)

Syphilis first presents as a pea-sized chancre and was called "the great pox," not because it was great fun to catch, but to differentiate it from smallpox. Syphilis progresses in several stages, some with and some without symptoms, but those who suffer the severe late stages of the disease could be covered with ulcers, become paralyzed, suffer from psychosis, or all three. By the end of the nineteenth century, an estimated 10 percent of Europeans had syphilis, and by the early twentieth century, an estimated one-third of all patients in mental institutions were suffering from late-stage syphilis, according to Irwin W. Sherman in *Twelve Diseases That Changed Our World*.

Early treatments for "the just rewards of unbridled lust" usually included mercury applied externally with grease to sores. The same treatment had been used for leprosy. Mercury salts were also given in pills mixed with perfume and fruit flavors. Other patients were subjected to "therapeutic fumigation" of mercury in a steam environment.

Italian physician Girolamo Fracastoro's 1530 classic, *Syphilis, or The French Disease*, was written in rhyming verse and is credited with giving the disease its modern name. (Recall he also theorized germs as the source of disease long before Pasteur and others proved it.) The text was translated into English from the original Latin in 1686, and in it he referenced the four humors along with mercury and other cures. It includes verses like these:

> With these Ingredients mix'd, you must not fear
> Your suffering Limbs and Body to besmear,
> Nor let the foulness of the Course displease,
> Obscene indeed, but less than your Disease

and

> The greater Part, and with success more sure,
> By Mercury perform the happy Cure;
> A wondrous virtue in that Mineral lies,
> Whether by force of various Qualities
> Of Cold and Heat, it flies into the Veins,
> And with a fiercer Fire their Flame restrains,
> Conqu'ring the raging Humours in their Seat,
> As glowing Steel exceeds the Forge's heat

The poem mentions several herbal preparations as well, including guaiacum, a family of shrubs and trees native to Central America. The botanical treatments for syphilis came from the belief that cures for diseases could be found near their sources. Thus, New World plants including guaiacum, sassafras, and sarsaparilla proved popular options. Guaiacum water was given to the sufferer, and then the patient was subject to a routine of sweating over many days while "keeping himself from women and wine especially," according to the book *Joyfull Newes Out of the New-found Worlde* from 1577, originally written in Spanish.

The same book listed preparations of sarsaparilla (sometimes mixed into a syrup with jujube, prunes, borage, barley flour, and syrup of violets) and sassafras root. Sassafras was a popular cure for syphilis and just about everything else, for it was "as good as cinnamon" in its pleasant smell and taste as well as medicinal features. Among other things, it treated the pox and was supposed to build the appetite, reduce headache, soothe stomach issues, purge kidney and other stones, "provoke urine," and cure toothache, gout, and "griefs of women."

For a brief time, sassafras root was an extremely valuable commodity, with special expeditions sent from England specifically to gather it. Guaiacum fell out of favor as a cure for venereal disease in the sixteenth century, but sassafras and sarsaparilla were still recommended in 1801. Just after 1900, the early chemotherapy agent Salvarsan was used to cure syphilis (more on that in chapter 8), but it was replaced by antibiotics that came into use in the 1940s. One of the first people to receive the new drug penicillin in America was bootlegger Al Capone in 1942. He had been released early from his Alcatraz prison sentence, as his advanced syphilis resulted in "paralytic dementia," but the disease was too advanced for penicillin to be effective. It killed him less than ten years out of prison at age forty-eight in 1947.

PENICILLIN

2 ounces (60 ml) blended scotch whiskey

0.75 ounce (20 ml) lemon juice

0.75 ounce (20 ml) ginger-honey syrup*

0.25 ounce (8 ml) smoky Islay scotch whiskey

Add ingredients except for Islay scotch to
an ice-filled shaker. Shake and strain into an
ice-filled Old-Fashioned glass. Top with
Islay scotch and garnish with candied
ginger or lemon twist. Adapted
from a recipe by Sam Ross.

· · · · ·

Root beer evolved from a small beer made fizzy by fermentation into a syrup added to fizzy soda water at the fountains. It became very popular. In *Fizz: How Soda Shook Up the World*, Tristan Donovan writes, "Soon sarsaparilla was one of the most popular flavors at the fountains, providing an early indication of how the soda business would soon embrace both the cookbook of quack medicine and its advertising rulebook too."

Drugstore and soda fountain owner Charles Elmer Hires created Hires Root Beer in 1876; and it is now thought to be the second-oldest

---

*Ginger-honey syrup: To a blender, add 1 cup each honey and hot water with about a 2 inch (50 mm) piece of ginger, diced. Blend and strain; store in refrigerator between uses.

extant soda after Vernors ginger ale. Hires claimed that the root beer would "purify the blood," as did most syphilis cures. Another ad stated, "It gives New Life to the Old Folks, Pleasure to the Parents, Health to the Children."

The 1906 book for operators of soda fountains, *The Standard Manual of Soda and Other Beverages*, mentions at the beginning of a chapter on "medicinal drinks" that "drinks of a presumably medicinal character occur not only in this chapter but in some the others as well. For example, tonic, tonic beer, coca, coca vanilla, gentian, moxie, malto, ginger, ginger tonic, kola coca, kola vanilla, lactart, and tamarind syrups of Chapter VIII are of more or less medicinal character. The same may be stated of phosphates and lactarts, and all of the mineral waters, many the egg, cream and milk, and fancy drinks."

Moxie soda was created in 1876 as Moxie Nerve Food, a nostrum (quack medicine) made with a secret miracle plant from the Strait of Magellan that was supposedly able to cure brain and nervous exhaustion, loss of manhood, imbecility and helplessness, paralysis, and softening of the brain. It would also promote appetite and was a cure for alcoholism. The truth of the matter is that Moxie was flavored with wintergreen and gentian, the bittering agent found in Angostura bitters and many amari. In 1884 Moxie was relaunched as a fountain syrup. During World War I, the company led an advertising campaign claiming, "What this country needs is plenty of Moxie," which helped turn the brand's name into a generic word for courage or spunk.

Other medicinal ingredients also became soda fountain staples. Phosphoric acid was considered a pick-me-up, served in the form of acid phosphate mixed with mineral salts. Horsford's Acid Phosphate was recommended for "Mental, Nervous, and Physical Exhaustion. Distress After Meals." Phosphates became a category of soda fountain drinks, with acid phosphate mixed with flavors to make cherry, chocolate, citrus, and other phosphates. Phosphoric acid is still used in colas, while lemon-lime sodas mostly use citric acid.

The soda fountain industry was prone to fads and trends in the 1900s as it had been with root beer the previous century. Beyond cherry phosphates, egg creams, malted sodas, and ice cream sodas and floats were all new trends at one point. Fountain flavors would grow popular at one shop, then all the others in a city would rush to capture the zeitgeist, much like bubble tea shops in recent years chasing trends like matcha and cheese tea.

COCAINE DRINKS

Cocaine was isolated from coca leaves in 1855 and became the exciting (literally) new medicine on the scene. It was recommended by Sigmund Freud as an antidepressant, by the Hay Fever Association as a remedy for that condition, and used in ear, throat, and nose surgery. It would supposedly cure morphine addiction, tuberculosis, and impotency. It eased Ulysses S. Grant's throat cancer and kept him lucid enough to write his memoirs in his final days.

In 1859 an Italian doctor, Paolo Mantegazza, wrote about his experiences chewing the coca leaf in Peru, saying that while he was under the influence of the drug he wrote 77,438 words, "each more splendid than the one before." In the text, he recalled: "I mocked the poor mortals condemned to live in this valley of tears," and concluded that "God is unjust because he made man incapable of sustaining the effect of coca all life long. I would rather have a life span of ten years with coca than one of 10,000,000 (and here I inserted a line of zeros) centuries without coca."

With this sort of enthusiasm behind the drug, cocaine quickly made its way into beverages. In 1863 a Corsican chemist living in Paris named Angelo Mariani (1838–1914) created Vin Mariani, a red wine and cocaine mixture that was marketed as a luxury health tonic. The wine had fans and public endorsers including popes Leo XIII and Saint Pius X, Thomas Edison, Queen Victoria, writer Jules Verne, and actress Sarah Bernhardt. Many of them appeared in ads for the product.

Vin Mariani was advertised this way: "Fortifies and refreshes body and brain. Restores health and vitality." Other ads mentioned that it "hastens convalescence especially after influenza," "may be given indefinitely, never causing constipation," and "is especially adapted, on account of its nice taste, for children." It was also available in the forms of cordials, lozenges, and pastilles. A spirits-based elixir version contained triple the cocaine.

In purely medicinal preparations, cocaine was often included as an anesthetic. Lloyd Manufacturing Company produced Cocaine Toothache Drops that were advertised with a pair of children playing on the ad. Allen's Cocaine Tablets were promoted for their use in treating colds, sore throats, nervousness (it is unclear how it would have helped with that), sleeplessness (same), heartburn, and flatulency, among other conditions. Its ointment form was recommended for everything from sunburn to mosquito bites. Burnett's Extracts advertised a cocaine product as "the best hair dressing. It kills dandruff, promotes the growth of hair, cures scald head and all irritation of the scalp."

Vin Mariani inspired many imitators, which in turn inspired Vin Mariani to run ads warning readers not to be fooled by them. One of these imposters was Pemberton's French Wine Coca, which claimed it could treat nerve trouble, dyspepsia, exhaustion, wasting diseases, constipation, and other ailments.

Its creator, Atlanta-based John Pemberton (1831–1888), attended medical college and initially became a "steam doctor" who promoted an alternative medical treatment recognizable today as sweating out toxins. Pemberton later sold his own cough syrup and blood purifiers. In 1886 Atlanta passed a local prohibition against alcohol, so Pemberton developed a nonalcoholic version of French Wine Coca, a soda fountain syrup named Coca-Cola.

Like the coca leaf, the kola nut was also thought to be medicinal, and was used to treat guinea worm, soothe stomachache, make childbirth less painful, and relieve fatigue. The latter is the work of the caffeine, of course. Kola was already being used in health tonics and sold in fizzy drinks, including one by Schweppes. Beyond the coca and kola, the syrup had vanilla, nutmeg, citrus, cinnamon, and cassia. It was advertised as being refreshing, exhilarating, and invigorating.

But just a couple years after its launch and with a new owner, the amount of cocaine and kola were reduced in the formulation, while the company focused on selling patent medicines. While the anti-alcohol abstinence movement grew in the US, so too were there campaigns against both cocaine and caffeine. In 1902 a *Los Angeles Times* story announced: THEY THIRST FOR COCAINE: SODA FOUNTAIN FIENDS MULTIPLYING. Around 1903 Coca-Cola syrup became cocaine-free.

CUBA LIBRE

2 ounces (60 ml) rum

4 ounces (120 ml) Coca-Cola

Pour over ice in a highball glass and
garnish with a lime wedge.

• • • • •

A surprising number of the most popular soda flavors that are still
around today were created by drugstore owners and pharmacists.
Vernors (originally "Vernor's") was created in 1866 by a pharmacist,
as was Dr Pepper in 1885, Pepsi in 1893, and Canada Dry ginger ale
in 1900. Orangina was created in 1933 by a Spanish pharmacist.

"The public can rest assured that Dr Pepper is non-alcoholic and
that it contains nothing detrimental or injurious to the most delicate
system," according to one ad. Dr Pepper was created in Waco, Texas,
by the pharmacist Charles C. Alderton (1857–1941) at a soda fountain in 1885, and it was promoted for giving "Vim, Vigor, Vitality."
Ads claimed that "Every Drop [Is] Pure and Healthful." It was an
alternative to colas that contained cocaine or caffeine, because it did
not—at least initially.

It was promoted as "Free from caffeine and drugs" and with "No
caffeine. No dope. No heart-depressing drug" and even more dramatically: "Dr Pepper stands alone on the bridge defending your
children against an army of caffeine doped beverages, as the great
Horatius defended Rome." Despite its initial point of differentiation,
caffeine was later added to the formula from 1917 to 1938. It was then

replaced with vitamin B$_1$, but this failed to gain traction, and the caffeine went back in.

Today we think of sodas as guilty pleasures or perhaps as contributors to obesity and diabetes, but most were marketed for their health-giving properties. Pepsi-Cola's name alluded to its use in aiding indigestion, also known as "dyspepsia." Orange Crush from 1911 was promoted as a source of vitamin C because it contained orange juice, rather than orange extracts.

During US Prohibition from 1920 to 1933, the soda fountain was proclaimed "the new American bar" while another publication announced, "The bar is dead, the fountain lives, and soda is king!" Some soda formulas were adjusted to mimic the kick missing from alcohol with pepper, salt, and chilies.

Launched in 1929, 7UP's initial formula included lithium citrate, and its original name was Bib-Label Lithiated Lemon-Lime Soda. You can see why the company changed it to 7UP Lithiated Lemon-Lime shortly thereafter. Unlike other sodas it was sold only in bottles, since its flavor was hard to standardize at fountains. During Prohibition, it was specifically advertised to soothe hangovers with a "7Up for 7 Hangovers" campaign. Those hangovers were from overeating, underdrinking (dehydration), overworking, mental lassitude, overdrinking, overworrying, and oversmoking. The *Woodland Daily Democrat* in California in 1932 ran a notice: "Woodland Ice & Bottling Works is distributing a new lithiated soda called '7 Up,' said to be the last word as an antidote for 'hang overs.' In other words, '7 Up' is good for one down."

After Prohibition, 7UP was advertised as a mixer to pair with alcohol that "tames whiskey" and "glorifies gin." As to its signature ingredient, lithium is sometimes used today as a mood stabilizer to treat bipolar disorder, but after World War II it was used as a supposedly healthy alternative to hypertension-causing salt. Lithium salts were banned around 1949 following reports of serious side effects, and they were removed from 7UP's formulation.

The soda fountain declined rapidly after World War II. According to *Fizz*, before the war every small town had a soda fountain, but in 1965 only half of them did. Sodas were sold in bottles and at fast-food restaurants that catered to car culture, rather than at sit-down bars inside other stores.

In the many years since lithium was outlawed for beverages, sodas continue to be promoted for "Vim, Vigor, and Vitality," just using other terms. 7UP once advertised its "alkaline reaction" and with a slogan, "That's the way to slenderize." In the 1950s, a few sugar-free diet sodas were on the market, but when Diet-Rite rebranded in 1962 from a beverage for people with diabetes sold in the medical section of drugstores to a soda for the general audience, the category really took off. Diet-Rite became the fourth-largest-selling soda in the US at this time, and all the other brands released diet formulations. Today Diet Coke is the third-bestselling soda in the US, after Coke and Pepsi.

Sports drinks, though usually noncarbonated like Gatorade (created in 1965 by the University of Florida College of Medicine scientists specifically as a fluids-replacement drink for football players), became everyday drinks. Then energy drinks like Red Bull (created in 1987) upped the ante with their allusions to "extreme sports."

Naturally, most diet and sports drinks are not exclusively consumed by dieters and athletes but by regular boozers using them both as mixers and for curing hangovers. Every now and then, someone combines the two into one product. Hop'n Gator Lemon-Lime

Lager was a combination of beer and Gatorade launched in 1969, soon reformulated as a "tropical-flavored malt liquor," and then shortly discontinued after that. Toward 2020 a new batch of "wellness beers," typically low in alcohol and with added mineral electrolytes, hit the market, as did vitamin-laced hard seltzers. Hop'n Gator was just ahead of its time.

KALIMOTXO

3 ounces (90 ml) dry red wine

3 ounces (90 ml) Coca-Cola

Add both to an ice-filled glass. Squeeze
a lemon wedge into the drink.

PATENT MEDICINES

The Smithsonian's National Museum of American History has an online and on-site display collection of patent medicines. The oldest one dates to roughly 1650 and is Knoxit Liquid, a mercuric chloride ointment that could have been used to treat syphilis. Most of the "Balm of America: Patent Medicine Collection" is from the mid-1800s and later, though, and includes Dr. John Hooper's Female Pills, Dr. Mead's Female Regulating Remedy, Dr. D. Jayne's Sanative Pills, True Cephalic Snuff, Dr. McMunn's Elixir of Opium, Bailey's Vermifuge, Hollis' Jaundice Bitters, Dr. Guild's Green Mountain Asthmatic Compound, Doct. Herricks Sugar Coated Vegetable Health Pills, Cherokee Liniment, Hanson's Magic Corn Salve, Dr. Shiloh's System

Vitalizer, and Dr. G. H. Tichenor's Antiseptic Refrigerant. The latter is 67.5 percent alcohol with arnica and peppermint.

The term "patent medicine" originated in England from "patents of royal favor" awarded to those who provided medicine to the royal family, but it came to refer to heavily advertised over-the-counter nostrums or quack medicines created by often-fictitious doctors. The advertising dollars from these medicines funded newspapers and magazines, and some brands sponsored entire "medicine shows" that were traveling vaudeville-style entertainment with a sales pitch at the end.

Very few patent medicines were actually patented, though some were trademarked. They can be grouped into categories such as medications for indigestion; pills for fever, chills, and malaria; laxatives; health tonics and bitters; "nerve drugs"; women's health products; vermifuges (intestinal worm expellers); cough and cold medicines; and drugs to help the liver and kidneys. They weren't all advertised as cure-alls, but many were promoted as cure-mosts.

The word "tonic" in health tonics did not imply tonic water as it does today but referred to an all-over heath enhancer. That said, many tonics of the 1800s did contain quinine, which gives its bitter flavor to tonic water. In the old American West the combination of quinine, strychnine, and iron was fairly standard in tonic medicines, infused in a base of alcohol. The quinine was to treat fever and chills, the iron was to fight anemia or "low blood," and the strychnine, which is poisonous in larger doses, was used like caffeine as an energy stimulant, mental booster, and laxative.

Most of the liquid patent medicines contained alcohol ranging from a few percent alcohol by volume (enough to extract medicinal herbs) up to 60 percent or more, at which point they were basically sanitizer. Patent medicines contained cocaine, opium, cannabis, to-bacco, mercury, and many other since-prohibited substances.

Opium had been used in medicine from ancient times, including as an ingredient in mithridate and theriac and in later plague remedies. Morphine, extracted from opium, was isolated in the early 1800s and used in a huge number of medicines both legitimate and not. Lauda-num, which is opium dissolved in alcohol, was used in patent medi-cines, though it took on some solid forms in its history, such as a 1618 formulation with castor, saffron, ambergris, musk, and nutmeg. It was often perfumed with other spices like cloves, licorice, and cin-namon because it was said to smell so foul on its own. Opium-containing medicines were often mixed with or prescribed alongside rhubarb root, a laxative (found in many amari) to counter opium's well-known side effect of constipation.

Opiates were used primarily against pain, coughing, and diarrhea, but they were prescribed for ailments including alcoholism, bronchitis, cancer, cholera, colic, cough, delirium tremens, diabetes, dysentery, earache, epilepsy, typhoid fever, gallstones, gonorrhea, gout, hemor-rhoids, hysteria, rheumatism, measles, mumps, pneumonia, whooping cough, and more. Many of the health issues treated by opiates, such as coughs and diarrhea, were caused by diseases that flourished in the dirty and crowded living conditions of the Industrial Revolution in the late 1700s and early 1800s, including cholera, dysentery, and tuberculosis.

Ingham's Vegetable Expectorant Nervine Pain Extractor was a pat-ent medicine with opium and 86 percent alcohol that claimed, "If sick it will do good; if well it will do no harm." Hardly. Mrs. Winslow's Soothing Syrup was one of many teething and colic medicines for chil-dren that included alcohol and morphine. Alcohol and opium would certainly have quieted fussy babies, but it also killed many of them.

A great summation of the state of patent medicines comes from a prohibitionist book, *Alcohol, a Dangerous and Unnecessary Medicine*, published in 1900 by Martha Meir Allen, the superintendent of the Department of Medical Temperance at the Woman's Christian Temperance Union (WCTU). She wrote:

> A careful compilation of manufacturers' announcements list 1,806 so-called patent medicines sold in open markets, in which alcohol, opium or other toxic drugs form constituent parts. 675 of the preparations are known as "bitters," stomachics, or cordials, and alcohol enters into their composition in quantities varying from fifteen to fifty per cent.; 390 are recommended for coughs and colds, nearly all of which contain opium. Sixty remedies are sold for the relief of pain, and no other purpose. 120 are for nervous troubles, and of this number, sixty-five have entering into their composition coca leaves, or kola nut, or both, or are represented by their respective active principles, cocaine or caffeine. 129 are offered for headaches, and kindred ailments, and usually with a guarantee to give immediate relief. In these are generally compounded phenacetine, caffeine, antipyrine, acetanilid, or morphine, diluted with soda, or sugar of milk. Dysentery, diarrhœa, cholera morbus, cramp in bowels, etc., have 185 quick reliefs or "cures" to their credit, nearly all of which contain opium, many of them in addition, alcohol, ginger, capsicum or myrrh in various combinations, and there are numerous cases on record where children and adults have been narcotized by their excessive use.

Snake oils were a category of patent medicines, some of which may have contained actual snake extracts at one time. One theory is that actual snake oil was introduced to America via Chinese railroad laborers in the mid-1800s as a folk medicine used to soothe joint pain. It contained oil from water snakes, which is rich in omega-3 fatty acids. These acids reduce inflammation, including that caused by arthritis, among other benefits. Lacking in Chinese water snakes, American medicine makers substituted rattlesnakes, which are useless for inflammation.

The most infamous of these was Clark Stanley's Snake Oil Liniment. Stanley (born c. 1854) credited Hopi tribe members for the formula, not Chinese railway workers. He gutted and boiled a live rattlesnake in a demonstration at the 1893 World's Columbian Exposition in Chicago to show how the product was supposedly made. However, it was later analyzed after the 1906 Pure Food and Drug Act passed, and results showed that the liniment contained mineral oil, capsicum (chili pepper extract), beef fat, and perhaps turpentine and camphor. Stanley was fined for his dishonest branding, and "snake oil salesman" became a generic term for a charlatan, while "snake oil" came to be a term for a worthless medicine.

Many snake oils became famous, or at least well advertised enough to enter the popular culture. Benjamin Brandreth's Vegetable Universal Pill was mentioned in *Moby-Dick* and in Edgar Allan Poe's satirical story "Some Words with a Mummy." Daffy's Elixir, a cure-all patent medicine with a base of alcohol, was noted in Charles Dickens's *Oliver Twist* and William Makepeace Thackeray's *Vanity Fair*.

MANHATTAN

2 ounces (60 ml) rye whiskey

1 ounce (30 ml) sweet vermouth

3 dashes Angostura bitters

Stir all ingredients with ice in a stirring pitcher
and strain into a cocktail glass. Garnish
with a maraschino cherry.

· · · · ·

While many of these patent medicines were just flavored alcohol, one
brand made a case for its medicine being *exclusively* alcohol. Duffy's
(no relation to Daffy's) Pure Malt Whiskey was marketed as "abso-
lutely pure and unadulterated" whiskey in the last decades of the 1800s.
Founder Walter B. Duffy (1840–1911) claimed in advertising that
it "makes the weak strong" and was a cure for consumption (tuberculosis), malaria, dyspepsia, "lost vitality," "sluggish blood," and more.
Testimonials in ads featured people like Abraham E. Elmer, of Utica,
New York, who is "vigorous at 119 years old," and Mr. John McGrath,
of 441 East 82nd Street, New York City, who is "smart at 102 years of
age." He is quoted as saying, "Duffy's Pure Malt Whiskey is my only
stimulant and tonic; it is both food and drink. It tones up my system,
stimulates my blood, as well as keeping me proof against coughs and
colds. . . . I shave myself, so you see I am not feeble."

By claiming his whiskey was medicine, Duffy could avoid paying
beverage alcohol tax on it. When a tax was later imposed on medicines and Duffy was forced to pay it, he used the opportunity to

advertise his as "the only whiskey recognized by the government as medicine." A few years after that, a trial showed that Duffy's did not have any additional medicinal ingredients and was nothing more than sweetened whiskey—so it was neither "pure" nor medicine— and it became subject to the higher beverage alcohol tax.

Many of Duffy's ads had endorsements from priests, doctors, and nurses, which was a common practice in patent medicine advertising. But many of these too were outright fabrications, and some endorsers who appeared in ads without their permission sued the company in response. Yet the ads were successful enough to grow the brand tremendously, and the company that began in Rochester, New York, expanded to include the George T. Stagg Company and another distillery in Kentucky.

In response to the unchecked false advertising and dangerous ingredients of patent medicines, *Collier's* magazine published an extensive multipart exposé by Samuel Hopkins Adams (1871–1958) called "The Great American Fraud," starting in 1905. The opening quote of the series is the epigraph for this chapter. The articles in the series attack quack medicines that were full of opiates, alcohol, and adulterants. Adams calls out Duffy's by name several times. "It pretends to be a medicine and to cure all kinds of lung and throat diseases. It is especially favored by temperance folk," he wrote. The series was compiled into a book of the same name released the next year, and it significantly contributed to the passing of the Pure Food and Drug Act in 1906.

In addition to all the quack medicines, there were plenty of quack medical devices purporting to use new technology to improve health, including Sanche's Oxygenator, Macaura's Pulsocon Vibrating Massager (renamed Macaura's Blood Circulator), Pulvermacher's Medical Electric Belts, and the Electric Corset. There were also quack physical therapies, some as intrusive as grafting goat and monkey testicles onto those of men in order to cure "sexual weakness" and render youthfulness anew. While these didn't involve cocktails, they inspired one: the Monkey Gland was created by famed bartender Harry McElhone of Harry's New York Bar in Paris in the 1920s.

MONKEY GLAND

1.5 ounces (45 ml) gin

1.5 ounces (45 ml) orange juice

1 teaspoon (5 ml) grenadine

1 dash absinthe

Add all ingredients to an ice-filled shaker.
Shake and strain into a chilled cocktail glass.

THE PURE FOOD AND DRUG ACT

If the adulterated whiskey and laudanum-laced medicine in post–Civil War America wasn't bad enough, the food was often in worse shape. This was a time of great economic and social transformation, with massive immigration into the country and industrialization of its industries resulting in mass migration to cities and fewer people living on farms close to food sources. Assembly-line processes came to be applied to food production in canning factories and in places like Chicago's stockyards.

At the time, the technology of canning was known but home refrigeration was uncommon, so untested chemical preservatives were used to keep canned food looking and smelling fresh. Fresh food also had its life span extended: milk was watered down, preserved with the embalmer formaldehyde, colored white with plaster of Paris or chalk, and the float of cream on top of the jug was mimicked with pureed calves' brains. Tainted milk killed hundreds, if not thousands, of children in the 1800s in the United States.

Formaldehyde was also used in canned beef, and borax household cleaner kept ham and butter from spoiling longer. Both wine and beer had their shelf lives extended with salicylic acid. And when those chemicals didn't do a good enough job, there was always copper sulfate to make peas green, alum to bleach flour white, ash to make coffee (actually sawdust) brown, and ground-up insects to mimic brown sugar.

One colorant still permitted for use in foods today also comes from insects. Cochineal, which can be labeled by that name or as "carmine" or "E120," has a bright red color (though it can be manipulated into a range of other variants like purple) and is frequently used to dye dried shrimp, sausage, and red-colored fruit in yogurt and jams. It is also used in red cosmetics. The color comes from a dried, crushed scale insect called cochineal that lives on the prickly pear cactus.

The insect was native to the Western Hemisphere and used by Aztecs to cure wounds and treat head, heart, and stomach problems, according to *A Perfect Red*, by Amy Butler Greenfield. After it was "discovered" by the imperial powers of Europe, cochineal was used as both fabric dye and medicine. It was considered an antidepressant that could cool fevers, produce sweat, and prevent infection. It was recommended in *The Country Housewife's Family Companion* circa 1750 for jaundice. Cochineal was given to England's Charles II in an enema, which must have proved alarming upon exit.

In modern times, cochineal is considered a natural food coloring, if not a vegetarian one. It's probably still used by many companies so that they can avoid the phrase "artificial coloring" on their labels. Cochineal was used to give Campari its signature bright red color, though it has been replaced with artificial coloring in many parts of the world, including the US. Cochineal is still employed by other red aperitif liqueurs though, including St. George Spirits' Bruto Americano, Leopold Bros. Aperitivo, and Cappelletti Aperitivo.

NEGRONI SBAGLIATO

1.5 ounces (45 ml) Campari
1.5 ounces (45 ml) sweet vermouth
1.5 ounces (45 ml) dry sparkling wine

Add all ingredients to an ice-filled Old-Fashioned
glass. Garnish with an orange slice.

• • • • •

At the St. Louis World's Fair of 1904, many canned and bottled foods were on display, and many of them contained artificial colorants. Chemists from the National Association of State Dairy and Food Departments were also present at the fair and set up their own booth. They took dyes extracted from canned foods and then used those dyes to color pieces of fabric to show consumers what they were really eating. The goal was to gain consumer support behind the need for pure food laws.

Manufacturers were not obligated to disclose adulterants at this time, nor to tell the truth in advertising. While England and several European countries passed food safety laws in the last half century of the 1800s, in the United States these laws were considered anti-business or anticapitalist. Powerful consolidated food manufacturer groups influenced government policies to keep it that way.

Some government agents and agencies were working for good, however. The US Department of Agriculture's chief chemist Harvey W. Wiley (1844–1930) spent thirty years, from 1882 to 1912, trying to expose the toxic properties of chemical food adulterants. He pressured legislators and progressive president Theodore Roosevelt to pass national food safety laws. Those laws protected not only food and medicine, but also beer, wine, and spirits. One initiative Wiley took was to form a group of human trial subjects known as the Poison Squad to systematically test chemicals used in food production. ("Test" is a nice way of saying "eat.") They experimented with chemicals including borax, salicylic acid, formaldehyde, saccharin, sodium benzoate, and copper salts. Squad members were given measured quantities of food with the various additives, then subjected to physicals and lab tests to show the impact of the potential toxins on the human body.

Adding to the momentum of the *Collier's* "Great American Fraud" exposé of patent medicines, fellow muckraker Upton Sinclair's book *The Jungle* had a tremendous impact on public support for food safety legislation. The novel described the Chicago meatpacking industry's horrific conditions for both the cows and the humans working in the processing factories. In the book, rats, fingers, and other unsavory objects ended up in the meat.

Though *The Jungle* was fiction based on Sinclair's research, government inspectors were sent out to see by how much conditions were exaggerated, only to confirm just what Sinclair described. In response,

President Roosevelt pushed for the quick passage of both the Pure Food and Drug Act and the Meat Inspection Act the same year the book was published, 1906. Sinclair meant the book to be about the need for socialism and to shed light on horrible labor conditions endured by the workers, but instead readers were more concerned for their consumer products. He conceded, "I aimed at the public's heart, and by accident I hit it in the stomach."

The 1906 Pure Food and Drug Act, largely a false-labeling law, was the beginning of a series of laws and enforcements building up to the Federal Food, Drug, and Cosmetic Act of 1938, which helped establish and empower the Food and Drug Administration. This changed which additives food, beverages, medicine, and other products could contain, how they could be labeled and advertised, and how they could be sold. After the act, a lot of patent medicines with false advertising went out of business. A lot but not all: patent medicines didn't disappear entirely (and things like morphine, opium, cocaine, and cannabis were still allowed in them), but they became more accountable, and their formulas were made less toxic or at least less potent.

Just before this, toward the year 1900, Congress investigated American whiskey to find that two million gallons of unadulterated whiskey were being sold, compared with 105 million gallons of "whiskey" mixed with neutral spirits and adulterants. Though the Bottled-in-Bond Act of 1897 allowed for a segment of whiskey to be certified as additive-free, the 1906 Pure Food ruling meant the rest of the whiskey on the market must be labeled truthfully as to its contents.

But the act didn't define "bourbon" let alone "whiskey." This caused a temporary kerfuffle as rectifiers now had to label their products as "imitation whiskey," "compound whiskey," or "blended whiskey." They were very displeased and set upon government officials they'd been sponsoring to pressure them to reverse the ruling. The Taft Decision of 1909 then clarified matters and allowed rectifiers to avoid those terms, as long as they were used truthfully. "Pure whiskey" was no longer allowed on labels, and even to this day, the Alcohol and Tobacco Tax and Trade Bureau seems reluctant to allow the word "pure" anywhere near a liquor label.

Harvey Wiley's Department of Agriculture became the enforcer of the Pure Food and Drug Act, and his department seized falsely labeled whiskey that did not "contain enough whiskey to give it character," rye whiskey that contained no rye whiskey, and dyed neutral spirit labeled as whiskey.

Wiley also went after Coca-Cola, but not because of the cocaine. He thought the soda was too high in caffeine, as well as habit forming, and that the "brain tonic" marketing was false advertising. Wiley believed that caffeine was fine for adults in tea and coffee, but he criticized Coke for marketing to children. The "soda fiends" were addicted to fountain beverages, and there were rumors of "soldiers driven wild by mixing whiskey and Coke," according to *Fizz*. Rather than caffeine-laced sodas, Wiley thought that people "should be contented with water." He provided quotes for the WCTU's *Alcohol, a Dangerous and Unnecessary Medicine*, warning of the addictive nature of patent medicines.

Wiley's department seized a shipment of Coca-Cola syrup in 1909, and two years later, the trial against the company was sensationalized in the media. Wiley's side brought in "Coke fiends" who testified to their addiction. Coke brought in scientists who showed it was healthy. Coke won.

Many people in the country thought that he had gone too far in his pursuit of product safety (for Wiley was a celebrity government crusader). He had begun his mission by protecting children from drinking embalming fluid in milk but was now battling fun by trying to ban America's favorite nonalcoholic beverage. After pressure, Wiley retired from government service.

Fortunately he was then hired by *Good Housekeeping* magazine as the director of "food, health, and sanitation." In that role, he had a column in the magazine and a laboratory at the office. He tested products to determine if they were worthy of earning one of the most iconic American food certifications: the Good Housekeeping Seal of Approval.

PROHIBITION

Now that whiskey was subject to truth-in-labeling laws and forbidden from containing harmful adulterants, Americans decided to outlaw it entirely. But prohibition of alcohol was neither a medical nor a food safety movement. President Herbert Hoover called it "a great social and economic experiment, noble in motive and far-reaching in purpose."

Problems with alcoholism were mentioned in the argument to ban booze but usually in the context that drunk men can't take care of their families or be trusted to vote properly. Alcoholic men might abuse their wives; alcoholic women might resort to sex work.

The temperance movement dates to the early 1800s and was supported by a number of organizations with different motivations but the same goal. Early temperance advocates were opposed only to distilled spirits rather than beer and wine (reminiscent of the absinthe abolitionists in France), which were usually seen as healthy everyday beverages. Some brewers joined the antialcohol movement against the distillers, not realizing they'd soon be lumped in with them.

Groups such as the Anti-Saloon League were not necessarily in favor of banning all alcohol everywhere but were opposed to the existence of saloons where men would get up to drinking, gambling, and visiting sex workers away from their families. Other prohibitionists sought to reduce crime and poverty, assuming that people who consume alcohol wasted their money at the bar rather than spending it on wholesome milk and meat.

Former baseball player and evangelist Reverend Billy Sunday claimed that an America without alcohol would be free of slums and "turn our prisons into factories and our jails into storehouses and corncribs." The WCTU was in favor of complete abstinence as part of other social reform issues, including the women's right to vote, which passed as the Nineteenth Amendment right after Prohibition.

WHITE LADY

2 ounces (60 ml) gin
0.75 ounce (45 ml) Cointreau
0.75 ounce (45 ml) lemon juice

Add all ingredients to an ice-filled shaker.
Shake and strain into a cocktail glass.

• • • • •

Anti-immigrant groups protested the new "foreign invasion of undeveloped races" who liked to socialize in the saloon (Irish) or at the family beer garden (Germans) as they would back home. World War I (1914–18) gave Americans further motivation to shun German and German-sounding beer. The Ku Klux Klan supported the passage of Prohibition, and the group grew in size in the 1920s as self-appointed enforcers of the law.

Industrialists like Henry Ford wanted sober employees to work harder and faster. Rural Southerners tended to support Prohibition, while city residents opposed it. Temperance propaganda (including the threat of spontaneous human combustion of alcoholics) was taught in schools, much like D.A.R.E. was used as propaganda in the "war on drugs" in the 1980s and 1990s.

The Eighteenth Amendment to the United States Constitution was a nationwide ban on the production, importation, transportation, and sale of intoxicating liquors. It lasted from 1920 to 1933. "Intoxicating" was later defined as greater than .5 percent alcohol by volume, much to the chagrin of some beer drinkers and even brewers who supported the amendment, not knowing that their favorite beverage would be outlawed as well.

There were exceptions to the rule, however. Consuming alcohol was still allowed, so anything hoarded before the law went into effect was fair game. The Yale Club reportedly stockpiled enough booze to last its members throughout the entire period of Prohibition. "Non-intoxicating cider and fruit juices" were allowed to be produced for home consumption, though home-brewed beer was not.

Much of the wine industry pivoted to selling unfermented grapes and grape juice rather than fermented wine, and vineyard acreage actually increased during Prohibition. Some wineries began selling "grape bricks" by brand names like Vine-Glo. The bricks were made of dried grapes that could be mixed into a gallon of water to make grape juice. They came with strict instructions not to leave the jug of reconstituted grape juice in a cool place for a few weeks, with sugar added to taste, lest it turn into wine. Wink, wink. Sacramental wines for religious services were also allowed (many people suddenly became religious around 1920), and vineyards that supplied the churches profited well during Prohibition.

Another way to drink legally during Prohibition was by prescription. The American Medical Association had delisted alcohol from its approved medicines just a few years before, but in 1922 it surveyed its members to find how many believed that alcohol was medicinally necessary. A small majority agreed that it was. It has been noted that if the association had asked members whether it was medicinally *useful* instead, the answer may have come out more strongly in favor. The conditions for which alcohol was medically necessary according to the survey included, among other conditions, asthma, high blood pressure, diabetes, shock, cancer, certain kinds of poisoning, insomnia, and snakebites.

The whiskey available by prescription was expensive, but it was guaranteed to be of quality since the medicinal whiskey aged in government-bonded warehouses. It was bottled at one hundred proof and sold in pint-sized bottles, and patients were limited to one pint every ten days for much of Prohibition. If that did not prove sufficient, dentists and veterinarians could also prescribe medicinal alcohol. Perhaps one's hamster had a case of snakebite.

Several years into Prohibition, stocks of aging whiskey in bonded warehouses began to run low, so specific licensed distillers were permitted to distill again in controlled amounts. Brandy and rum were available by prescription in addition to whiskey; patients had their choice of medication when they got to the pharmacy. Beyond distillers, doctors and pharmacists profited from the business in prescribing and fulfilling prescriptions for medicinal alcohol.

Many drugstores specialized in just the one drug during Prohibition. Walgreens expanded from nine pharmacies in 1916 to over five hundred by the end of the 1920s, though the company website credits its invention of the malted milkshake in 1922 for the success.

Patent medicines that survived the Pure Food and Drug Act could still contain alcohol (now labeled to show the amount contained) and be purchased without a prescription. Many people bought their medicinal alcohol in the form of "gripe water" for colic in babies or as Lydia E. Pinkham's Vegetable Compound, which was advertised as being useful in treating female complaints. The latter medicine contained about 20 percent alcohol in this era. It is still available for sale today in the form of Lydia Pinkham Herbal Liquid Supplement (at a lower proof) and still contains two of its old advertised medicinal ingredients—pleurisy and black cohosh root.

It was not the only patent medicine to survive to the modern day. Moxie and many other sodas evolved from them. Black Draught laxative, Smith Brothers cough drops, Sanatogen vitamins, Mentholatum ointment, Fletcher's Laxative, Father John's Medicine cough syrups, and Carter's Little Pills all still exist and date back to patent medicine time, though none of these were alcohol based.

The patent medicine Jamaica Ginger Extract, known as "jake," was a favorite source of "medicinal" alcohol for drinkers in dry counties, is said to have contained up to 80 percent alcohol. During Prohibition, one of its components was replaced by a plasticizer that when combined with the alcohol created a neurotoxin. Imbibers of jake ended up with a condition called "jake leg," "jake walk," or "gingerfoot," which was a strange way of walking ("like a marionette") due to paralysis of muscles below the knee. Jake leg impacted over thirty thousand people, most of them poor immigrants, and many never recovered from the condition.

MOSCOW MULE

2 ounces (60 ml) vodka

0.5 ounce (15 ml) lime juice

4 ounces (120 ml) ginger beer

Add all ingredients to an ice-filled glass or
copper mug. Garnish with a lime wheel.

MOONSHINE

However, most of the toxic alcohol consumed during Prohibition was of the illegal variety. Illicit alcohol was either imported from abroad or distilled clandestinely at home. From abroad, alcohol came into the country overland from Mexico, on boats from Canada across the Great Lakes or down either coast of the US, or from the Caribbean to the beaches of Florida.

Distilling liquor within the US without a license was risky. Moonshiners could be spotted by Prohibition enforcement agents by the trails of smoke from the fires used to heat their stills. Seeking to avoid raw grains that needed to be cooked before fermentation (requiring additional fire and smoke), moonshiners would more often ferment cane sugar or malt syrup, which could be done at room temperature.

The equipment used for illicit distillation might be made from scrap metal and held together with poisonous lead solder, with a cooling condenser made from a repurposed car radiator. Traditionally, distillers make "cuts" (discarding the beginning and end of the run) of the liquid out of the still to ensure they remove the natural acetaldehyde, methanol, and fusel oils that form during fermentation. During Prohibition, distillers often skipped that step to save money, since they were already committing an illegal act and not putting their names on the bottles anyway.

Methyl alcohol or methanol, also known as "wood alcohol," is a natural by-product of distillation for beverage (ethyl) alcohol, or it can be distilled from wood without fermentation. On its own, methyl alcohol is used for all sorts of nondrinking purposes, including as an ingredient in antifreeze, as a solvent or fuel, and in resins, pharmaceuticals, perfumes, paints, and insecticides.

Many people died of methanol poisoning during Prohibition, and not all owing to bootlegged liquor: To dissuade its citizens from drinking the industrial ethanol meant for cleaners, cosmetics, and the like, the US government required that this alcohol be rendered undrinkable, or "denatured." This was accomplished with the addition of poisonous methanol or with other adulterants that were intolerably bitter tasting or smelling. A modern example of denatured alcohol is rubbing alcohol sold as a topical antiseptic: it can be made either from isopropyl alcohol or be ethanol based, but in the latter case it is denatured with "bitterants."

Problematically, methanol is flavorless, and the deadly impacts of drinking it can occur days later. If ingested, methanol slowly converts into more dangerous by-products like formaldehyde and formic acid. The symptoms of methanol poisoning include headache, weakness, loss of coordination, vomiting, blindness, and death. Some estimate that ten thousand people were killed from government-poisoned alcohol alone.

Bootleggers purchased denatured industrial ethanol and tried to renature it, employing chemists and distillers to figure out how to do so. They could filter it, redistill it, or add things to it to render the undrinkable industrial alcohol back into drinkability. This was done both on a large scale by mob-owned distilleries, and on a smaller scale by housewives paid by the mob to run alcohol cookers in their kitchens to remove poisons from industrial alcohol. Seeking to thwart these practices, the government experimented with a range of additives that were meant to be too challenging to identify and renature, including benzene, pyridine, iodine, zinc, mercury salts, nicotine, ether, chloroform, and acetone. But methyl alcohol was supposedly the most effective adulterant, as it is difficult to separate from ethanol. Officials later required that the methanol levels be doubled in industrial alcohol, up to as much as 10 percent.

SCOFFLAW

2 ounces (60 ml) rye whiskey

1 ounce (30 ml) dry vermouth

0.75 ounce (20 ml) lemon juice

0.75 ounce (20 ml) grenadine

2 dashes orange bitters

Add all ingredients to an ice-filled shaker. Shake and strain
into a cocktail glass, and garnish with an orange twist.

. . . . .

To stretch their supplies, bootleggers would thin out smuggled-in or home-distilled potable alcohol with industrial alcohol (renatured or not), or water it down. They would also fake its heat and flavor using all the tricks employed before the Pure Food Act was in place, like adding pepper or ginger to make it hot and coloring to make it look like aged whiskey. Gin was produced with juniper oil mixed with ethyl alcohol and watered down, as it had been in the Gin Craze of the 1700s. Some cocktails served at hidden speakeasy bars no doubt helped disguise the flavor of bad alcohol.

Prohibition was a law meant to improve not the health of drinkers but the health of society. However, it negatively impacted both the health of people who continued to drink alcohol and the peace of mind of those who didn't. A New York judge presiding over a trial of a speakeasy break-in (as noted in Deborah Blum's *The Poisoner's Handbook*) said, "Prohibition is a joke. It has deprived the poor working-man of his beer and it has flooded the country with rat poison." Because of the many loopholes for circumnavigating the law, the crime and corruption it fostered, uneven enforcement (many regions simply didn't enforce Prohibition at all), plus the onset of the Great Depression that began in 1929, the "noble experiment" was considered a failed one, and the Eighteenth Amendment was repealed with the passing of the Twenty-First Amendment.

Unfortunately, dangerous adulterated alcohol did not suddenly disappear from the market upon repeal. Shortly after Prohibition in 1939, *The Gentleman's Companion*, by Charles H. Baker Jr. (1895–1987), was published, based largely on the author's global drinking adventures during the previous decade. Though mostly a cocktail book, there are some party-hosting and etiquette tips inside, including instructions "to salvage a guest from the effects of hanging—by rope, not the morning after." One wonders how often suicide was attempted at Baker's parties given that he felt the need to include the advice, and also what it says about him as a party host.

Perhaps a more common problem at parties in this era, though, was adulterated alcohol. Baker included advice "to alleviate apparent death from toxic poisonings, and especially should, in any happenstance, the quality of the liquor be suspect." He offers three recipes for emetics to cause the victim to vomit poisonous liquor.

Today thousands of people are sickened and killed by toxic illegal alcohol each year. Sometimes individual moonshiners injure themselves, but often, hundreds of people become ill all at once as a batch of methanol-loaded moonshine enters the market via crime networks. This happens particularly in developing nations and those where alcohol is illegal or not socially accepted. In 2020 there were a reported 5,876 hospitalizations and at least 800 deaths in less than two weeks in Iran, as a rumor spread that drinking high-proof alcohol would kill the coronavirus.

Not every legacy of Prohibition is negative, though. NASCAR stock car racing evolved from the practice of Appalachian bootleggers' modifying small cars for better speed and handling to evade capture. Before Prohibition, bars (at least saloons) were limited to men only, but the speakeasies were open to women and, in a few cases, people of color. After Prohibition, many bars stayed integrated.

NASCAR SPRITZ

1 bottle Miller High Life beer

1 ounce (30 ml) Aperol

Drink an ounce of the beer. Pour in Aperol and
a long lime twist. Recipe from Chad Arnholt.

. . . . .

Two of the most significant laws impacting the safety of medicine
and alcohol in the US were the Pure Food and Drug Act and Prohibition. Before the former, sick and thirsty people couldn't be sure
that what they thought they had purchased was what they had ingested. Prohibition ensured that legal prescription liquor was safe to
drink, and that illegal booze was usually not, but people drank it
anyway. Both were intended for the good of American society, but
one failed so completely that even one hundred years later we look
back on it with incredulity.

PITT'S
PATENT TONIC WATER,

28A, WHARF ROAD,
CITY ROAD, LONDON, N.

———o———

CHEMICAL AND MICROSCOPICAL LABORATORY,
74, *Wimpole Street, Cavendish Square, W.,*
19th December, 1860.

Report on PITT'S PATENT TONIC WATER, by Dr. HASSALL.

I HAVE carefully analysed Pitt's Tonic Water.

The idea of combining a tonic like Quinine with an aerated water is a good one, and the practical difficulties in the way of carrying it out have been entirely overcome in this preparation.

It is a pleasant, refreshing tonic, and invigorating beverage, strengthening to the digestive organs, and calculated to promote appetite. It is also an excellent restorative to the stomach weakened by any excess or indulgence.

From its composition and properties, Pitt's Tonic Water ought to a great extent to supersede the use of soda and other aerated waters.

(Signed)   ARTHUR HILL HASSALL, M.D. Lond.,
Analyst of "The Lancet" Sanitary Commission;
Author of "Food and its Adulterations,"
"Adulterations Detected," and other works.

N.B. Numerous first-class Medical and other Testimonials to be had on application.

TONIC

MALARIA, MOSQUITOES, *and* MAUVE

The gin and tonic has saved more Englishmen's lives,
and minds, than all the doctors in the Empire.

—*Winston Churchill*

M alaria has been around for one hundred million years or so, and the ancestors of mosquitoes and the parasites they carry may have also infected dinosaurs. Dinosaurs evolved into birds, one of several animal species that suffer from malaria, as do monkeys, bats, lizards, antelopes, and other vertebrates.

The written history of malaria in humans dates back millennia, with intermittent summer fevers and enlarged spleens the two telltale symptoms of the disease. Descriptions of malarial-type fevers have appeared in most of the medical texts referenced in previous chapters. They were described in the Chinese medical text *Huangdi Neijing* (Yellow Emperor's Inner Classic) purportedly from 2700 BCE but probably written much later. The text also made the association between the fevers and splenomegaly. Malarial symptoms were mentioned in Indian Vedic texts from 1500 BCE, and in the Ebers papyrus from around the same time in Egypt. Hippocrates described different types of recurring malarial fevers. Galen thought that the varieties of fever (quotidian, tertian, quartan, which reoccurred at different rates) were controlled by different humors, and thus the recommended treatment would be different for each. On the other hand, Paracelsus's opinions on malaria are hard to find, which is surprising given how enthusiastic he was to share his thoughts about everything else.

The word "malaria" comes from the Italian "mal'aria," meaning "bad air." It was long thought to be caused by miasma, like cholera, yellow fever, the plague, and most infectious diseases. People knew that malaria came from areas with swamps, marshes, and stagnant water, but didn't figure out that mosquitoes (rather than the air itself) caused it until almost 1900. By that point, the cure for it had been established for 250 years already.

Though today it is a disease of warm climates, malaria has turned up in nearly every part of the world at one point, having made its way as far north as Siberia and Norway, and at least as far south as Patagonia.

In 1740 a visitor to the Vatican wrote, "There is a horrid thing called mal'aria that comes to Rome every summer and kills one." It was known as the fever, summer fever, intermittent fever, marsh fever, the ague, fever 'n' ague, quotidian ague, tertian ague, quartan ague, Roman intermittent fever, Chickahominy fever, Roman marsh fever, pioneer shakes, and African remittent fever, among other names. The disease is characterized by fever and ague, which refers to cycles of shivering and sweating, and it was often named for where you caught it.

Rome was bordered by outlying farmland and marshes, and the

entire region was riddled with malaria from its ancient days through the 1930s. In the summers, the city became insufferable. Those who could afford to relocated to the breezier hills for the season. For farmers, fall harvesttime often proved deadly.

Malaria likely killed Pope Innocent VIII (in 1492), Pope Alexander VI (1503), Pope Adrian VI (1523), Pope Sixtus V (1590), and Pope Gregory XV (1623), all in July, August, or September. When a pope died, a papal conclave was called, and the cardinals returned to Rome to elect a new one. If this took place in the summer, many of the cardinals (potential new popes) would catch malaria and die as well. In 1287 a ten-month-long conclave resulted in the death of six cardinals before the rest fled the city.

Beyond the all-purpose medical cures of bloodletting, amputation, and wearing of amulets, the early purported cures for malaria were many and varied. They included applying split pickled herrings to the feet, throwing a patient headfirst into a bush, mixing the patient's urine with flour and throwing that on an anthill, avoiding melons, and drinking viper's broth, crab's eyes mixed with radishes, wolf's eyes, cabbage, or brandy mixed with cat's blood and pepper. No recipe for the latter is included here.

THE FEVER TREE

The Jesuit order, a congregation of the Catholic Church specializing in evangelization and education, was founded in 1534, and their missionaries were established in Peru from the mid-1500s. They learned of the Indigenous practice of ingesting cinchona tree bark as a cure for fevers or shaking around 1630, and being familiar with Roman fevers, they sent some of it back to Italy. The bark was effective against the fevers there too.

It should not have been. There is no good evidence that human-infecting malaria existed in the New World before the Europeans arrived. To survive in a new environment, the malaria parasite needs to infect both humans and certain species of mosquitoes, and this has to happen in warmish weather in which the mosquito can survive. Historians believe that malaria didn't transfer to the West when humans migrated over the Bering land bridge from Siberia to Alaska thirteen thousand years ago—it was too cold.

So the Indigenous cure for local fevers in Peru must have been treating another underlying disease or condition with similar feverish symptoms, or merely treating the symptoms. This discovery is like finding out that the aspirin used to soothe a hangover headache also cures a headache symptomatic of brain cancer . . . as well as the brain cancer.

WHITE PORT AND TONIC

2 ounces (60 ml) white port

4 ounces (120 ml) tonic water

Add to an ice-filled glass and garnish
with a lemon wedge.

· · · · ·

We use the word "malaria" for both the disease and the parasite that causes it. The parasite isn't mosquito venom like a snakebite, but a separate, single-celled organism (plasmodium) that lives inside of both mosquitoes and humans. Mosquitoes are the vectors, or agents, that transmit the parasite to humans when they suck our blood. A female anopheles mosquito carrying malaria parasites bites a human and releases those parasites into them. The parasites travel to the human's liver to mature, replicate, and multiply asexually, and infect red blood cells. In the blood, they multiply, and some change again into male and female forms, while giving the human the symptoms of malaria illness. Humans infected with the parasite can then return it to mosquitoes when another one bites that human. The mosquito sucks up some of the parasites along with the blood it is after. The parasites change form yet again in the mosquito's stomach, multiply, and infect its salivary glands. The next time the mosquito bites a human, it will inject the parasites into them, and the cycle starts over again.

When the malaria parasite is in a human's blood, the fever and ague come. Quinine, an alkaloid in cinchona tree bark, disrupts the growth and reproduction of malaria in the blood, and can cleanse it of the parasite. However, the plasmodium also lives in the human liver in a different form, and infected people may be asymptomatic when it does.

People with malaria not only have cyclical bouts of fever every few days, they can also suffer recurring fevers months and even years after first being infected as the parasites pour back into the blood from the liver. Eventually this can wear people down and kill them, if they didn't die from the initial infection. But others who catch malaria over and over can become somewhat immune to it.

The name of the cinchona tree comes from the Countess of Chinchón from Spain, who, legend had it, caught a fever and was given the cure by the Indigenous peoples when her husband was the viceroy in Peru. She supposedly returned home and shared the miracle cure with the world. In 1742, the father of modern taxonomy, Carolus Linnaeus, made the official name for the tree "cinchona," leaving off the first "h."

But as it turns out, there were two Countesses of Chinchón: The first died in Spain three years before her husband was appointed viceroy of Peru. The second died in Colombia, possibly of yellow fever, so she couldn't have returned to Europe with the cure. The error was only discovered in the early 1900s, long after the nomenclature was permanent.

The efficacy of the bark was proportional to the amount of quinine contained within it, and this varied wildly depending on the cinchona species and where the trees grew. Furthermore, the ideal quantity and frequency of cinchona bark administration was not well established or understood, so doctors struggled to determine the proper dosage even with the best bark. Plus, too much bark comes with some nasty side effects that could be mistaken for the malaria itself.

Also unknown to doctors was that the bark could be merely a temporary relief from the symptoms of malaria, which can recur again and again. The cure worked, but not all the time nor always to the same degree, so many doctors had doubts as to whether it was really a cure at all.

The name "quinine," for the antimalarial chemical compound in the bark, is derived from the Indigenous peoples' name for the tree, quina. This bark and name were often confused with the Peruvian balsam tree, named quinaquina, according to the authors of *Just the Tonic*.

Over time the tree and bark were known by other names, including calisaya, Peruvian bark, fever tree, countess's powder, fever bark, cardinal's powder, Jesuits' powder, and Popish powder. The latter names are due to the bark's first importer into Europe: the Jesuits.

Given its inconsistent effectiveness, Protestants of the 1600s denounced the "Catholic cure" as quackery or evil magic, and many medical practitioners in Protestant countries tried to invent their own remedies. One such person was Robert Talbor (1642–1681), a British apothecary apprentice who railed against the Peruvian bark in favor of his own medicine, which he called "the English Cure." Talbor published a pamphlet claiming that his alternative was just as effective as the Jesuits' bark, and he gained fame and reputation after curing the fevers of royals including King Charles II of England, the queen consort Marie Louise of Spain, and the child of Louis XIV of France.

Louis XIV purchased the formula for the English Cure for 3,000 gold crowns under the condition that he would not publish it until after Talbor's death, which occurred shortly thereafter. When the formula was made public in 1681, Talbor's fraud was revealed: his secret recipe was powdered cinchona bark in wine, disguised by flavoring it with various botanicals like parsley, anise, rose petals, and lemon juice in different preparations.

But by Talbor's deception the bark's medicinal value was confirmed, and soon cinchona tree bark was used as a cure and preventative for malaria by all the great colonizing empires of the era. This allowed for exploration and exploitation of previously inaccessible parts of the world including much of Africa and India. The superpowers' increased exploitation of the Western Hemisphere also spread malaria from Europe into the New World. There, the mosquitoes bred, followed waterways inland, and conquered new territories of their own.

In the young United States, malaria was as problematic as anywhere else. The English are believed to have introduced it to Jamestown, Virginia, in 1607. George Washington suffered hearing loss due to quinine toxicity. In the Lewis and Clark expedition from 1803 to 1806, the explorers brought along fifteen pounds of powdered Peruvian bark designated not only to treat malaria but also to be mixed with gunpowder in poultices for both snakebites and gunshot wounds.

During the US Civil War of the 1860s, more than a million cases of malaria were reported, and deaths were about ten thousand, mostly among the Union troops who had less acquired immunity. In the historical fiction book *Little House on the Prairie*, set in Kansas around 1870, the whole family comes down with the mysterious and deadly fever 'n' ague. Ma thinks they caught it from eating a watermelon.

DRINKING BARK

Cinchona tree bark and the quinine within it are very bitter, which is probably a natural defense of the tree against burrowing insects. The bark was traditionally pulverized and served as a powder to be mixed with liquids, and in the days when beer and wine were safer to drink than water, those were the liquids of choice.

Beyond water, beer, and wine, we find references to cinchona bark being served or recommended to be served with other beverages including hot chocolate (1730s England), rum (1771 British Royal Navy), sherry (1856 Niger), whiskey (1860s American Civil War), arrack (1863 India), and pink lemonade (early 1900s Panama). Most of these beverages were sweetened with sugar, which counteracts the bitterness of the quinine.

ESPRESSO TONIC

■

2 ounces (60 ml) espresso

0.5 ounce (15 ml) simple syrup

0.5 ounce (15 ml) lime juice

4 ounces (120 ml) tonic water

Add first three ingredients to an ice-filled glass.
Stir and fill with tonic water.

· · · · ·

In the 1800s about two hundred years after the global importance of cinchona bark was discovered, the Dutch, British, and Spanish superpowers that relied on it began to take a stronger interest in the plant's biology. They sought to learn which varieties of cinchona trees were the most effective against malaria and to plant those varieties in their own colonies rather than purchasing bark from newly independent South American countries.

Throughout this century, many expeditions of botanists and explorers were sent to Peru, Bolivia, and Ecuador to collect cinchona seeds and saplings. This was dangerous work, because the governments (both Peru and Bolivia had won independence in the 1820s) wisely protected their precious commodity by forbidding export of any seeds or whole plants that could be grown elsewhere—under penalty of death.

Nonetheless, the Dutch were successful in acquiring seeds and planted them on the island of Java in Indonesia, but unluckily the trees were mostly low-quinine varieties. British explorer Sir Clements Robert Markham led a massive expedition around 1860 to collect five different types of trees, and he managed to bring back several hundred saplings and seeds from different regions of the continent. But, according to *Just the Tonic*, none of the seedlings survived planting in India. Other British-backed expeditions were successful and trees with relatively low quinine content were planted in India, largely for local use.

The most successful pilfering of cinchona seeds was by a British alpaca salesman named Charles Ledger (1818–1905). Ledger's Bolivian friend and assistant Manuel Incra Mamani identified the proper trees from which to collect seeds, for which he was later imprisoned, dying shortly after release. Mamani managed to smuggle out forty pounds of seeds overall. Ledger failed to sell the seeds to the British but managed to sell one pound to the Dutch.

The resulting plants from those seeds contained more quinine than other known varieties, so the Dutch grafted the saplings onto their existing trees in Java in the 1870s. Plantations in India produced powdered bark for local consumption, but the Javanese tree plantations were used to make higher-quality processed quinine for the export market. The trees performed so well that by the 1930s, around 95 percent of the world's supply of cinchona bark came from trees grown on Java, rather than from India or their native lands. Botanists named the species of cinchona tree for its "discoverer": *Cinchona ledgeriana*.

The offspring of Ledger's bounty traveled again. In 1933 the Dutch gave a gift of cinchona seeds from Java to King Albert I of Belgium. His son donated them to start a plantation in what was once called the Belgian Congo. This plantation remains today, and at least one tonic water brand, Fever Tree, sources its quinine from it. Other brands, including Q Tonic, source cinchona from Peru and other parts of South America, and brands including East Imperial buy theirs from plantations in Indonesia.

Quinine was first isolated from cinchona bark in France in 1820, allowing those who could afford it to take a compact pill form of the medicine instead of ground-up bark in a liquid. Dr. John Sappington (1776–1856), the great-great-great-grandfather of Hollywood actress and dancer Ginger Rogers, sold quinine sulfate pills in the United States to fight malaria in the form of Sappington's Anti-Fever Pills. His was one of the most successful patent medicines in America in the early 1800s, selling five hundred thousand boxes in 1844 alone. The same year he also published *The Theory and Treatment of Fevers*, known as the first medical book written west of the Mississippi River. In it he gave away his formula, as he was already wealthy and wanted to spread the cure freely. The formula was "one grain quinine each, three-fourths of a grain of liquorice, and one-fourth grain of myrrh, to which was added just so much of the oil of sassafras as would give to them an agreeable odor."

Quinine showed up in many other products, including cod-liver oil with quinine, and "granulated effervescing citrate of quinine" to be added to one's beverage of choice like Alka-Seltzer. Cinchona and its quinine became known not just for curing fevers (and not only malarial ones) but for all sorts of other conditions; it was a sort of panacea.

The American Herbal from 1801 listed Peruvian bark as

> a very celebrated remedy in many diseases, as in the "intermitting" fever, and those of a malignant, putrid kind; contagious "dysenteries," smallpox, measles, gangrene, "mortifications," hemorrhages, nervous and convulsive complaints, spitting of blood, pleurisy, peripneumony, emphysema, ill

conditioned ulcers, phthisis, scrophula [inflamed lymph nodes in the neck due to tuberculosis], rickets, scurvy, dropsy, &c. It strengthens the stomach, helps digestion, diffuses wind, raises the pulse, increases the elasticity of the vessels, promotes the peristaltic motion of the intestines, the circulation of the fluids, resists putrefaction, helps menstrual obstructions from debility, strengthens the solids, and invigorates the system in general by giving new life and vigor to the circulatory vessels. In short, it is an excellent medicine, which has saved the lives of millions of the human species. . . . The best mode of administering of it, is in substance, in wine, brandy, and water, sweetened, or in any other convenient vehicle.

This helps explain why quinine ended up in so many beverages beyond tonic water: it was the electrolytes or provitamin of its day. Calisaya Bitters ("calisaya" being a common term for cinchona in the US) were advertised as "preventative for all malarious diseases" as well as "for loss of appetite dyspepsia and general debility." Elixir of Calisaya was a liqueur of bark often with other flavorings like orange peel, cinnamon, coriander, fennel, caraway, or cardamom, which was dyed red with cochineal. It was available by the 1830s and served at drugstore soda fountains in the US where there was some moral panic about it. It earned the nickname "the red menace" (owing to the cochineal coloring), and its users were called "calisaya fiends." Likely it was just high in alcohol, and the panic was similar to that about absinthe on a smaller scale. An 1898 headline warned: MAD POLICEMAN USED CALISAYA INORDINATELY AND WAS A SLAVE TO ITS HORRORS. TOOK TWENTY DRINKS A DAY.

Other countries produced quinine or cinchona beverages as well, many of them familiar to us today as amari with origins as cure-alls and digestif tonics from Italy and France. They include Amaro Sibilla, Amer Picon, Averna, Barolo Chinato, Bigallet China-China, Bonal Gentiane-Quina, Byrrh, Fernet-Branca, Kina Lillet, and Ramazzotti. Many of these contained other health- and digestion-enhancing bittering agents previously discussed, like wormwood, gentian, and rhubarb.

BLACK MANHATTAN

2 ounces (60 ml) rye whiskey

1 ounce (30 ml) Averna amaro

1 dash Angostura bitters

1 dash orange bitters

Stir all ingredients with ice in a stirring pitcher
and strain into a cocktail glass. Garnish with
a maraschino cherry. Created by Todd Smith.

TONIC WATER

As discussed in chapter 4, artificially carbonated waters were created in the late 1700s to replicate naturally fizzy, supposedly medicinal mineral water spas like Pyrmont and Selters. In England, soda waters tended to be sold in bottles, and the flavored soda syrups like lemon were added to the bottles directly and sold combined. As these were considered healthy beverages, it is no great surprise that

quinine was also added to soda water for general health or specifically to combat malaria.

The first known bottled carbonated water with quinine was a
short-lived product made by Hughes & Company, as seen in an 1835
advertisement. This was followed by Pitt's Aerated Tonic Water from
1858. It was created by London soda manufacturer Erasmus Bond after he obtained a patent around 1850 for "aerated tonic liquid." Jacob
Schweppe had retired in 1799 and died in 1821, long before his company Schweppes released its first tonic water. The Schweppes company started producing tonic water with quinine in the 1870s.

The cinchona tree bark had been exported by Italians living in
South America, the trees replanted in the Dutch property of Indonesia,
the bark processed in Amsterdam, and the resulting quinine put into
carbonated bottled tonic water by the British. Gin had Dutch origins
as genever and was modernized as gin by the English. And yet the Gin
and Tonic seems to have first come together in India.

The British East India Company controlled India from 1757 to
1858, and the British Raj governmental rule lasted until 1947. Malaria
was endemic to India, and locals usually cured their malaria with
homegrown quinine bark after transplanted trees took hold there,
while the British ruling class took their quinine in pill and tonic
water form.

In an advertisement in *The Lancet London* from 1861, a testimo-
nial for Pitt's Aerated Tonic Water states, "In some cases, a small
portion of wine or French brandy may be required to be added to the
'Tonic Water' Wine in those more easily stimulated, and brandy
where a more potent adjunct is requisite, as in some instances all ef-
fervescent beverages are apt to produce a sense of weight and cold-
ness in the stomach, with flatulency or spasms."

As with other simple highballs like Rum and Coke and Vodka Soda, we'll never really know the first person to have mixed gin and tonic water together. The earliest record of the Gin and Tonic found so far is from 1868, by which time the Brits in India had clearly started to *enjoy* the taste of the quinine-juniper combination and drank it recreationally. From *The Oriental Sporting Magazine*:

> Independent of the lotteries, there was plenty of betting, and our modest fiver went on *Polly*, more for the sake of backing her rider than thinking of what class she was. Loud cries of "gin and tonic," "brandy and soda," "cheroots," & c., told us the party was breaking up for the night, and we wended our way home (only a short distance from the mess, luckily), feeling certain we could lay 2 to 1 we named the winner of each race on the morrow, only that it would be a very rash bet to make.

Though earlier references to the first combination of gin with tonic water will surely be found, the drink's popularity in India really took off in the 1880s, judging by its mention in newspapers and magazines of the time. By the first years of the 1900s, the references to the drink start showing up in Buenos Aires, Argentina, where both the British and malaria also had footholds.

MOSQUITO DISCOVERY AND ERADICATION

We now know that mosquitoes transmit malaria, but it was about 250 years between the discovery of the cure for malaria in 1630 and the proof of its cause. Over the millennia, various scholars theorized that mosquitoes were the real cause of the disease, but this was not widely accepted. In 1854 a French doctor in Venezuela observed malaria and mosquitoes in an area with no swamps, so he suspected the mosquito was the cause, and "introduces a poison which has properties akin to a snake venom." Close.

In the United States, Dr. Albert Freeman Africanus King (1841–1914), previously known for helping to carry dying president Abraham Lincoln after he was shot at Ford's Theatre to a house across the street, outlined in 1882 a list of nineteen reasons why mosquitoes caused malaria. He further proposed covering the entire American capital (which is surrounded by rivers) in a wire net as tall as the Washington Monument to keep mosquitoes out.

From 1880 to 1900, scientists working independently and in collaboration around the world revealed the mechanisms of the disease. In the 1880s in Algeria, the malaria parasite was first observed in blood thanks to improved microscopy. Malaria-infected blood has granules of black pigment that are sure signs of the disease in both humans and birds, and the path of infection and spread of malaria could now be tracked more easily. In 1881 in Havana, scientists had strong evidence for mosquito transmission of malaria. And finally in 1898 in Calcutta, the incredibly complicated life cycle of the malaria parasite—which feeds on both humans and mosquitoes—was explained.

As soon as mosquitoes were proven to be the transmission vectors of malaria, government leaders knew they had to figure out better ways to kill the insects. Civil engineers began mosquito-eradication projects, including getting rid of all possible stagnant water in which mosquitoes lay their eggs, spraying oil over water pools to prevent mosquito reproduction, and using mosquito nets and window screens to prevent infection and transmission of malaria.

The first major successful mosquito-eradication project was in the construction of the Panama Canal, in which American engineers nearly eliminated mosquito-spread disease, including yellow fever (called "the saffron scourge"), using the aforementioned measures. These actions were replicated the world over, with the greatest success in wealthy countries with good infrastructure. In the 1930s, after all those centuries of malaria, the Pontine Marshes south of Rome were pumped dry. Without the mosquitoes to spread malaria parasites from an infected person to an unaffected one, the disease was quickly limited to those who already had it. And there was quinine for that.

MAUVE

In 1856 in London, young chemist William Perkin (1838–1907) was attempting to create synthetic quinine from the raw material of coal tar, a waste product in the making of gas for lamps called "the first large-scale industrial waste." The tar was boiled and distilled to become creosote (a wood preservative that contains benzene and aniline) and pitch (used to make asphalt). Perkin failed at making quinine, but in the process he found that a brilliant purple substance was created.

Until this point, purple had been a valuable color only available to the rich and royalty, coming from natural dyes like Tyrian purple made from the glandular mucus of sea snails. Perkin was aware of this, so he refined his process and went into the fabric dye business.

His discovery became one of the first synthetic pigments, named mauve or mauveine.

The new color was a sensation. Both the wife of Napoleon III, Empress Eugénie, and Queen Victoria in Britain wore similarly colored dresses, and mauve came into great demand. For a while, anyway, because fashion is fickle. By 1890, Oscar Wilde in *The Picture of Dorian Gray* wrote, "Never trust a woman who wears mauve, whatever her age may be, or a woman over thirty-five who is fond of pink ribbons. It always means that they have a history."

Perkin's discovery helped kick off the aniline (coal tar–derived) dye industry with surprising, far-reaching consequences. Aniline dyes became crucial as microscopy stains, which allowed scientists to better observe cellular structures, bacteria, and parasites. Coal tar derivatives were manipulated into other materials, including sweeteners, laxatives, detergents, anesthetics, cosmetics, and resins.

Robert Koch (1843–1910), who isolated the anthrax bacterium in 1876 and is cocredited with establishing the germ theory of disease, used aniline dyes and other new technology to identify bacteria responsible for suppuration (staph infection), tuberculosis, and cholera in less than ten years. The organism responsible for syphilis was identified in 1905 by other researchers. From the disease's appearance post-Columbus near 1500 through to 1900, syphilis had been mostly treated with mercury, with some doctors switching to bismuth salts in the last decades of the 1800s.

German scientist Paul Ehrlich (1854–1915) studied aniline dyes against diseases with the intention of developing "magic bullets" that would kill harmful bacteria without harming human cells. He realized that if these dyes could bind differently to various cellular structures to make them show up under the microscope, they might do the same for different types of organisms, and also kill those organisms.

He first experimented with African sleeping sickness using trypan red dye, which was successful in mice but didn't cure the illness in humans. Ehrlich then began manipulating arsenic-containing compounds that were believed to be safer and effective in the same disease, and he theorized that these compounds might also be useful against syphilis.

Ehrlich and Sahachiro Hata from his laboratory found an arsenic-derived compound in 1909 that attacked the syphilis spirochete directly; it was named Compound 606 after that number of experiments leading to the successful one. It was commercialized under the name Salvarsan. For this discovery, Ehrlich is known as the father of chemotherapy, the treatment of disease using chemical substances.

This new drug lessened the severity of syphilis symptoms in many people but did not always cure the disease. Late-stage syphilis can paralyze, blind, or cause paralytic dementia as it spreads to the brain and nervous system. With the high percentage of sufferers in Europe and the intensity of these symptoms, late-stage syphilis remained an important problem to solve.

Physicians noticed by studying the now-observable causative organism, *Treponema pallidum*, under the microscope that it could not withstand high heat, and that patients who came down with high fevers in late-stage syphilis had improved health. This led Austrian physician Julius Wagner-Jauregg (1857–1940) in 1917 to try something desperate and brilliant: giving late-stage syphilitics a transfusion of blood from people suffering from malaria. The patient with syphilis would come down with the well-studied malarial fever. The fever would heat the blood enough to kill off the syphilis, then after a few rounds of fever, the doctor would cure the malaria with quinine. Though the trick wasn't 100 percent effective, it did stop disease progression in many people and saved lives. Wagner-Jauregg, Ehrlich, and Koch were each awarded Nobel Prizes in different years.

Salvarsan and its successors were still the best available treatment for syphilis for decades, until antibiotics were discovered and then employed in the 1940s. Antibiotics are chemotherapeutic agents produced by other microbes rather than by human chemical synthesis.

To summarize, the quest to make synthetic quinine to cure malaria led to the discovery of aniline dyes that led to the identification of microbes that caused syphilis and other diseases, as well as to the birth of chemotherapy. Early chemotherapy was effective in treating syphilis but in desperate cases had to be supplemented by giving patients the disease malaria and its cure, quinine.

Aniline dyes had other impacts specific to cocktails and spirits. Artificial colorings used in many foods, spirits, and liqueurs are also aniline dyes (now derived from petroleum rather than coal tar), including FD&C Yellow No. 5 in the US (E102 in the EU), which gives Midori melon liqueur its signature green color.

We owe the clown-red color of typical maraschino cherries to an aniline dye, FD&C Red No. 40 in the US (E129 in the EU). Historically, jarred cherries to go in cocktails and on sundaes were preserved in maraschino liqueur that was likewise distilled from cherries. They were supplanted by cheaper versions that are bleached in the brining process and dyed bright red with E129. In 1911 a writer complained, "It is a tasteless, indigestible thing, toughened and reduced to the semblance of a formless, gummy lump by long imprisonment in a bottle." In the modern craft-cocktail revival, bartenders have reclaimed the original style of maraschino cherry made without the artificial coloring, manufactured by brands like Luxardo, which dates to about 1905.

AVIATION

2 ounces (60 ml) gin

0.5 ounce (15 ml) maraschino liqueur

0.25 ounce (8 ml) crème de violette

0.75 ounce (20 ml) lemon juice

Add all ingredients to an ice-filled shaker.
Shake and strain into a cocktail glass. Garnish
with a maraschino cherry; may as well
make it one of the bright red ones.

COMING TO AMERICA

Though mosquito eradication was successful in many parts of the world in the early 1900s, antimalarial medicine was still desperately needed. World War II nearly ended disastrously owing to the fragility of the global quinine supply system. As more than 95 percent of the world's commercial supply of quinine was then grown on Dutch-controlled Java, when the Japanese captured the island in 1942 the world's main cinchona tree bark source then became unavailable to the Allies.

Two years earlier, the Germans had captured Amsterdam, where the supplies of refined quinine were stored. The Axis powers had captured nearly all the available quinine on earth. Luckily, before the war ended (and before cinchona trees on new plantations on US-controlled islands were able to mature), synthetic quinines such as atabrine and chloroquine were developed.

Meanwhile, other scientists were trying to kill the mosquitoes. Swiss chemist Paul Hermann Müller (1899–1965) discovered the insecticidal properties of DDT (dichlorodiphenyltrichloroethane) in 1939. When sprayed aerially, DDT was used to combat typhus (spread by external parasites such as lice, fleas, and ticks), as well as dengue fever and malaria (both spread by mosquitoes).

Today we think of DDT as a toxin, but in many areas of the world it was a lifesaving substance, highly effective at eliminating malaria as part of a global spraying initiative from the 1940s through the 1960s. Later, an investigation of DDT by the author and naturalist Rachel Carson led to the publication of the book *Silent Spring* in 1962, which is usually considered the beginning of the environmental movement in the United States.

There are reports of a cocktail made with a pinch of powdered DDT in the United States in the 1950s. It was supposedly called the Mickey Slim and was a cocktail of gin with DDT that would make the drinker extra loopy. If it were true, it would make a nice way to tie up this section, but there is a lack of evidence to show that it ever really existed.

In the United Kingdom in the first half of the twentieth century, recreational drinking of Gin and Tonics was slowed by the world wars. Quinine and sugar, essentials for the troops, were both rationed, and

soda brands were not permitted to use either in some years. Schweppes
didn't let that stop it from advertising its unavailable product. One
campaign lamented, "If we had some gin we'd have a gin and tonic if
we had some Schweppes."

In America, the G&T didn't really take off until after World
War II, and it was at first treated like an exotic and still medicinal cocktail. The aforementioned American writer Charles H. Baker Jr. spent
a large portion of the years of US Prohibition cavorting in countries
where it was legal to consume alcohol, and his book *The Gentleman's
Companion* is full of stories of drinking cognac mixed with champagne
in central India, egg-laden beer toddies in Denmark, and crème de
menthe cocktails in Colombia. He wrote of the G&T that the drink
"still later became accepted over here by American hosts who wanted
to impress folk with having combed the orient."

The Gin and Tonic was heavily promoted in the 1950s and 1960s
by Schweppes, which had opened a bottling plant in the United States
in 1953. At the direction of David Ogilvy (1911–1999), the advertising world's biggest superstar, the company ran campaigns celebrating
the Britishness of the brand (and citing Schweppes as the only authentic tonic for the cocktail, naturally). One set of campaigns imagined
a county called Schweppshire in England, with attractions including
Schwepstow Castle, the Schwepping Forest, and suburbs of Ciren-
schwepster.

The medicinal history of tonic was left out of the advertising, and
additional campaigns by Schweppes, Canada Dry, and other tonic
brands played up the postwar, men's club, genteel, proto-yuppie aesthetic of golf and country club pools and plaid. While the Gin and Tonic
never went completely out of style after that, 1950s nostalgia came

back with a vengeance in the 1980s. *The Official Preppy Handbook* (1980) defined the G&T as "what you drink at the club before, during, and after a tennis game."

CINCHONISM

Unknown to Western medicine until relatively recently, a second natural cure for malaria was recorded in Chinese literature dating back two thousand years. The herb qinghao was used to reduce fevers, including malarial ones. Like quinine, this herb, it turns out, doesn't just treat the symptoms of malaria but likewise can be a cure.

Chinese scientists studied the herb and figured out how to extract its active compound in the 1970s. This herb is *Artemisia annua*, like wormwood and mugwort a member of the *Artemisia* genus, indigenous to Asia. The antimalarial drug extracted from the plant, artemisinin, is used in combination with other drugs in an antimalarial treatment regimen known as "artemisinin-based combination therapy." As malaria quickly develops immunity to drugs used against it, doctors combine single drugs into groups and continuously change them to outsmart the parasite. Grand wormwood and other varieties don't contain enough artemisinin to be effective against malaria, but it's nice to think that all the absinthe the French soldiers drank in North Africa wasn't a complete waste.

When taking quinine for malaria, both soldiers taking quinine pills and drinkers taking Gin and Tonics discovered that there could be too much of a good thing. Baker continued his description of the new and trendy Gin and Tonic in 1939, writing that the drink "originated to combat fevers, real or alleged, & which later became an established drink in India & the Tropical British East. . . . But we

must warn all those who embrace this drink to remember it is a medicine and not primarily a stimulant only. On more than one occasion
we have temporarily showed aberration on this subject, with the result that our ears rang unmercifully and next day we felt like Rame-
ses II, réchauffé."

It was unusual for Baker to recommend any level of caution, and
yet he noted, "We suggest from 2 to 4 drinks of gin and tonic as
being plenty for any one sitting." For Baker, that would be a *very*
quiet night. Midcentury author David A. Embury also warned in
The Fine Art of Mixing Drinks (1948), "Remember that this is not
merely a thirst quencher but also a tonic. It *does* contain real quinine,
and too much quinine, while not intoxicating in the ordinary sense,
nevertheless can produce a head that feels like a fully inflated bal-
loon. Take due notice and govern yourself accordingly."

The condition they're talking about is not a hangover but cinchonism: poisoning from excess quinine. Early tonic waters were likely
therapeutic in strength, given the reported side effects, and not designed solely for refreshment. Symptoms of cinchonism include sweaty
skin, ringing of the ears (tinnitus), blurred vision, impaired hearing
or high-frequency hearing loss, headache, vertigo, dizziness, nausea,
vomiting, and diarrhea. Major overdoses can trigger lethal cardiac ar-
rhythmia.

The currently allowed quantity of quinine in beverages by the
United States Food and Drug Administration is eighty-three parts
per million, which translates to eighty-three milligrams per liter. That
must be a tiny fraction of what it was in Baker and Embury's day,
but some modern scientists decided to perform an experiment to
see if drinking tonic water at today's quinine levels could provide protection against malaria. An article in the journal *Tropical Medicine and*

International Health announced the results of giving volunteers one-half or a full liter of tonic to drink quickly, and then measured the blood impact. They found that "considerable quantities of tonic water may, for a short period of time, lead to quinine plasma levels at the lower limit of therapeutic efficacy and may, in fact, cause transitory suppression of parasites. However, continuous levels that are appropriate for malaria prophylaxis cannot be maintained with even large amounts of tonic." One can only drink so many G&Ts.

Other experiments, of sorts, have been run by bartenders. Beginning around 2007, American bartenders started buying cinchona tree bark in small chunks or as powder with which to make tonic syrup. This syrup is then added to sparkling water for vintage-style tonic as in the soda fountain days. These bartenders may be unaware that the first bottled tonic waters were created decades after quinine had already been isolated from the bark, so their brown, earthy tonic waters may not be so historically authentic.

Stores and websites that sell small quantities of cinchona bark (it is a homeopathic remedy for leg cramps, but the US Food and Drug Administration recommends against its use for this) do not list the percent of quinine and other alkaloids contained in the bark, so bartenders cannot be sure of safe amounts to use in their preparations. Purified quinine is typically available for sale only to beverage production facilities as well as medical ones in the US and is not available for the home or restaurant bartender.

While the homemade tonic waters may not be historically authentic, the side effects of tonic syrups sure are. Both bartenders experimenting with their cinchona bark syrup recipes and a few unfortunate bar customers have in recent years reported suffering from the symptoms of cinchonism once again.

The quinine in tonic water provides a direct link to the beverage's medicinal history, as does the wormwood in vermouth, the gentian in bitters, and the rhubarb in amaro. Ingesting too much of them will remind the drinker that medicine can be dangerous in high doses, if the alcohol alone hasn't made the point clear already.

GIN AND TONIC

2 ounces (60 ml) gin

5 ounces (150 ml) tonic water

Add a lime wheel to the bottom of a double Old-Fashioned glass. Fill glass with ice and press down, then pour liquids over the top.

. . . . .

The Gin and Tonic was likely created in India by the British and made up of many medicinal parts: the lime for scurvy, the fizzy water for anemia and other conditions, the quinine for malaria, and the gin as a diuretic. The combination, as we know, is outstanding. Today we'd call the G&T a cocktail, now a catchall term for a mixed drink. But the cocktail was once a mixed drink with specific ingredients and was intended to soothe a specific condition.

MIXOLOGY

MIXED DRINKS *and* MODERN MEDICINE

> It must be confessed that American drinks are as
> far ahead of English as a glass of Laurent-Perrier
> champagne is above a glass of the gooseberry article,
> and it might be profitable to take a lesson or two from
> the transatlantic experience.
>
> —Pharmaceutical Formulas, *published in 1902 in London*

Despite its poisoned food, adulterated whiskey, and ineffective patent medicine, the US of the 1800s was a great place to get a mixed drink. Books and articles written by visitors to the young country inevitably contain some praise along the lines of "if you come to America, you simply must try the juleps."

An 1807 Englishman commented, "the first craving of an American, in the morning, is for ardent spirits, mixed with sugar, mint, or some other hot herb; and which are called slings."

In the 1853 *Travels in South and North America*, by Alexander

Marjoribanks of Scotland, the author introduces a section on drinks: "If the French have been long proverbial for their science in the discovery of cooking, the Americans are no less celebrated for their discoveries in the science of drinks, and their skill in mixing them." He then cites the popular drinks of the time, such as the Sherry Cobbler, Mint Julep, Brandy Smash, Brandy Cocktail, Brandy Skin, plus the categories of punches, toddies and slings, sangarees, and eggnogs.

Others commented more on the *quantity* of alcohol. In 1861 a London war correspondent in America wrote, "In the matter of drinks, how hospitable the Americans are! I was asked to take as many as would have rendered me incapable of drinking again; my excuse on the pleas of inability to grapple with cocktails and the like before breakfast, was heard with surprise, and I was urgently entreated to abandon so bad a habit."

Charles H. Baker Jr., wrote in 1939, "America has invented, and always will invent, more of the world's good mixed drinks than all the rest of humanity lumped together."

BITTERS

Today any mixed drink, be it a Rum and Coke or a Cosmopolitan, is called a cocktail, but originally a cocktail was a specific new drink format separate from the ones before it. The earliest known reference to the term "cocktail" in a drink context dates to England in 1798, where it is mentioned as a ginger beverage. The name likely comes from the cocked tail of a horse—a horse that had ginger stuck up its butt. This violation of the animal was a trick to make the horse act perky and high-spirited to command a better sale price. (Reportedly before ginger was used for this purpose, the choice of suppository was a live eel. It could be worse.)

The beverage "cocktail" referred to a drink made spicy with ginger or hot pepper. As a beverage, the hot ingredients would perk up the drinker, particularly if consumed in the morning. None of this was mentioned in descriptions of the drink in its day; cocktail historian David Wondrich has only recently pieced it together.

The cocktail soon came to America, and its first mention was in 1806 in a newspaper from Hudson, New York, called *The Balance Columbian Repository*, which noted, "Cocktail is a stimulating liquor composed of spirits of any kind, sugar, water, and bitters." Around 1835, a visitor to New Orleans confirmed this as he wrote, "Now the difference between a brandy-cocktail and a brandy-toddy is this: a brandy-toddy is made by adding together a little water, a little sugar, and a great deal of brandy—mix well and drink. A brandy cocktail is composed of the same ingredients, with the addition of a shade of Stoughton's bitters; so that the bitters draw the line of demarcation."

In America the spicy ginger drink had evolved into a drink with bitters. According to Wondrich, the spicy ginger or pepper was replaced with more shelf-stable bitters (Stoughton's being an early popular brand), but the drink performed the same role. It was a breakfast drink to perk up or revive a person, particularly in the morning from the effects of the previous evening's drinking.

The book *Cooling Cups and Dainty Drinks*, published in 1869, specifies that "cocktails are compounds very much used by 'early birds' to fortify the inner man, and by those who like their consolations hot and strong."

A cocktail was a format that could accommodate any base spirit:

gin, brandy, rum, and whiskey, or even wines. So a Whiskey Cocktail (known today as an Old-Fashioned) and a Champagne Cocktail are directly related. The Martini may have been so named originally as a cocktail made with Martini & Rossi vermouth.

CHAMPAGNE COCKTAIL

1 sugar cube

4 dashes Angostura bitters

4 or so ounces (120 ml) champagne

On a spoon, coat sugar cube with bitters.
Drop into a flute and fill with champagne.
Garnish with a lemon twist.

. . . . .

Bitters were a type of patent medicine formulated from bitter botanicals used specifically for stomach conditions, and in England they were consumed in alcohol such as gin or brandy or even wine as a hangover cure early in the 1700s. These wines and spirits were often sweetened, so these beverages were close to a cocktail about a century before that name was assigned to the mixture.

Baker wrote in *The Gentleman's Companion*, "However, as is so often the case with truly worth-while ventures, fate stuck her tongue in cheek, and decreed that the bitters invented for health should prove not only to be one of the best titillaters of the jaded appetite, but by far the best priceless ingredient in all sorts of cocktails and mixed drinks; as well as in many of the tastiest exotic food receipts we have sampled around the world."

One of the oldest and initially most popular bitters is Stoughton Bitters, which dates to 1690 in London. They were officially named Elixir Magnum Stomachicum or Stoughton's Great Cordial Elixir. Most patent medicines were not patented, but Stoughton's actually did receive a British royal patent in 1712. Stoughton's had a base of brandy and an infusion of gentian, which is the backbone of nearly all bitters today. It was advertised for many ailments as was typical of patent medicines, but specifically "to recover and restore a weakened stomach or lost appetite occasioned by hard drinking."

Published replicas of Stoughton's recipe mostly included gentian, bitter orange peel, and chamomile. Some have wormwood and many have snakeroot. The latter ingredient has been used medicinally but can be unsafe, as Americans learned the hard way: when cows feed on white snakeroot, they can cause "milk sickness" in the humans who drink their milk. Snakeroot-poisoned milk may have killed Abraham Lincoln's mother.

The Stoughton's brand (and many unauthorized reproductions of it) was sold in America and was consumed as a digestive and for hangovers, as well as in cocktails. But there were as many kinds of bitters as there were other patent medicines, claiming to cure a wide variety of ailments. The bitters among the Smithsonian's National Museum of American History collection of patent medicines include Dromgooles Bitters ("a uterine tonic, sedative and antispasmodic; aids in the relief of periodic pain and distress"), Atwood's Bitters ("temporary constipation, gas in the stomach, sour stomach and flatulence"), Burdock

Blood Bitters ("dyspepsia and stomach troubles"), Cocamoke Bitters ("Anti-malarial, anti-dyspeptic tonic"), Lash's Bitters ("Original Tonic Laxative Bitters"), Peruvian Bitters ("dipsomania, chills, fever, and all malarial diseases. A delightful appetizer, giving tone and strength to the stomach."), Hostetter's Celebrated Stomach Bitters ("Dyspepsia, liver complaint, costiveness and indigestion, intermittent fever, fever and ague, a good anti-bilious, powerful recuperant, appetizer, strengthener of digestive forces, corrective and mild cathartic"), and N. K. Brown's Iron and Quinine Bitters ("dyspepsia, indigestion, nervous prostration, general debility, fever and ague, etc.").

Some of these bitters wound up in cocktails, but by the time the first cocktail books were published in the second half of the nineteenth century, a few brands emerged as bartenders' favorites. Beyond Stoughton's there were Angostura, Abbott's, Boker's, and Peychaud's. At one time, Abbott's Bitters was called Abbott's Angostura Bitters, but the brand was sued by Angostura over the name and lost. Boker's (misprinted in Jerry Thomas's 1862 *The Bar-Tender's Guide* as "Bogart's") was one of the most popular bitters in cocktail books of the 1800s, but both Abbott's and Boker's eventually disappeared from the market.

Both Angostura and Peychaud's bitters have stayed in production through to the present day. Peychaud's Bitters was created by pharmacist Antoine Amédée Peychaud (1803–1883), a Creole immigrant from Haiti. His bitters were launched in 1838 in New Orleans, where they were frequently served with brandy. They are essential in the New Orleans classic Sazerac, which is a cocktail by definition (spirit, sugar, water, bitters), with an extra splash of absinthe.

SAZERAC

■

2 ounces (60 ml) rye whiskey

0.5 ounce (15 ml) simple syrup

2 dashes Peychaud's bitters

1 dash absinthe

Rinse a rocks glass with absinthe and discard.
In a stirring pitcher, stir the remaining ingredients
with ice, then strain into the rocks glass.
Garnish with lemon twist.

. . . . .

Angostura Aromatic Bitters was created by Johann Siegert (1796–
1870), a German doctor living in Angostura, Venezuela, as the surgeon
general in Simón Bolívar's army. In 1824 he released his proprietary
blend of botanicals (angostura tree bark not among them; it was
named for the town) as a tonic to help with tropical stomach ailments
for Bolívar's army. It was also sold to sailors for seasickness and became one of the two ingredients in the Pink Gin meant to calm shipboard nausea. (Angostura for a time bottled a Pink Rum that was
premixed rum and bitters.)

The production of Angostura bitters moved from Venezuela to
Trinidad, where they are still produced. They were advertised as a
"useful remedy in all complaints arising from weakness and sluggish-
ness of the digestive organs, malaria, colic, diarrhea, and colds." The
current label lists only culinary uses: beyond cocktails, they are suggested as an additive to cooked fruits, French dressing, mincemeat

or pumpkin pie filling, and fish chowder. It could probably use an update.

Old liqueur formularies list recipes for imitation Angostura bitters. One lists as ingredients calisaya (cinchona) bark, gentian, galangal, zedoary, angelica root, red saunders (a tree often used for its coloring), bitter orange peel, tonka bean, cardamom, cinnamon, cloves, and ginger, with alcohol, water, wine, and coloring caramel.

Angostura bitters contain 44.7 percent alcohol, which can be quite a wallop if consumed as a shot. Doing so is a long-held tradition at the bar Nelsen's Hall and Bitters Club on Washington Island in Lake Michigan. There a practice of doing shots of Angostura dates back to Prohibition circa 1920. More often, "Ango" is only used in dashes in the Pink Gin, the Champagne Cocktail, the Old-Fashioned, and the Manhattan. They have a Christmas spice (clove, cinnamon, ginger) aroma that ties drinks together; some bartenders compare using bitters in cocktails to using a pinch of salt to perfect a soup.

In an 1874 letter from Mark Twain to his wife, the famous humorist wrote, "Livy my darling, I want you to be sure & remember to have, in the bath-room, when I arrive, a bottle of Scotch whisky, a lemon, some crushed sugar, & a bottle of Angostura bitters. Ever since I have been in London I have taken in a wine-glass what is called a cock-tail . . . before breakfast, before dinner, & just before going to bed. . . . To it I attribute the fact that up to this day my digestion has been wonderful—simply perfect. It remains day after day & week after week as regular as a clock."

Many bitters that did survive the Pure Food and Drug Act of 1906 and its related regulations did not survive Prohibition. Some people still take bitters somewhat medicinally—Bitters and Soda is a popular stomach soother for hangovers and an alternative for people cutting down on drinking. A common cure for the hiccups is sucking on a lemon wedge soaked with Angostura. A 1981 *New York Times* story covered this important issue, noting: "David S. Nolan, the bartender, and Dr. Jay Howard Herman wrote in a letter to *The New England Journal of Medicine* that the remedy cured hiccups in 14 of the 16 people they tried it on, 'including two cases of initial treatment failure that was overcome after a second treatment within five minutes.' That is a success rate of 88 percent."

Cocktail bitters that are used in drops and dashes share many of the same ingredients, particularly gentian and cinchona, with potable digestifs like Averna and Becherovka. In recent years, a few brands of bitters and amari have expanded into the opposite format: Angostura now makes Amaro di Angostura, and Peychaud's Bitters has released Peychaud's Aperitivo. Instead of drops and dashes, these bitter digestifs can be consumed on their own or over ice. In the other direction, Suze gentian liqueur came out with a range of gentian-laced cocktail bitters.

EVOLUTION OF THE COCKTAIL

Bitters were the ingredient that defined cocktails, but mixed drinks were around for a long time before cocktails came into the picture. From the later 1600s to the early 1800s, punch ruled the day. Roughly distilled and usually unaged spirits were softened and sweetened with sugar or fruit-flavored syrup, citrus, and spices sometimes including tea. As time went on, the bowl of punch evolved into the single-serving personal punch for the on-the-go drinker (specifically in on-the-go America), including the Pisco Punch, Milk Punch, and Sixty-Ninth Regiment Punch. Punches evolved into fixes (an individual punch with fancy garnish) and sours (without the fancy garnish), including the Whiskey Sour and Pisco Sour.

With a splash of soda water, a punch became a collins like a Tom Collins (if it was served "tall" in a highball glass with ice) or a fizz (a short version with no ice meant to be drunk quickly as a hangover cure or morning zester). The Morning Glory Fizz is a type of silver fizz (a fizz with added egg white) that used scotch and absinthe together. Author Harry Johnson (1845–1930), in his 1882 *New and Improved Bartender's Manual*, wrote, "The author respectfully recommends the above drink as an excellent one for a morning beverage, which will give a good appetite and quiet the nerves."

MORNING GLORY FIZZ

2 ounces (60 ml) blended scotch whiskey

0.5 ounce (15 ml) lemon juice

0.5 ounce (15 ml) lime juice

0.5 ounce (15 ml) simple syrup

3 dashes absinthe

1 egg white

1–2 ounces (30–60 ml) soda water

Add all ingredients except soda to a shaker and shake
once without ice and then again with ice. Strain into
a juice glass without ice and top with soda.

. . . . .

The most famous silver fizz, however, is the Ramos Gin Fizz dating to around 1888 in New Orleans. The bar that made it popular employed thirty-five bartenders just to do the shaking, which was reportedly done for a wholly unnecessary twelve minutes per drink. A golden fizz was made with egg yolk rather than egg white, and a royal fizz was made with the whole egg.

The aforementioned sour category is a drink of spirit, citrus, and sugar. A daisy is a sour with a flavored syrup or liqueur (such as curaçao or grenadine) and often a splash of soda water. The Margarita ("daisy" in Spanish) is a tequila daisy that grew popular after 1940. It is made without the fizzy water, as you well know from your last visit to Chili's.

But back to the cocktail: Joining it as a morning drink in the early 1800s is the toddy (spirit, sugar, water), which could be served hot or cold depending on the season; the sling (same thing but usually with ice); and the julep (more on that in the ice section). The sling was probably so named for "slinging one back" before breakfast.

Morning cocktails took on nicknames, including antifogmatics, pick-me-ups, eye-openers, bracers, smashers, and corpse revivers. The most famous of the corpse revivers (published in 1930) is the Corpse Reviver No. 2, as found in *The Savoy Cocktail Book*, by Harry Craddock. The Corpse Reviver No. 1 (sweet vermouth, apple brandy, grape brandy) is described as "to be taken before 11AM, or whenever steam and energy are needed," while the Corpse Reviver No. 2 (lemon juice, Lillet Blanc, Cointreau, gin, and absinthe) comes with more of a warning: "Four of these taken in swift succession will unrevive the corpse again."

CORPSE REVIVER NO. 2

1 ounce (30 ml) gin

1 ounce (30 ml) Cointreau

1 ounce (30 ml) Lillet Blanc

1 ounce (30 ml) lemon juice

1 dash absinthe

Add all ingredients to an ice-filled shaker.
Shake and strain into a cocktail glass. Garnish
with a lemon twist or orange twist.

· · · · ·

Cocktails also evolved into more elaborate affairs. Rather than plain sugar, bartenders employed flavored liqueurs like curaçao, maraschino liqueur, and then later absinthe. The new categories of drinks with these liqueurs were called "fancy" and "improved" cocktails like the Fancy Brandy Cocktail and Improved Holland Gin Cocktail. Often, multiple flavored liqueurs were used in one cocktail, and to some curmudgeonly drinkers (for there are always curmudgeonly drinkers) things had gotten out of control. Just as drinkers in the 1990s and early 2000s disdained "martinis" that came in flavors like sour apple and chocolate, drinkers of the 1880s found these fancy and improved cocktails way over-the-top. So, in rebellion, they might request an old-fashioned Whiskey Cocktail without all the bells and whistles, much as we might have to specify a classic Martini or Daiquiri without the preparation in a blender today.

After the world wars, the preparation of an Old-Fashioned slipped again. It was commonly made with an orange slice and cherry muddled into the bottom of the glass with the sugar cube and bitters (sometimes with a splash of soda water or Sprite). In the modern craft-cocktail renaissance after 2000, the new curmudgeons had to request an "Old-Fashioned Old-Fashioned." Today the no-fruit original-style Old-Fashioned is once again the standard in better cocktail bars.

OLD-FASHIONED, ALSO KNOWN AS WHISKEY COCKTAIL, ALSO KNOWN AS THE OLD-FASHIONED OLD-FASHIONED

2 ounces (60 ml) bourbon

1 sugar cube

2 dashes Angostura bitters

In an Old-Fashioned glass, muddle the sugar
and bitters with a splash of water if needed.
Add ice and bourbon, then stir. Garnish
with an orange twist.

. . . . .

Vermouth also made a major impact as a cocktail ingredient. The slightly bitter, fortified, and aromatized wine was imported into the US in the mid-1800s but entered cocktails in the last decades of the century, giving us the Martini and the Manhattan, among other drinks. Initially, both these cocktails also included bitters in their recipes.

These new vermouth-laden cocktails continued to be morning drinks, but far from exclusively. In 1895 the *Atlanta Constitution* reported of the habits of a Confederate general: "Before breakfast he enters the saloon, and resting his elbow upon the counter, says, 'A Manhattan cocktail.' His order is useless, for every barkeeper in Lynchburg knows the general's drink, and many of them begin concocting the Manhattan as soon as he is seen entering the door. A dozen times a day or more he imbibes the drink, and swallows it with an evident relish."

The "hair of the dog" remedy of drinking in the morning to mitigate the impacts of drinking too much at night is probably as old as drinking alcohol. The Hippocratic author of *Epidemics* wrote, "If, following intoxication, there is a headache, drink a cotyle [about one-third liter] of undiluted wine."

To avoid a hangover, seventh-century Greek physician Paul of Aegina recommended the following: "When one has drunk [excessively], it is not proper to take much of any other food; but while drinking, one should eat boiled cabbage, and taste some sweetmeat, particularly almonds. These things relieve headache, and are not difficult to vomit."

If vomiting became a bit too easy, Pliny recommended a dissuasion tactic for alcoholics: "The eggs of an owlet administered to drunkards three days in wine are productive of a distaste for that liquor."

AMERICAN AND OTHER ICED DRINKS

When the cocktail was defined, it was spirit, sugar, bitters, and *water*, not ice. The first known recipe (rather than description) for a cocktail was printed in 1833 and still calls for water, but by the time Jerry

Thomas's *Bar-Tender's Guide* came out in 1862, the recipe specified ice. This gives a fairly narrow time range in which ice came into common use.

Ice had been employed medicinally where available for centuries, as an anti-inflammatory against swelling in wounds and broken bones; to reduce muscle spasms, cramping, and pain from injuries and in arthritis; to reduce the pain of sores and lesions externally; and to reduce fevers both internally and externally.

Iced *beverages* had been a historical hit or miss. At different times and places there were prejudices against putting ice in drinks, and often against cold beverages in any form. In Roman times, some mixed their wine with snow rather than water, but Pliny protested that cold drinks with ice added were unnatural, as it went against the seasons. Adding ice or snow directly to wine or water was thought by different cultures to cause colic, convulsions, paralysis, blindness, madness, and sudden death.

Often when beverages were chilled, the ice was used on the outside of the vessel rather than in direct contact with the liquid. In the 1600s in Spain and Italy, glass vessels were made with pockets for filling with snow or ice to chill without mixing. Decorative cooling devices held bottles of wine in an ice bath. A Polish poem set in 1811 tells of vodka cooling in snowdrifts to be served after a hunting shoot.

The method of making ice cream by stirring salt and snow or ice water on the outside of a conductive bowl or bottle was used to chill beverages from the outside as well. Even after refrigeration became available, *Cooling Cups and Dainty Drinks*, in its recipe for "Claret Cup a la Brunow for a Party of Twenty," started with the instructions to "put into a large vessel imbedded in a mixture of ice and salt."

Throughout the world, ice to cool food and drinks was collected in the wintertime from lakes and mountaintops and stored in caves, underground cellars, and insulated icehouses to last as long as possible through the summers. Wealthy people in Europe built icehouses as part of their estates.

Artificial refrigeration was first demonstrated in the 1700s, but one of the first people to build a working refrigeration device was the American John Gorrie in the 1840s. He did so with the plan to cool the rooms of patients suffering from malaria and yellow fever, which he had first accomplished with a sort of air-conditioning using blocks of lake ice. But these blocks were not always available for purchase in Florida where he practiced.

Cooling Cups and Dainty Drinks promised that "the author has given especial attention to the subject of Refrigeration—almost a new art among us—as well as to that of aerated waters, and other draughts so much sought after in the summer season."

In American soda fountains, ice was often used to cool the tanks for soda water rather than put into the drinks themselves. *The Standard Manual of Soda and Other Beverages* from 1906 states, "Some dealers put shaved ice into the soda water when served. It is a tedious process to grind the ice on a shaver, and makes the process of serving drinks much slower; ice is usually impure, and the beverage is really not fit to drink; and lastly, the beverage quickly loses its gas and tastes flat." The manual also includes many recipes for ice cream, but these are mixed with water then frozen, rather than relying on pond ice. Vintage drawings show people sipping Coca-Cola from small, U-shaped glasses that fit into the hand, rather than the ice-filled Big Gulp familiar today. Ice was generally treated with suspicion.

The person credited for making ice an ingredient inside beverages in America is Boston-based Frederic Tudor (1783–1864). Beginning in the first decade of the 1800s, his workers cut up frozen lakes, including Walden Pond (Henry David Thoreau described the ice harvest in *Walden* in 1854), and shipped it off to ports both foreign (including Martinique, Cuba, India, and Brazil) and domestic (Charleston, Savannah, New Orleans, and others). A Boston newspaper in 1806 wrote, "No joke. A vessel has cleared at the Custom House for Martinique with a cargo of ice. We hope this will not prove a slippery speculation." He sold it for medicinal use to doctors in the tropics, but the real profits came from its use for food and drink.

Tudor offered bartenders free ice to get their customers hooked on cooling drinks. He wrote, "It is a matter of certainty that the love of cold drinks and refreshments in warm weather is nearly universal and that the prejudice against them wears away more and more every year. At places where ice is first introduced as a novelty, in the course of years its use becomes general. . . . Thus when people are able to get cool drinks for the same price as the warm, the prejudice against cold drinks will be overcome. The object is to make the whole population use cold drinks instead of warm or tepid and it will be effected in the course of three years." Elsewhere he wrote, "A man who has drank his drinks cold at the same expense for one week can never be presented with them warm again."

He was right. Tudor's big bet eventually paid off, after he lost all his money a few times along the way. Not only did ice become popular in American beverages, it also became a signature ingredient. Englishwoman Sarah Mytton Maury (1803–1849) toured the US in the 1840s and wrote effusively about the use of ice: "Of all the luxuries in America I most enjoyed the ice. . . . It is customary when you pay a visit, for the attendant immediately on your arrival to present you with ice water or iced lemonade."

When ice came to England, it was imported from the States. Wenham Lake Ice in Massachusetts was marketed as the purest and best product, and ice from this lake became a fashionable luxury. The company deliverymen wore uniforms with American eagles on the buttons, reflecting its provenance. In 1845 *Wilmer and Smith's European Times* reported: "This commodity which was first introduced to the notice of the English public a short time ago . . . is so rapidly advancing in popularity in the metropolis that no banquet of any magnitude is considered complete without it. . . . Not only is the Wenham Lake ice coming into vogue as a luxury among the aristocracy, but it is also recommending itself to the middle classes as a necessity, and even to the humbler ranks of life as an article of economy."

The new availability of ice in America resulted in the creation of new categories of drinks including cobblers and juleps, and the idea of "cooling drinks" in general. The cobbler, including the Sherry Cobbler, took hold in the middle 1800s following the popularity of ice. It is essentially a Sherry Sour over cobblestone-size ice.

Maury recalled a dinner party conversation on her visit to the States: "'Whenever you hear America abused' observed a lady to me as she presented a glass of sparkling Sherry cobbler, with the huge crystals floating about in the exquisitely co-mingled cup, 'remember the ice.'"

SHERRY COBBLER

3 ounces (90 ml) amontillado sherry

0.5 ounce (15 ml) simple syrup

1 orange half wheel

Muddle the orange wheel with the syrup in the
bottom of a cocktail shaker. Fill with ice and
sherry and shake, then strain into a julep or
juice glass filled with fresh crushed ice.
Garnish with an an additional orange wheel.

· · · · ·

The Mint Julep has origins that predate iced cocktails by nine hundred
years, give or take. In the Islamic Golden Age, the scholars who were
distilling rose water ("julab" is the Arabic word for for rose water)
also made floral syrups and sweetened drinks for medicinal purposes.
Sweetened juleps followed the path of knowledge from Persia into Europe and over to the New World. In 1753, after "malignant fevers"
impacted Rouen, France, a doctor noted in his case report that "many
did well with a simple julep of sugar and water, and a little wine."

The same year, *The New English Dispensatory* defined the drink:
"Julep is an agreeable liquor, designed as a vehicle for medicines of
greater efficacy, or to be drank after them, or to be taken occasionally as an auxiliary." It was the spoonful of sugar that helped the
medicine go down. The *Dispensatory* includes a recipe for a "Stomachic
Julep" that is six ounces of cinnamon water, one ounce each of nutmeg

water and stomachic tincture, and half an ounce of orange peel syrup. It is listed among other juleps for poisons and infections, flatulence, hysteria, and a weak heart.

Through to at least the mid-1800s, the julep was still a medicine, at least in Europe. But at that time in America, the name julep had already become a jokey term for an alcoholic drink, like calling Valium "mother's little helper." References to mint in the drink pop up just before 1800, and it became a sweetened, aromatic, and not-at-all medicinal drink, unless one was using it to cure a hangover.

A julep could be made with rum or whiskey, but the Mint Julep specifically referred to a brandy-based version in its early days. It also didn't start out with the hailstone-sized bits of ice that practically define the drink today. The beverage probably originated in Virginia and made its way to New York, where it was popularized there by bartenders including Cato Alexander (1780–1858), a former enslaved person who offered a julep variation called the Hail-Storm: a Mint Julep with ice. Alexander was not the first person to add ice to the drink, however. David Wondrich cites 1807 as the first known reference to its inclusion, and because of it he has deemed the Mint Julep "the first true American drink."

PRESCRIPTION JULEP

2 ounces (60 ml) cognac

1 ounce (30 ml) rye whiskey

0.75 ounce (20 ml) simple syrup

5 mint leaves

Bruise mint leaves with syrup in bottom of julep
cup, then add alcohol. Fill cup with crushed ice and
swirl until cup frosts. Top with more ice to form
a mound and plant several more mint sprigs in it.
The name is a joking reference to the drink's
medicinal history, as published in 1857.

. . . . .

Iced beverages had become standard in the US after the 1830s, but not
so everywhere. In 1880 Mark Twain commented on the lack of them
in *A Tramp Abroad*, writing, "Europeans say ice-water impairs digestion. How do they know?—they never drink any." In 1902 a book
entitled *Recipes of American and Other Iced Drinks* was published in
England, further demonstrating that ice was an imported concept.

To this day, many cultures of the world shun iced beverages. In
an opinion piece in *The New York Times* in 2011, Alina Simone wrote,
"As the daughter of émigrés from Ukraine, I was raised on room-
temperature beverages and always associated ice with a raft of great
American stuff other kids were allowed to have but I wasn't: puppies,
sheet cake, fun. My own grandmother would cringe from a glass of
ice water as if it were a syringe of Ebola virus. To this day I have no

idea what disease she associated with the consumption of cold liquids. Pneumonia? Athlete's foot? Chlamydia?"

Many practitioners of both Indian Ayurvedic medicine and traditional Chinese medicine avoid iced beverages as they are said to create digestive imbalance. Some modern guidebooks for Chinese visitors to America warn that iced beverages are the default at bars and restaurants, so drinkers should be sure to specify that they don't want it. A visitor to the United States writes on a travel blog (translated): "What I don't understand is why the Americans like to drink drinks with ice so much? No matter what kind of drink you want to buy, the waiter will put some ice cubes in the paper cup for you without discussing it, and then add the drink. Several of us can't enjoy this 'blessing' for our stomachs, so we must declare in advance every time we buy a drink, thank you for your kindness, and ask for the 'procedure' of ice cubes to be exempted!"

MODERN MEDICINE

In the many years since ice and vermouth came to cocktails, most drink trends have not been medicinal in nature. Between and after the world wars, tiki drinks and bars proliferated. Martinis were made with less and less vermouth, until (according to filmmaker Luis Buñuel) "allowing a ray of sunlight to shine through the bottle of Noilly Prat before it hits the bottle of gin" was the preferred amount. From the 1970s through the 1990s, artificially colored liqueurs and vodka-laden sugar bombs were the most popular drinks. Around the year 2000, the Cosmopolitan and the flavored "martinis" ruled the night; these were similar vodka-laden sugar bombs but served up in a cocktail glass. Some innovative bartenders chose to use fresh juice in their drinks once again, a baby step on the way to the classic- and craft-cocktail renaissance. Within a decade bartenders and drinkers were rediscovering the classics as they were originally made.

After 2000, bartenders found it necessary to make many of their own ingredients, like homemade versions of vintage bitters that no longer existed, absinthe (until the ban was lifted), and flavored syrups without high-fructose corn syrup. A new era of creativity in mixology is afoot. But there is a small downside: although today we can be relatively certain that our packaged foods no longer contain opium or boiled snake, when bartenders re-create vintage recipes, some now-known-unsafe ingredients sneak in.

As previously discussed, activated charcoal, cinchona bark, rhubarb leaves, tonka beans, and wormwood are all potentially dangerous or regulated ingredients, and these have recently made their way back into some homemade cocktail ingredients. A few other resurrected ingredients have proven problematic as well. Safrole, a compound in the root beer (and one time syphilis cure) ingredient sassafras, was banned in the US in 1960 for its suspected role in causing cancer.

Calamus, also known as sweet flag, is an aromatic marsh herb used in some liqueurs, as well as in scented beauty products and potpourri. Vintage recipes in old formularies for liqueurs, including Campari, frequently call for calamus. In the United States, calamus is expressly prohibited for food as it is "procarcinogenic," but in other countries it is allowed if the beta asarone it contains is kept beneath a certain level. Some brands of vermouth and likely other liqueurs include calamus in their formulation for Europe but leave it out for the US market.

Bitter almonds contain a cyanide precursor that turns toxic and potentially deadly in the body. In old detective movies and in noir books, the coroner often concludes something like "her breath smelled of almonds, she was poisoned!" Today bitter almond liqueurs like Disaronno tend to be made from the pits of stone fruit, including peaches, cherries, and apricots. The pits also contain the same cyanide precursor as in bitter almonds, but it is removed during the production of the liqueur.

AMARETTO SOUR

1.5 ounces (45 ml) amaretto liqueur

1 ounce (30 ml) bourbon

1 ounce (30 ml) lemon juice

0.25 ounce (8 ml) simple syrup

1 egg white

Shake ingredients in a cocktail shaker first
without ice and then with ice. Strain over fresh
ice in an Old-Fashioned glass. Garnish with a
lemon twist and maraschino cherry. Adapted
from a recipe by Jeffrey Morgenthaler.

· · · · ·

In recent years, apricot kernels have developed a reputation as a natural cancer cure, though there is no scientific evidence to support it. In 2017 an Australian man poisoned himself by eating the kernels to keep his prostate cancer in remission. Bartenders have been warned not to make their own amaretto for this reason.

A surprising ingredient to find regulated is licorice, specifically the glycyrrhizin compound it contains. Licorice root lends a subtle, soft sweetness to some liqueurs and gins. Glycyrrhizin can cause potassium levels in the body to fall, leading to abnormal heart rhythms as well as high blood pressure, edema (swelling), lethargy, and congestive heart failure. Typical cases requiring medical intervention for glycyrrhizin overdoses tend to be from adults drinking large amounts of licorice tea daily, but different levels of glycyrrhizin are allowed in various foods and beverages.

There has been a renewed attention to "healthy" cocktails and spirits in the past few years, which is a bit of a false flag when alcohol is involved. Many of these commercial products are reduced in proof, like "skinny" vodkas that are just lower ABV and sometimes flavored with healthy-sounding botanicals, such as mint and cucumber. Some embrace pseudoscience, like a vodka with an ingredient that claims to "protect DNA from alcohol-induced damage," another vodka made with "purified hyper-oxygenated water," and Collagin, which is, as it sounds, a gin with added skin, hair, and joint supplement collagen.

Daily it seems there is a news article reporting (or misreporting) about alcohol's impact on human health—it increases one kind of cancer or decreases cognitive ability; it destroys the life of a former child star, or an elderly person credits their long life to a daily glass of whiskey. Much like medicine, alcohol can have a positive health impact or a very negative one, and this is not new information. Ancient Ayurvedic texts pointed out that alcohol was medicine in moderation and poison in excess.

As Amitava Dasgupta writes in *The Science of Drinking*, be it over a single night or many years, a little bit of alcohol is not bad for one's health and may even improve it, while excess alcohol leads to all

sorts of problems. In the short term—while one is consuming it—
alcohol reduces anxiety, promotes energizing feelings, triggers the
release of endorphins (the body's natural painkillers), and can help
people get to sleep. Yet at higher doses over one drinking session,
alcohol causes cognitive function decline and loss of motor control;
impairs the ability to store new memories and to learn; can quash the
libido; slows the central nervous system (it doesn't kill brain cells,
though—that turns out not to be true); causes restless sleep and in-
hibits REM sleep; and can lead to accidents, high-risk behaviors, alcohol poisoning, and death by overdose.

Over the long term, moderate consumption (a serving or two of
alcohol per day) seems to have plenty of positive impacts: it lowers
the risk of heart attacks (particularly red wine) and reduces the risks
of stroke, heart disease, heart failure, diabetes, gallstones, arthritis,
age-related dementia, and Alzheimer's disease. It may even reduce
the chances of catching the common cold (especially red wine, again).
People who drink are hospitalized less than abstainers. Moderate consumption may reduce incidences of gastric cancer, lung cancer, bladder cancer, kidney cancer, and head and neck cancer.

Higher rates of regular consumption (usually defined as four or
more servings per day) are associated with increased risks for liver
disease, brain damage, heart damage, stroke, bone damage, high blood
pressure, malnutrition, immune system suppression, catching infectious diseases, premature menopause, birth defects in offspring, and
depressed testosterone levels in men. Excessive drinking may increase
incidences of cancer in the mouth, throat, liver, colon, stomach, lung,
and pancreas. And, of course, alcohol is an addictive drug for many
people.

Other studies have shown that moderate consumption of alcohol can lead to not only a higher quality of health but a longer life versus people who abstain entirely. This was first pointed out by Johns Hopkins biologist Raymond Pearl, who noted in 1926 (in the middle of US Prohibition) that "the moderate drinking of alcoholic beverages did not shorten life. On the contrary moderate steady drinkers exhibited somewhat lower rates of mortality, and greater expectation of life than did abstainers. . . . It certainly gives no support to the almost universal belief that alcohol always shortens life, even in moderate quantities." More recent studies have sought to figure out why this is, and the answer doesn't have anything to do with the medicinal qualities of alcohol: People who consume alcohol tend to be more social. Moderate drinkers tend to have more close friends than abstainers and are more likely to be married, while nondrinkers tend to be at greater risk for depression. These factors have shown to correlate with a longer life span, leading many scientists to conclude that moderate consumption of alcohol helps us develop relationships and that relationships are beneficial for our mental and physical health.

This is not to say that anyone should start consuming alcohol if they do not already, in the hopes of living longer; it just serves as an explanation for why a little bit of liquor has been shown to have a positive impact on life span. As with medicine, the dose makes the poison.

NOTES AND FURTHER READING

This material is meant to complement the bibliography and identify where some specific sources were used when not otherwise mentioned in the text.

CHAPTER 1. FERMENTATION: GREEKS, GALEN, AND GUINNESS

Particularly useful books and notes for this section were Lucia, Salvatore Pablo, *A History of Wine as Therapy* (Philadelphia: J. B. Lippincott Company, 1963); Jouanna, Jacques, *Greek Medicine from Hippocrates to Galen* (Leiden, Netherlands: Brill, 2012); and the notes from the talk by Grivetti, Louis E., "Wine: Medical and Nutritional Attributes," Robert Mondavi Winery, April 29–May 5, 1991, accessed 2021, https://nutritionalgeography.faculty.ucdavis.edu/wp-content/uploads/sites/106/2014/11/Wine.Medical.Nutrition.Attributes.NapaCalifornia.pdf.

The history of alcohol comes from many sources, but Curry, Andrew, "Our 9,000-Year Love Affair with Booze," *National Geographic*, February 2017, 30–53, is a great roundup of other works.

Pyramid builders not being enslaved people is from, among other places, Betz, Eric, "Who Built the Egyptian Pyramids? Not Slaves," *Discover*, February 1, 2021, https://www.discovermagazine.com/planet-earth/who-built-the-egyptian-pyramids-not-slaves.

Pathogens in beer and wine is from Menz, G., Aldred, P., and Vriesekoop, F., "Growth and Survival of Foodborne Pathogens in Beer," *Journal of Food Protection* 74, no. 10 (October 2011): 1670–75, https://doi.org/10.4315/0362-028X.JFP-10-546; and Møretrø, Trond, Daeschel, M. A., "Wine Is Bactericidal to Foodborne Pathogens"

(Abstract), *Journal of Food Science* 69 (2004): M251–M257, https://doi.org/10.1111/j .1365-2621.2004.tb09938.x.

Washing wounds is from Broughton, G., 2nd, Janis, J. E., and Attinger, C. E., "A Brief History of Wound Care," *Plastic and Reconstructive Surgery* 117, no. 7, supplement (June 2006): 6S–11S, https://doi.org/10.1097/01.prs.0000225429.76355.dd.

Xenophon quote is from Nelson, Max, "Did Ancient Greeks Drink Beer?" *Phoenix* 68, no. 1/2 (2014): 27–46, accessed May 3, 2021, https://doi.org/10.7834/phoe nix.68.1-2.0027.

"The main points in favor of . . . white strong wine" is from Grivetti, "Wine."

Columella quote "When we shall have" is from Rasmussen, Seth C., *The Quest for Aqua Vitae* (Heidelberg, Germany: Springer Science & Business, 2014).

"A mixture of three wines" and "When a man is entering upon his fortieth year" quotes are from Grivetti, "Wine."

"The healing art of Hippocrates was transformed" is from Lucia, *History of Wine as Therapy.*

"Old men must not eat much of starches" is from Flandrin, Jean-Louis, Montanari, Massimo, and Sonnenfeld, Albert, *Food: A Culinary History from Antiquity to the Present* (New York: Columbia University Press, 1999).

Medicinal use of spices is from, among other sources, Howes, Melanie-Jayne, Irving, Jason, and Simmonds, Monique, *The Gardener's Companion to Medicinal Plants* (London: Quarto Publishing, 2016).

Antimicrobial spices information is from D'Souza, S. P., Chavannavar, S. V., Kanchanashri. B., and Niveditha, S. B., "Pharmaceutical Perspectives of Spices and Condiments as Alternative Antimicrobial Remedy," *Journal of Evidence-Based and Complementary Alternative Medicine* 22, no. 4 (2017): 1002–10, https://doi.org/10.1177 /2156587217703214.

Theriac section is from Hudson, Briony, "Theriac: An Ancient Brand?" Wellcome Collection, October 18, 2017, https://wellcomecollection.org/articles/Wc5IP ScAACgANNYO.

Pliny quote "There is an elaborate mixture" is from *Pliny's Natural History*, accessed at Wayback Machine, last updated February 2, 2009, https://web.archive .org/web/20161229101439/http://www.masseiana.org/pliny.htm.

Invalid Stout is from Elsdon, Sam, "'Nourishment and Flavor': The Invalid Stout Comes Ontario," SPEED/ERAMOSA, July 2, 2016, http://www.speedanderamosa .com/blog/2016/7/2/the-beer-of-office-workers-the-invalid-stout-in-ontario.

CHAPTER 2. QUINTESSENCE: ALCHEMY AND AQUA VITAE

I found alchemy quite challenging to summarize. Some of the most useful books to me were Taylor, Frank Sherwood, *The Alchemists* (New York: Barnes & Noble Books, 1992); Cobb, Cathy, Fetterolf, Monty, and Goldwhite, Harold, *The Chemistry of Alchemy* (Amherst, NY: Prometheus Books, 2014); and Maxwell-Stuart, P. G., *The*

Chemical Choir (London: Continuum, 2012). For distillation history, Moran, Bruce T., *Distilling Knowledge* (Cambridge, MA: Harvard University Press, 2005); and Rasmussen, Seth C., *The Quest for Aqua Vitae* (N.p.: Springer Science & Business, 2014), which includes a summation of the challenging work by Forbes, R. J., *Short History of the Art of Distillation* (Hayward, CA: White Mule Press, 2009). Paracelsus comes up in a lot of books, but my main source was Ball, Philip, *The Devil's Doctor* (New York: Farrar, Straus and Giroux, 2006).

Chapter epigraph is from *The National Popular Review* 4, no. 1 (January 1894): 42, https://books.google.com/books?id=fYHrIYMx6dUC&dq.

Philosopher's stone instructions are from Melton, J. Gordon, *Encyclopedia of Occultism and Parapsychology* (Detroit: Gale Research, 1996).

Information on distillation in India and China is from Allchin, F. R., "India: The Ancient Home of Distillation?" *Man* 14, no. 1 (1979): 55–63, https://www.jstor.org/stable/2801640; and Lu Gwei-Djen, Needham, Joseph, and Needham, Dorothy, "The Coming of Ardent Water," *Ambix* 19, no. 2 (1972): 69–112, https://doi.org/10.1179/amb.1972.19.2.69.

"In this way one can distill wine using a water-bath" is from Freely, John, *Light from the East: How the Science of Medieval Islam Helped to Shape the Western World* (New York: Palgrave Macmillan, 2011).

The Thousand and One Nights quote is from "The Book of the Thousand Nights and a Night," Wikisource, last edited August 30, 2018, https://en.wikisource.org/wiki/Page:The_Book_of_the_Thousand_Nights_and_a_Night_-_Volume_5.djvu/250.

"Wine is the best facilitator" is from Abu-Asab, Mones, Amri, Hakima, and Micozzi, Marc S., *Avicenna's Medicine* (Rochester, VT: Healing Arts Press, 2013).

Women in medicine information is from Anderson, Bonnie S., and Zinsser, Judith P., *A History of Their Own: Women in Europe from Prehistory to the Present* (New York: Harper & Row, 1988).

"Place in the cucurbita" is from Stillman, John Maxson, *The Story of Early Chemistry* (New York: Dover Publications, 1960).

Distilling could render "the fragile indestructible" is from Taape, T., "Distilling Reliable Remedies: Hieronymus Brunschwig's Liber de arte distillandi (1500) between Alchemical Learning and Craft Practice," *Ambix* 61, no. 3 (August 2014): 236–56, http://europepmc.org/article/PMC/5268093.

"Aqua vitae is commonly called the mistress of all medicines" is from Rasmussen, *Quest for Aqua Vitae*.

Li Shizhen's quote is from "Mellified Man," Wikipedia, Wikimedia Foundation, last edited November 8, 2021, https://en.wikipedia.org/wiki/Mellified_man.

Mumia "is a spice found in the sepulchers of the dead" is from Parra, J. M., "Europe's Morbid 'Mummy Craze' Has Been an Obsession for Centuries," *National Geographic*, December 10, 2019, https://www.nationalgeographic.com/history/magazine/2019/11-12/egyptian-mummies-in-european-culture/.

"A resinous, hardened, black shining surface" is from Dawson, Warren R., "Mummy as a Drug," *Proceedings of the Royal Society of Medicine*, November 2, 1927, https://www.ncbi.nlm.nih.gov/pmc/articles/PMC2101801/pdf/procrsmed01192-0163.pdf.

"The blood too of gladiators" is from *Pliny's Natural History*, Wayback Machine, last updated February 2, 2009, https://web.archive.org/web/20161229101439/http://www.masseiana.org/pliny.htm.

Irn-Bru information is from "Our History," AG Barr, 2021, https://www.agbarr.co.uk/about-us/our-history/timeline.

Ferro China information is from the talk notes "Iron Amaro," by Philip Duff and Fulvio Piccinino, https://www.slideshare.net/philipduff/iron-amaro-philip-duff-fulvio-piccinino; and "Ferro China Amari," by Simon Difford, https://www.diffordsguide.com/beer-wine-spirits/category/1291/ferro-china-amari.

CHAPTER 3. MONKS: MONASTIC LIQUEURS AND THE MIDDLE AGES

Oliver, Garrett, *The Oxford Companion to Beer* (Oxford, UK: Oxford University Press, 2011) was a main resource for all parts of beer history in this book. For the history of the monastic orders, Zarnecki, George, *The Monastic Achievement* (New York: McGraw-Hill, 1972) was the most useful, with Seward, Desmond, *Monks and Wine* (New York: Crown, 1979) covering the overlap of monks and wine. For Chartreuse, the brand book *Chartreuse the Liqueur*, by Caliano, Martine, et al. (n.p., 2020), was very useful, as well as the brand's website, www.chartreuse.fr, and interviews with Tim Master of US importer Frederick Wildman and Sons. Mintz, Sidney W., *Sweetness and Power* (New York: Viking, 1985) was a main resource for sugar history. Information on mummies and other corpse medicine largely came from Sugg, Richard, *Mummies, Cannibals, and Vampires* (New York: Routledge, 2011).

Saint Benedict epigraph is from "Chapter 40: The Proper Amount of Drink," Monastery of Christ in the Desert, 2021, https://christdesert.org/prayer/rule-of-st-benedict/chapter-40-the-proper-amount-of-drink.

"Once distilled, keep it" is from Groopman, Jerome, "The History of Blood," *The New Yorker*, January 14, 2019, https://www.newyorker.com/magazine/2019/01/14/the-history-of-blood.

Plague background information is from Armstrong, D. (director), "The Black Death: The World's Most Devastating Plague," 2016, and *The Black Death* [video file], The Great Courses, retrieved June 29, 2020, from Kanopy, https://www.kanopy.com/product/black-death-1.

The surviving recipe for plague water is from "Plague Water," Alcohol's Empire, Minneapolis Institute of Art, 2019, https://artsmia.github.io/alcohols-empire/recipes/plague-water/.

"Wine windows" is from Harvey, Lisa, "One of Florence's 'Wine Windows' Is Open Once More," *Atlas Obscura*, August 14, 2019, https://www.atlasobscura.com/articles/florence-wine-windows.

The Compleat Herbal of Physical Plants is cited from Early English Books, accessed December 24, 2021, https://quod.lib.umich.edu/e/eebo/A53912.0001.001.

Information about the International Trappist Association can be found at https://www.trappist.be/en/.

For other monastic liqueurs, a much larger selection can be found in Seward, *Monks and Wine.*

Centerbe information is from "The Centerbe," Italy Heritage, 1998–2021, https://www.italyheritage.com/traditions/food/centerbe.htm.

Stellina information is from Coldicott, Nicholas, "This Obscure Liqueur May Save Your Soul," *Japan Times*, October 23, 2009, https://www.japantimes.co.jp/life/2009/10/23/food/this-obscure-liqueur-may-save-your-soul, as well as the brand's website, http://www.stellina.fr/secrets-expertise.html.

Bénédictine additional history is from email communication with Sébastien Roncin.

Bénédictine information about Singapore and confinement is from "No One Likes Benedictine DOM in Their Kailan but This Is Why We Eat It Anyway," Confinement Diaries, April 11, 2018, accessed 2022, https://web.archive.org/web/20210114200013/https://confinement-diaries.com/benedictine-dom-singapore.

Buckfast information is from several online news sources, including Lyall, Sarah, "For Scots, a Scourge Unleashed by a Bottle," *The New York Times*, February 3, 2010, https://www.nytimes.com/2010/02/04/world/europe/04scotland.html; Harris, Elise, "England's Popular Monastic Wine Has a Backstory, and a Bite," *Crux*, August 19, 2018, https://web.archive.org/web/20180819082235/https://cruxnow.com/church-in-uk-and-ireland/2018/08/19/englands-popular-monastic-wine-has-a-backstory-and-a-bite/; and Jeffreys, Henry, "Buckfast: A Drink with Almost Supernatural Powers of Destruction," *The Guardian*, February 27, 2015, https://www.theguardian.com/lifeandstyle/2015/feb/27/buckfast-drink-with-supernatural-powers-destruction.

Buckfast "linked to 6,500 reports" is from Morley, Katie, "Monks Could Lose Charitable Status over Production of 'Dangerous' Buckfast Wine," *The Telegraph*, April 11, 2017, https://www.telegraph.co.uk/news/2017/04/11/monks-could-lose-charitable-status-production-dangerous-wine/.

£12 million tax-free is from Frost, Natasha, "How a Tonic Wine Brewed by Monks Became the Scourge of Scotland," *Atlas Obscura*, June 7, 2017, https://www.atlasobscura.com/articles/buckfast-scotland.

CHAPTER 4. SCIENCE: PHLOGISTON, PYRMONT, PASTEUR, AND PATHOGENS

Primary sources for the science and scientists in this chapter included Partington, James Riddick, *A Short History of Chemistry* (Mineola, NY: Dover Publications, 1989); Taylor, Frank Sherwood, *A Short History of Science and Scientific Thought* (New York: W. W. Norton, 1963); and Geison, Gerald L., *The Private Science of Louis*

Pasteur (Princeton, NJ: Princeton University Press, 1995). For natural spas, Chapelle, Frank, *Wellsprings: A Natural History of Bottled Spring Waters* (New Brunswick, NJ: Rutgers University Press, 2005) was a useful source. For germ theory, main sources included Fitzharris, Lindsey, *The Butchering Art* (New York: Scientific American; Farrar, Straus and Giroux, 2017); and Wootton, David, *Bad Medicine* (Oxford, UK: Oxford University Press, 2007).

Additional information on phlogiston is from Brancho, Jimmy, "Oxygen's Alchemical Origins: The Phlogiston Story," *Tree Town Chemistry*, February 4, 2016, http://treetownchem.blogspot.com/2016/02/oxygens-alchemical-origins-phlogis ton.html.

"I would not interfere with the providence of the physician" is from Priestley, Joseph, *Directions for Impregnating Water with Fixed Air* (London: Printed for J. Johnson, 1772), accessed 2021, https://wellcomecollection.org/works/bs6kgbcq/items.

"For having learned from Dr. Black" is from Thorpe, Thomas Edward, *Joseph Priestley* (London: J. M. Dent, 1906), accessed 2021 via Google Books, https://www .google.com/books/edition/Joseph_Priestley/uAwFAAAAYAAJ?hl=en&gbpv=0.

"By this process may fixed air be given to wine" is from Priestley, *Directions for Impregnating Water*.

For bottled water histories, most came from the websites of each brand.

Additional information about Lady Mary Wortley Montagu is from "Lady Mary Wortley Montagu," Wikipedia, Wikimedia Foundation, last edited December 8, 2021, https://en.wikipedia.org/wiki/Lady_Mary_Wortley_Montagu.

"When I read Pasteur's article" is from Fitzharris, *Butchering Art*.

Additional information on Listerine is from "Listerine," National Museum of American History, accessed December 21, 2021, https://americanhistory.si.edu/col lections/search/object/nmah_1170944.

CHAPTER 5. BITTERSWEET: APERITIF, ABSINTHE, AND AMARO

Good reads on the science of taste are Prescott, John, *Taste Matters: Why We Like the Foods We Do* (London: Reaktion Books, 2012); and Shepherd, Gordon M., *Neurogastronomy* (New York: Columbia University Press, 2012). For vermouth, Adam Ford's *Vermouth: The Revival of the Spirit That Created America's Cocktail Culture* (Woodstock, VT: Countryman Press, 2015) is a primary source, backed up with Piccinino, Fulvio, *The Vermouth of Turin* (Turin, Italy: Graphot, 2018); and Berta, P., and Mainardi, G., *The Grand Book of Vermouth Di Torino: History and Importance of a Classic Piedmontese Product* (Canelli, Italy: OICCE, 2019). Adams, Jad, *Hideous Absinthe* (Madison: University of Wisconsin Press, 2004); and absinthes.com were useful sources for absinthe information.

The discussion of scent receptors is from "Humans Can Distinguish At Least One Trillion Different Odors," Howard Hughes Medical Institute, March 20, 2014, https:// www.sciencedaily.com/releases/2014/03/140320140738.htm.

"Very good for old age" is from Lucia, *History of Wine as Therapy*.

"Antidote to the mischief of mushrooms" is from Culpeper, Nicholas, *The Complete Herbal* (London: Thomas Kelly, 1835), accessed 2021 via Google Books, https://books.google.com/books?id=z0qd6D8-jGYC.

"[Hopping beer] may be in every respect as well performed" is from Buhner, Stephen Harrod, *Sacred and Herbal Healing Beers* (Boulder, CO: Brewers Publications, 1998).

Fortified wine information is largely from Epstein, Becky Sue, *Strong, Sweet and Dry* (London: Reaktion Books, 2019).

Information on fennel and other herbal uses is from Howes, Irving, and Simmonds, *Gardener's Companion to Medicinal Plants*.

"Drunkenness used not to be a French vice" is from book 2 of Brown, Jared McDaniel, and Anistatia Renard Miller, *Spirituous Journey* (self-published, 2010).

Thujone overdose case is from Weisbord, Steven D., Soule, Jeremy B., and Kimmel, Paul L., "Poison on Line—Acute Renal Failure Caused by Oil of Wormwood Purchased through the Internet," *New England Journal of Medicine* 337 (1997): 825–27, https://www.nejm.org/doi/full/10.1056/nejm199709183371205.

Discussion of anise liqueurs is from Zavatto, Amy, "Everything You Need to Know about Anise-Flavored Spirits," Liquor, November 2, 2020, https://www.liquor.com/anise-spirits-5085280.

Information on some medicinal uses of gentian is from Mirzaee, F., Hosseini, A., Jouybari, H. B., Davoodi, A., and Azadbakht, M., "Medicinal, Biological and Phytochemical Properties of Gentiana Species," *Journal of Traditional and Complementary Medicine* 7, no. 4 (2017): 400–408, published online January 28, 2017, https://www.ncbi.nlm.nih.gov/pmc/articles/PMC5634738/.

Much of the information about amaro brands and which ones contain gentian, wormwood, rhubarb, etc., comes from Parsons, Brad Thomas, *Amaro* (Berkeley, CA: Ten Speed Press, 2016).

CHAPTER 6. SPIRITS: GRAPES, GRAIN, AGAVE, AND CANE

In this chapter, the books I found most useful are usually named in the text of each section.

"Forty Virtues of Armagnac" was provided by the Bureau National Interprofessionnel de l'Armagnac via email. Much information on scurvy is from Harvie, David I., *Limeys* (Gloucestershire, UK: Sutton Publishing, 2005).

Charles II of Navarre information is largely from "Charles II of Navarre," Wikipedia, Wikimedia Foundation, last edited December 10, 2021, https://en.wikipedia.org/wiki/Charles_II_of_Navarre.

Cognac history is largely from Faith, Nicholas, *Cognac*, 3rd revised and updated ed. (Oxford: Infinite Ideas, 2016); and Jarrard, Kyle, *Cognac* (Hoboken, NJ: John Wiley & Sons, 2005).

"Unless the doctor has a bottle or so" and "Its prime use was as a cardiac stimulant" quotations are from Guly, H., "Medicinal Brandy," *Resuscitation* 82, no. 7 (2011): 951–54, https://www.ncbi.nlm.nih.gov/pmc/articles/PMC3117141.

Saint Bernard information is from Curtis, Wayne, "The Myth of the St. Bernard and the Brandy Barrel," *The Daily Beast*, February 5, 2018, https://www.thedailybeast.com/the-myth-of-the-st-bernard-and-the-brandy-barrel.

Elisabetta Nonino information is from a personal interview in 2019.

John Timbs's *Popular Errors Explained and Illustrated* (London: David Bogue, 1856) can be found via Google Books, https://books.google.com/books?id=KK5j AAAAcAAJ.

Pokhlebkin's vodka history is shown disproven in Schrad, Mark Lawrence, *Vodka Politics* (New York: Oxford University Press, 2014).

"Some water which is called aqua vite" is from "Akvavit," Wikipedia, Wikimedia Foundation, last edited December 23, 2021, https://en.wikipedia.org/wiki/Akvavit.

Rum and distillation history in India is from Wondrich, David, "Forget the Caribbean: Was Rum Invented in India?" *The Daily Beast*, July 9, 2018, https://www.thedailybeast.com/forget-the-caribbean-was-rum-invented-in-india.

"A booster, a medicine, a salve" is from Broom, Dave, *Rum: The Manual* (London: Mitchell Beazley, 2016).

Information on kidney disease in cane workers is from Santos, Ubiratan Paula, Zanetta, Dirce Maria T., Terra Filho, Mario, and Burdmann, Emmanuel A., "Burnt Sugarcane Harvesting Is Associated with Acute Renal Dysfunction," *Kidney International* 87, no. 4 (2015): 792–99, https://www.sciencedirect.com/science/article/pii/S0085253815301988.

A True and Exact History of the Island of Barbados was accessed via Text Creation Partnership, 2021, https://quod.lib.umich.edu/e/eebo/A48447.0001.001/.

Robert Dossie's *An Essay on Spirituous Liquors* (London: J. Ridley, 1770) quotation was accessed via Google Books, https://books.google.com/books?id=ibxY AAAAcAAJ.

"A very general but erroneous opinion" is from Beatty, William, *Authentic Narrative of the Death of Lord Nelson* (London: T. Davison, 1807), accessed 2021, https://www.gutenberg.org/files/15233/15233-h/15233-h.htm.

The molasses tsunami is from Sohn, Emily, "Why the Great Molasses Flood Was So Deadly," History, January 15, 2019, https://www.history.com/news/great-molasses-flood-science.

"No workingman ever drank" is from Rorabaugh, W. J., *Prohibition: A Concise History* (Oxford, UK: Oxford University Press, 2018).

Guifiti information is from "Guifiti," Arzu Mountain Spirit, October 6, 2015, http://www.arzumountainspirit.com/blog/2015/10/8/guifiti.

Mamajuana information is from Perry, Kevin E. G., "Mamajuana, the 'Dominican Viagra,' Has Big Turtle Dick Energy," *Vice*, March 7, 2019, https://www.vice.com/en/article/panvw7/mamajuana-the-dominican-viagra-has-big-turtle-dick-energy.

Information on Dr. Livingstone's body is from "Zambia Honors Dr. Livingstone on 100th Anniversary of His Death," *The New York Times*, May 12, 1973, https://www.nytimes.com/1973/05/12/archives/zambia-honors-dr-livingstone-on-100th-anniversary-of-hisdeath-sense.html.

For whiskey, many books were consulted, with the following cited the most: Broom, Dave, *Whisky: The Manual* (London: Mitchell Beazley, 2014); Maclean, Charles, *Malt Whisky* (London: Octopus Publishing, 2010); Mitenbuler, Reid, *Bourbon Empire* (New York: Penguin, 2015); and Minnick, Fred, *Bourbon: The Rise, Fall, and Rebirth of an American Whiskey* (Minneapolis, MN: Voyageur Press, 2016).

Gunn, John C. *Gunn's Domestic Medicine*, 13th Edition (Pittsburgh, PA: J. Edwards & J. J. Newman, 1839), accessed 2021 via Google Books, https://books.google.com/books?id=6a8hAQAAMAAJ.

The Manufacture of Liquors, Wines, and Cordials without the Aid of Distillation is from HathiTrust Digital Library, accessed December 24, 2021, https://catalog.hathitrust.org/Record/007681147.

Rock and rye discussion is from Japhe, Brad, "Everything You Need to Know about Rock and Rye," *Whisky Advocate*, April 29, 2019, https://www.whiskyadvocate.com/need-to-know-rock-and-rye.

Baijiu statistics are from "Baijiu Booms as China's Bull Run Grows," *The Drinks Business*, December 14, 2020, https://www.thedrinksbusiness.com/2020/12/the-baijiu-boom; and Bellwood, Owen, "The 10 Most Valuable Spirits Brands in the World," *The Drinks Business*, June 7, 2021, https://www.thedrinksbusiness.com/2021/06/the-ten-most-valuable-spirits-brands-in-the-world.

Bruman, Henry J., *Alcohol in Ancient Mexico* (Salt Lake City: University of Utah Press, 2000) was very useful in the tequila and pulque section.

CHAPTER 7. POISON: PHOSPHATES, PATENT MEDICINES, PURE FOOD, AND PROHIBITION

Tristan Donovan's book *Fizz: How Soda Shook Up the World* (Chicago: Chicago Review Press, 2014) was particularly useful here for everything soda. Irwin W. Sherman's *Twelve Diseases That Changed Our World* (Washington, DC: ASM Press, 2007) was useful for syphilis. Information on Harvey Wiley and the Pure Food and Drug Act largely comes from Deborah Bloom's *The Poison Squad* (New York: Penguin Press, 2018), with additional information on poison alcohol during Prohibition from Blum's *The Poisoner's Handbook* (New York: Penguin, 2010).

"The first thing every American" is from Donovan, *Fizz*.

Syphilis nomenclature is from Tampa, M., Sarbu, I., Matei, C., Benea, V., and Georgescu, S. R., "Brief History of Syphilis," *Journal of Medicine and Life* 7, no. 1 (2014): 4–10, https://www.ncbi.nlm.nih.gov/pmc/articles/PMC3956094/.

Hires Root Beer information is from Armijo, Stephanie, "Hires Root Beer," History of the Soda Fountain, updated November 17, 2016, https://scalar.usc.edu /works/history-of-the-soda fountain/hires-root-beer.

Phosphoric acid information is from O'Neil, Darcy S., *Fix the Pumps* (N.p: Darcy O'Neil, 2009).

"God is unjust" comes from "Paolo Mantegazza," accessed December 24, 2021, https://www.erythroxylum-coca.com/mantegazza/index.html.

Vin Mariani ad copy is from Google Image searches.

Additional Coca-Cola information is from Standage, Tom, *A History of the World in Six Glasses* (New York: Bloomsbury, 2006).

"The public can rest assured that Dr Pepper is non-alcoholic" is from Rodengen, Jeffrey L., *The Legend of Dr Pepper/Seven-Up* (Fort Lauderdale, FL: Write Stuff Syndicate, 1995).

Information on the Smithsonian patent medicine collection can be found at "Balm of America: Patent Medicine Collection," National Museum of American History, accessed December 24, 2021, https://americanhistory.si.edu/collections/object -groups/balm-of-america-patent-medicine-collection.

Information on the medical uses for opium is from Hodgson, Barbara, *In the Arms of Morpheus* (Buffalo, NY: Firefly Books, 2001).

Snake oil information is from Graber, Cynthia, "Snake Oil Salesmen Were on to Something," *Scientific American*, November 1, 2007, accessed 2021, https://www .scientificamerican.com/article/snake-oil-salesmen-knew-something/, and Gandhi, Lakshmi, "A History of 'Snake Oil Salesmen,'" *Code Switch*, NPR, August 26, 2013, accessed 2021, https://www.npr.org/sections/codeswitch/2013/08/26/215761377 /a-history-of-snake-oil-salesmen.

Duffy's medicine information is from Haara, Brian F., *Bourbon Justice* (Lincoln, NE: Potomac Books, 2018).

"Vigorous at 119 years old" is from an advertisement viewed at Peachridge Glass, accessed December 24, 2021, https://www.peachridgeglass.com/wp-content/up loads/2013/05/DuffyMaltWhiskeyAd.jpg.

Information about cochineal in modern products is from English, Camper, "Bug-Based Coloring Makes a Comeback in Spirits," *SevenFifty Daily*, October 5, 2017, accessed 2021, https://daily.sevenfifty.com/bug-based-coloring-makes-a-comeback -in-spirits.

St. Louis World's Fair of 1904 information is from Smith, Andrew F., *The Oxford Encyclopedia of Food and Drink in America* (New York: Oxford University Press, 2004).

Grape bricks information is from Teeter, Adam, "How Wine Bricks Saved the U.S. Wine Industry during Prohibition," *VinePair*, August 24, 2015, accessed 2021, https://vinepair.com/wine-blog/how-wine-bricks-saved-the-u-s-wine-industry-dur ing-prohibition.

The survey of doctors as to the medicinal use of alcohol during Prohibition comes from Okrent, Daniel, "An Illegal Substance Sold Legally," *Los Angeles Times*, May 16, 2020, accessed 2021, https://www.latimes.com/archives/la-xpm-2010-may-16-la-oe-0516-okrent-prohibition-20100516-story.html.

Information on toxic alcohol in Iran is from Arnold, Carrie, "Tainted Sanitizers and Bootleg Booze Are Poisoning People," *National Geographic*, August 19, 2020, https://www.nationalgeographic.com/science/article/methanol-poisoning-bootleg-sanitizer-alcohol-how-to-protect-yourself-coronavirus-cvd.

CHAPTER 8. TONIC: MALARIA, MOSQUITOES, AND MAUVE

Of the many books on tonic, quinine, and malaria that I've read, the ones I refer to most often are Duran-Reynals, Marie Louise de Ayala, *The Fever Bark Tree* (London: W. H. Allen, 1947); Sherman, Irwin W., *Magic Bullets to Conquer Malaria* (Washington, DC: ASM Press, 2011); and Nesbitt, Mark, and Walker, Kim, *Just the Tonic* (Richmond, Surrey, UK: Kew Publishing, 2019). Information on syphilis is from Sherman, *Twelve Diseases*.

Text from *The Theory and Treatment of Fevers* was accessed at Swift, Gabriel, "Sappington's Theory and Treatment of Fevers," *Princeton Collections of the American West*, July 12, 2021, https://blogs.princeton.edu/westernamericana/2012/07/12/sappingtons-theory-treatment-of-fevers.

Information on calisaya fiends is from Stailey, Doug (LibationLegacy). "If you've dug around in old cocktail recipes . . ." May 17, 2018, 10:08 p.m. Tweet. https://twitter.com/LibationLegacy/status/997297967320137728.

Quinine in commercial beverages list is sourced in part from Parsons, *Amaro*.

The Hughes and Company quinine water reference comes from Nesbitt and Walker, *Just the Tonic*.

"In some cases, a small portion of wine" is from *The Lancet* (London: Elsevier, 1861). Accessed 2021 via Google Books, https://books.google.com/books?id=rRdAAAAAcAAJ.

The Oriental Sporting Magazine quote is no longer on Google Books, but a screen grab is visible in Nesbitt and Walker, *Just the Tonic*.

Maraschino cherry information is from Curtis, Wayne, "Mixopedia: The Maraschino Cherry," *Imbibe*, December 19, 2016, https://imbibemagazine.com/history-lesson-the-maraschino-cherry.

Information disproving the Mickey Slim cocktail was sourced from Koerner, Brendan I., "The Myth of the Mickey Slim," *MicroKhan*, June 9, 2010, http://www.microkhan.com/2010/06/09/the-myth-of-the-mickey-slim, as well as the comments on this blog post.

The *Tropical Medicine and International Health* article is from Meyer, Christian G., Marks, Florian, and May, Jürgen, "Editorial: Gin Tonic Revisited," *Tropical Medicine*

and International Health 9, no. 12 (December 2004): 1239–40, https://onlinelibrary
.wiley.com/doi/full/10.1111/j.1365-3156.2004.01357.x.

CHAPTER 9. MIXOLOGY: MIXED DRINKS AND MODERN MEDICINE

Much of the history of cocktails in America comes from Wondrich, David, *Imbibe!*
(New York: TarcherPerigee, 2015).

"It must be confessed that American drinks" is from *Pharmaceutical Formulas: A
Book of Useful Recipes for the Drug Trade* (London: The Chemist and Druggist, 1902),
accessed 2021 via Google Books, https://books.google.com/books?id=gdpNAQA
AMAAJ.

"If the French have been long proverbial" is from Majoribanks, Alexander, *Travels in South and North America* (London: Simpkin, Marshall, and Company, 1853),
accessed 2021 via Google Books, https://books.google.com/books?id=9RZwtDB
m7JMC.

"In the matter of drinks, how hospitable" is from Will-Weber, Mark, *Muskets and
Applejack* (Washington, DC: Regnery History, 2017).

"Now the difference between a brandy-cocktail" is from Grimes, William,
Straight Up or On the Rocks: The Story of the American Cocktail (New York: North
Point Press, 2001).

Mark Twain letter is from "The Remix; Recipe for Regularity | 1874 Letter from
Mark Twain to His Wife," *The New York Times*, December 3, 2006, https://www
.nytimes.com/2006/12/03/style/the-remix-recipe-for-regularity-1874-letter-from-mark
-twain-to-his.html.

The cure for hiccups story is from "A Bitter Medicine Cures the Hiccups," *The
New York Times*, December 31, 1981, https://www.nytimes.com/1981/12/31/style
/a-bitter-medicine-cures-the-hiccups.html.

New and Improved Bartender's Manual is from EUVS Vintage Cocktail Books, accessed December 24, 2021, https://euvs-vintage-cocktail-books.cld.bz/1882-Harry
-Johnson-s-new-and-improved-bartender-s-manual-1882/24.

"Before breakfast he enters" is from Greene, Philip, *The Manhattan* (New York:
Sterling Epicure, 2016).

"If, following intoxication, there is a headache" is from Jouanna, *Greek Medicine*.

"The eggs of an owlet" is from *The Natural History of Pliny*, trans. John Bostock
and H. T. Riley (London: Henry G. Bohn, 1856), accessed 2021 via Google Books,
https://books.google.com/books?id=1UoMAAAAIAAJ.

"It is a matter of certainty" is from "Supplementary Material on Frederick Tudor
Ice Project," *Bulletin of the Business Historical Society* 9, no. 1 (1935): 1–6, accessed
May 4, 2021, https://www.jstor.org/stable/3110750?origin=crossref&seq=1.

Wenham Lake Ice information is from Weightman, Gavin, *The Frozen Water
Trade* (New York: Hyperion Books, 2003).

Wilmer and Smith's European Times reference comes from Phillips, John C., *Wenham Great Pond* (Salem: Peabody Museum, 1938), accessed 2021, http://www.seeking myroots.com/members/files/H003116.pdf.

"Many did well with a simple julep" is from Mons. Le Cat, "An Account of Those Malignant Fevers, That Raged at Rouen, at the End of the Year 1753," *Philosophical Transactions (1683–1775)* 49 (1755): 49–61, accessed May 4, 2021, http://www.jstor .org/stable/104908.

"As the daughter of émigrés from Ukraine" is from Simone, Alina, "Why Do Russians Hate Ice?" *The New York Times*, August 3, 2011, https://opinionator.blogs .nytimes.com/2011/08/03/ice-enough-already/?ref=opinion.

"What I don't understand is why the Americans like" is from Tao, Yan, "American News Series: It Is Difficult to Drink Hot Water," March 9, 2015, https://www .douban.com/group/topic/73302265.

Ingredient safety information is from cocktailsafe.org.

"Australian man poisoned himself" is from Panko, Ben, "Man Poisons Himself by Taking Apricot Kernels to Treat Cancer," *Smithsonian Magazine*, September 13, 2017, https://www.smithsonianmag.com/smart-news/natural-health-treatment-poisons -man-180964870.

"The moderate drinking of alcoholic beverages did not shorten life" is from Gaffney, Rusty, "Wine Is Good News for Health in 2008," *Prince of Pinot* 7, no. 10 (January 14, 2009), https://www.princeofpinot.com/article/603.

Alcohol and longevity information is from Cloud, John, "Why Nondrinkers May Be More Depressed," *Time*, October 6, 2009, http://content.time.com/time/health /article/0,8599,1928187,00.html; and Cloud, John, "Why Do Heavy Drinkers Outlive Nondrinkers?" *Time*, August 30, 2010, http://content.time.com/time/magazine/arti cle/0,9171,2017200,00.html.

BIBLIOGRAPHY

Absinthes.com. "The Absinthe Encyclopedia by David Nathan-Maister—Absinthes
.com—The Definitive Guide to the History of Absinthe." Accessed 2021.

Abu-Asab, Mones, Hakima Amri, and Marc S. Micozzi. *Avicenna's Medicine*. Rochester, VT: Healing Arts Press, 2013.

Adams, Jad. *Hideous Absinthe*. Madison: University of Wisconsin Press, 2004.

Ahmed, Selena, Ashley Duval, and Rachel Meyer. *Botany at the Bar*. Boulder, CO:
Roost Books, 2019.

Allen, Martha Meir. *Alcohol, a Dangerous and Unnecessary Medicine*. New York: Department of Medical Temperance of the National Woman's Christian Temperance
Union, 1900. https://www.google.com/books/edition/Alcohol_a_Dangerous_
and_Unnecessary_Medi/Icw0AQAAMAAJ.

Baker Jr., Charles H. *Jigger, Beaker and Glass*. Lanham, MD: Derrydale Press, 1992.

Ball, Philip. *The Devil's Doctor*. New York: Farrar, Straus and Giroux, 2006.

Bamforth, Charles. *Grape vs. Grain*. New York: Cambridge University Press, 2008.

Barrios, Virginia B. De. *A Guide to Tequila, Mezcal and Pulque*. Mexico City, Mexico:
Minutiae Mexicana, 1984.

Bell, Madison Smartt. *Lavoisier in the Year One*. New York; London: W. W. Norton,
2006.

Berta, P., and G. Mainardi. *The Grand Book of Vermouth Di Torino*. Canelli, Italy:
OICCE, 2019.

Bethard, Wayne. *Lotions, Potions, and Deadly Elixirs*. Lanham, MD: Roberts Rine-
hart, 2013.

Blum, Deborah. *The Poisoner's Handbook*. New York: Penguin, 2010.

Blum, Deborah. *The Poison Squad*. New York: Penguin Press, 2018.

Bose, Dhirendra Krishna. *Wine in Ancient India*. Milan, Italy: Edizioni Savine, 2016.

Bowen, Sarah. *Divided Spirits*. Oakland: University of California Press, 2015.

Braun, Julius. *On the Curative Effects of Baths and Waters*. London: Smith, Elder, 1875. Accessed 2021. https://books.google.com/books?id=nOxhAAAAcAAJ.

Brock, Pope. *Charlatan: America's Most Dangerous Huckster, the Man Who Pursued Him, and the Age of Flimflam*. New York: Three Rivers Press, 2008.

Broom, Dave. *Gin*. London: Mitchell Beazley, 2020.

Broom, Dave. *Rum*. London: Mitchell Beazley, 2016.

Broom, Dave. *Whisky*. London: Mitchell Beazley, 2014.

Brown, Jared McDaniel, and Anistatia R. Miller. *The Distiller of London*. London: Mixellany Limited, 2020.

Brown, Jared McDaniel, and Anistatia R. Miller. *The Mixellany Guide to Vermouth and Other Aperitifs*. London: Mixellany Limited, 2011.

Brown, Jared McDaniel, and Anistatia R. Miller. *The Soul of Brasil*. UK: Anistatia Miller and Jared Brown, 2008.

Brown, Jared McDaniel, and Anistatia R. Miller. *Spirituous Journey*. Book 2. London: Mixellany Limited, 2009.

Bruman, Henry J. *Alcohol in Ancient Mexico*. Salt Lake City: University of Utah Press, 2000.

Brunschwig, Hieronymus. *The Virtuous Book of Distillation*. London, 1527. Reprint, Ann Arbor, MI: Text Creation Partnership, 2021. https://quod.lib.umich.edu/cgi/t/text/text-idx?c=eebo;idno=A03318.0001.001.

Bryan, Cyril P. *Ancient Egyptian Medicine*. Chicago: Ares Publishers, 1974.

Chapelle, Frank. *Wellsprings*. New Brunswick, NJ: Rutgers University Press, 2005.

Cobb, Cathy, Monty Fetterolf, and Harold Goldwhite. *The Chemistry of Alchemy*. Amherst, NY: Prometheus Books, 2014.

Conrad, Barnaby. *Absinthe*. San Francisco, CA: Chronicle Books, 1988.

Craddock, Harry. *The Savoy Cocktail Book*. London: Constable, 1930. Accessed 2021. https://euvs-vintage-cocktail-books.cld.bz/1930-The-Savoy-Cocktail-Book.

Curry, Andrew. "Our 9,000-Year Love Affair with Booze." *National Geographic*, February 2017, 30–53.

Curtis, Wayne. *And a Bottle of Rum*. New York: Three Rivers Press, 2018.

Dasgupta, Amitava. *The Science of Drinking*. Lanham, MD: Rowman & Littlefield, 2011.

David, Elizabeth. *Harvest of the Cold Months*. New York: Viking, 1995.

Delahaye, Marie-Claude. *Pernod Creator of Absinthe*. Auvers-sur Oise, France: Musée de l'Absinthe, 2008.

Dicum, Gregory. *The Pisco Book*. San Francisco: Cleargrape, 2011.

Donovan, Tristan. *Fizz*. Chicago: Chicago Review Press, 2014.

Dorfles, Gillo, Giorgio Fioravanti, and Marzio Romani. *Soc. Anon. Fratelli Branca Milano*. Milan, Italy: Fratelli Branca Distillerie, 2002.

Duran-Reynals, Marie Louise de Ayala. *The Fever Bark Tree*. London: W. H. Allen, 1947.

Edmunds, Lowell. *Martini, Straight Up*. Baltimore, MD: John Hopkins University Press, 1998.

Edwards, Griffith. *Alcohol*. New York: Thomas Dunne Books, 2002.

Embury, D. A. *The Fine Art of Mixing Drinks*. New York: Mud Puddle Books, 2008.

Epstein, Becky Sue. *Brandy*. London: Reaktion Books, 2014.

Epstein, Becky Sue. *Strong, Sweet and Dry*. London: Reaktion Books, 2019.

Faith, Nicholas. *Cognac*, 3rd revised and updated ed. Oxford, UK: Infinite Ideas, 2016.

Faith, Nicholas, and Ian Wisniewski. *Classic Vodka*. London: Prion Books, 1997.

Fitzharris, Lindsey. *The Butchering Art*. New York: Scientific American; Farrar, Straus and Giroux, 2017.

Flandrin, Jean-Louis, Massimo Montanari, and Albert Sonnenfeld. *Food*. New York: Columbia University Press, 1999.

Forbes, R. J. *Short History of the Art of Distillation*. Hayward, CA: White Mule Press, 2009.

Ford, Adam. *Vermouth*. Woodstock, VT: Countryman Press, 2015.

Fracastoro, Girolamo. *Syphilis, or A Poetical History of the French Disease Written in Latin by Fracastorius; and Now Attempted in English by N. Tate*. London: Jacob Tonson, 1686. Reprint, Ann Arbor, MI: Text Creation Partnership, 2021. http://name.umdl.umich.edu/A40377.0001.001.

French, John. *The Art of Distillation*. London: E. Cotes for Thomas Williams, 1653. Reprint, Ann Arbor, MI: Text Creation Partnership, 2021. https://quod.lib.umich.cdu/c/eebo/A40448.0001.001.

Galiano, Martine, Philip Boyer, Christian Delafon, Antoine Munoz, Jean-Marc Roget, and Philippe Bonnard. *Chartreuse the Liqueur*. N.p., 2020.

Garfield, Simon. *Mauve*. New York: W. W. Norton, 2002.

Geison, Gerald L. *The Private Science of Louis Pasteur*. Princeton, NJ: Princeton University Press, 1995.

Gerard, John. *The Herball, or, Generall Historie of Plantes*. London: John Norton, 1597. Accessed 2021. https://www.biodiversitylibrary.org/bibliography/51606.

Gosnell, Mariana. *Ice*. Chicago: University of Chicago Press, 2005.

Greene, Philip. *The Manhattan*. New York: Sterling Epicure, 2016.

Greenfield, Amy Butler. *A Perfect Red*. New York: HarperCollins, 2005.

Grivetti, Louis E. *Wine*. Robert Mondavi Winery. April 29–May 5, 1991. Accessed 2021. https://nutritionalgeography.faculty.ucdavis.edu/wp-content/uploads/sites/106/2014/11/Wine.Medical.Nutrition.Attributes.NapaCalifornia.pdf.

Haara, Brian F. *Bourbon Justice*. Lincoln, NE: Potomac Books, 2018.

Harvie, David I. *Limeys*. Gloucestershire, UK: Sutton Publishing, 2005.

Hauck, Dennis William. *The Complete Idiot's Guide to Alchemy*. New York: Penguin, 2008.

Herlihy, Patricia. *Vodka*. London: Reaktion Books, 2012.

Hiss, A. Emil. *The Standard Manual of Soda and Other Beverages*. Chicago: G. P. Engelhard & Company, 1906.

Hodgson, Barbara. *In the Arms of Morpheus*. Buffalo, NY: Firefly Books, 2001.

Hollingham, Richard. *Blood and Guts*. New York: Thomas Dunne Books, 2009.

Hornsey, Ian S. *A History of Beer and Brewing*. London: Royal Society of Chemistry, 2004.

Howes, Melanie-Jayne, Jason Irving, and Monique Simmonds. *The Gardener's Companion to Medicinal Plants*. London: Quarto Publishing, 2016.

Jarrard, Kyle. *Cognac*. Hoboken, NJ: John Wiley & Sons, 2005.

Jouanna, Jacques. *Greek Medicine from Hippocrates to Galen*. Leiden, Netherlands: Brill, 2012.

Joyce, Jaime. *Moonshine*. Minneapolis, MN: Zenith Press, 2014.

Kelly, John. *The Great Mortality*. New York: HarperCollins, 2005.

Kosar, Kevin R. *Whiskey*. London: Reaktion Books, 2010.

Lucia, Salvatore Pablo. *A History of Wine as Therapy*. Philadelphia: J. B. Lippincott, 1963.

Maclean, Charles. *Malt Whisky*. London: Octopus Publishing, 2010.

Maddison, R. E. W. "Studies in the Life of Robert Boyle, F.R.S. Part II. Salt Water Freshened." *Notes and Records of the Royal Society of London* 9, no. 2 (1952): 196–216. http://www.jstor.org/stable/3087215.

Martineau, Chantal. *How the Gringos Stole Tequila*. Chicago: Chicago Review Press, 2015.

Maury, Sarah Mytton. *An Englishwoman in America*. London: Thomas Richardson and Son, 1848. Accessed 2021. https://www.google.com/books/edition/An_Englishwoman_in_America/MH11AAAAMAAJ?hl=en&gbpv=0.

Maxwell-Stuart, P. G. *The Chemical Choir*. London: Continuum, 2012.

Mitenbuler, Reid. *Bourbon Empire*. New York: Penguin, 2015.

Minnick, Fred. *Bourbon*. Minneapolis: Voyageur Press, 2016.

Minnick, Fred. *Mead*. Philadelphia: Running Press, 2018.

Minnick, Fred. *Rum Curious*. Minneapolis: Voyageur Press, 2017.

Mintz, Sidney W. *Sweetness and Power*. New York: Viking, 1985.

Mitenbuler, Reid. *Bourbon Empire*. New York: Viking, 2015.

Monardes, Nicolas, and John Frampton. *Joyfull Newes Out of the New Found World*. London: W. W. Norton, 1580. Accessed 2021. http://fsu.digital.flvc.org/islandora/object/fsu%3A213358.

Moran, Bruce T. *Distilling Knowledge*. Cambridge, MA: Harvard University Press, 2005.

Morgan, Nicholas. *A Long Stride*. Edinburgh, Scotland: Canongate Books, 2020.

Multhauf, Robert P. "John of Rupescissa and the Origin of Medical Chemistry," *Isis* 45, no. 4 (December 1954): 359–67.

Nelson, Max. "Did Ancient Greeks Drink Beer?" *Phoenix* 68, no. 1/2 (2014): 27–46. https://doi.org/10.7834/phoenix.68.1–2.0027.

Nesbitt, Mark, and Kim Walker. *Just the Tonic*. Richmond, Surrey, UK: Kew Publishing, 2019.

O'Brien, Glenn. *Hennessy*. New York: Rizzoli International Publications, 2017.

Oliver, Garrett. *The Oxford Companion to Beer*. Oxford, UK: Oxford University Press, 2011.

O'Neil, Darcy S. *Fix the Pumps*. N.p.: Darcy O'Neil, 2009.

Parsons, Brad Thomas. *Amaro*. Berkeley, CA: Ten Speed Press, 2016.

Parsons, Brad Thomas. *Bitters*. Berkeley, CA: Ten Speed Press, 2011.

Partington, James Riddick. *A Short History of Chemistry*. Mineola, NY: Dover Publications, 1989.

Perry, Charles. *Scents and Flavors*. New York: New York University Press, 2017.

Piccinino, Fulvio. *The Vermouth of Turin*. Turin, Italy: Graphot, 2018.

Piercy, Joseph. *Slippery Tipples*. Cheltenham, UK: The History Press, 2011.

Prescott, John. *Taste Matters*. London: Reaktion Books, 2012.

Priestley, Joseph. *Directions for Impregnating Water with Fixed Air*. London: Printed for J. Johnson, 1772. Accessed 2021. https://wellcomecollection.org/works/bs6 kgbcq/items.

Rasmussen, Seth C. *The Quest for Aqua Vitae*. N.p.: Springer Science & Business, 2014.

Roach, Mary. *Stiff*. New York: W. W. Norton, 2003.

Rocco, Fiammetta. *Quinine*. New York: HarperCollins, 2004.

Rodengen, Jeffrey L.. *The Legend of Dr Pepper/Seven-Up*. Fort Lauderdale, FL: Write Stuff Syndicate, 1995.

Rogers, Adam. *Proof*. New York: Houghton Mifflin Harcourt, 2014.

Romanico, Niccolo Branca Di. *Branca*. New York: Rizzoli, 2015.

Rorabaugh, W. J. *Prohibition*. Oxford, UK: Oxford University Press, 2018.

Rowell, Alex. *Vintage Humour*. Oxford, UK: Oxford University Press, 2018.

Sandhaus, Derek. *Baijiu*. Melbourne, Australia: Penguin, 2014.

Sandhaus, Derek. *Drunk in China*. Lincoln, NE: Potomac Books, 2019.

Sandler, Merton, and Roger Pinder. *Wine*. Boca Raton, FL: CRC Press, 2002.

Schrad, Mark Lawrence. *Vodka Politics*. New York: Oxford University Press, 2014.

Seward, Desmond. *Monks and Wine*. New York: Crown, 1979.

Shepherd, Gordon M. *Neurogastronomy*. New York: Columbia University Press, 2012.

Sherman, Irwin W. *Magic Bullets to Conquer Malaria*. Washington, DC: ASM Press, 2011.

Sherman, Irwin. *Twelve Diseases That Changed Our World*. Washington, DC: ASM Press, 2007.

Simmons, Douglas A. *Schweppes, the First 200 Years*. N.p.: Springwood Books, 1983.

Smith, Andrew F. *The Oxford Encyclopedia of Food and Drink in America*. New York: Oxford University Press, 2004.

Solmonson, Lesley Jacobs. *Gin*. London: Reaktion Books, 2012.

Standage, Tom. *A History of the World in Six Glasses*. New York: Bloomsbury, 2006.

St. Clair, Kassia. *The Secret Lives of Color*. New York: Penguin, 2017.

Stearns, Samuel. *The American Herbal, or Materia Medica*. Walpole, NY: Thomas & Thomas, 1801. Accessed 2021. https://archive.org/details/2573006R.nlm.nih.gov.

Stewart, Amy. *The Drunken Botanist*. Chapel Hill, NC: Algonquin Books, 2013.

Stewart, Amy. *Wicked Plants*. Chapel Hill, NC: Algonquin Books, 2009.

Stillman, John Maxson. *The Story of Alchemy and Early Chemistry*. New York: Dover Publications, 1960.

Sugg, Richard. *Mummies, Cannibals, and Vampires*. New York: Routledge, 2011.

Taape, T. "Distilling Reliable Remedies: Hieronymus Brunschwig's Liber de arte distillandi (1500) between Alchemical Learning and Craft Practice." *Ambix* 61, no. 3 (August 2014): 236–56. http://europepmc.org/article/PMC/5268093.

Taylor, Frank Sherwood. *The Alchemists*. New York: Barnes & Noble Books, 1992.

Taylor, Frank Sherwood. *A Short History of Science and Scientific Thought*. New York: W. W. Norton, 1963.

Terrington, William. *Cooling Cups and Dainty Drinks*. New York: George Routledge & Sons, 1869. Accessed 2021. https://euvs-vintage-cocktail-books.cld.bz/1869-Cooling-Cups-and-Dainty-drinks-by-William-Terrington.

Thomas, Jerry. *The Bar-Tender's Guide*. New York: Dick & Fitzgerald, 1862. Reprint, New York: Cocktail Kingdom, 2013.

Thorpe, Thomas Edward. *Joseph Priestley*. London: J. M. Dent, 1906. Accessed 2021. https://www.google.com/books/edition/Joseph_Priestley/uAwFAAAAYAAJ?hl=en&gbpv=0.

Turner, Jack. *Spice*. New York: Random House, 2004.

Weightman, Gavin. *The Frozen Water Trade*. New York: Hyperion Books, 2003.

Williams, Olivia. *Gin Glorious Gin*. London: Headline Publishing, 2015.

Will-Weber, Mark. *Muskets and Applejack*. Washington, DC: Regnery History, 2017.

Wondrich, David. *Imbibe!* New York: TarcherPerigee, 2015.

Wootton, David. *Bad Medicine*. Oxford, UK: Oxford University Press, 2007.

Yenne, Bill. *Guinness*. Hoboken, NJ: John Wiley & Sons, 2007.

Zarnecki, George. *The Monastic Achievement*. New York: McGraw-Hill, 1972.

IMAGE CREDITS

Chapter 1: *Leslie's Weekly* 95 no. 2450 (August 21, 1902): 190, https://babel.hathitrust .org/cgi/pt?id=mdp.39015036655788

Chapter 2: *The Pharmaceutical Era* 12 (December 15, 1894): Supplement p. 5, https:// babel.hathitrust.org/cgi/pt?id=mdp.39015080402442

Chapter 3: *Leslie's Weekly* 95 no. 2465 (December 4, 1902): 548 and no. 2467 (Dec 18, 1902): 710, https://babel.hathitrust.org/cgi/pt?id=mdp.39015036655788

Chapter 4: *Canadian Journal of Medicine and Surgery* 40 no. 4 (October 1916): xxv, https://babel.hathitrust.org/cgi/pt?id=ucl.b5587172

Chapter 5: *Giornale della reale società italiana d'igiene* 6 (1884): Supplement p. 5, https://babel.hathitrust.org/cgi/pt?id=nyp.33433075972442

Chapter 6: *The Tammany Times* 31 no. 4 (July 27, 1907): 16, https://babel.hathitrust .org/cgi/pt?id=coo.31924065973467

Chapter 7: *Puck* 17 no. 417 (March 4, 1885): 141, https://babel.hathitrust.org/cgi/pt ?id=mdp.39015038641554

Chapter 8: *Puck* 17, no. 431 (June 10, 1885): 238, https://babel.hathitrust.org/cgi /pt?id=mdp.39015038641554

Chapter 9: *Puck* 17 no. 417 (March 4, 1885): 127, https://babel.hathitrust.org/cgi/pt ?id=mdp.39015038641554

INDEX